Your Mathematics Standards Companion
at a Glance

Indexes Cross-Referencing Your State Standards with the Common Core appear at the front of the book.

This column shows where to find instructional guidance for that standard or topic.

Indexes Cross-Referencing Your State Standards

Alaska Standards for Mathematics
Arizona's College and Career Ready Standards
Arkansas Mathematics Standards
Mathematics Florida Standards (MAFS)

Alaska	Arizona	Arkansas	Florida	Common Core Domain	Common Core Standard	Page(s)
Kindergarten						
K.CC.1	K.CC.A.1	K.CC.A.1	MAFS.K.CC.1.1	Counting and Cardinality	K.CC.A.1	5
K.CC.2	K.CC.A.2	K.CC.A.2	MAFS.K.CC.1.2		K.CC.A.2	6
K.CC.3	K.CC.A.3	K.CC.A.3	MAFS.K.CC.1.3		K.CC.A.3	7
K.CC.4	K.CC.B.4	K.CC.B.4	MAFS.K.CC.2.4		K.CC.B.4	9
K.CC.5	K.CC.B.5	K.CC.B.5	MAFS.K.CC.2.5		K.CC.B.5	10
K.CC.6	K.CC.C.6	K.CC.C.6	MAFS.K.CC.3.6		K.CC.C.6	12
K.CC.7	K.CC.C.7	K.CC.C.7	MAFS.K.CC.3.7		K.CC.C.7	14
K.OA.1	K.OA.A.1	K.OA.A.1	MAFS.K.OA.1.1	Operations and Algebraic Thinking	K.OA.A.1	26
K.OA.2	K.OA.A.2	K.OA.A.2	MAFS.K.OA.1.a/1.2		K.OA.A.2	27
K.OA.3	K.OA.A.3	K.OA.A.3			K.OA.A.3	28
K.OA.4	K.OA.A.4	K.OA.A.4	MAFS.K.OA.1.4		K.OA.A.4	29
K.OA.5	K.OA.A.5	K.OA.A.5	MAFS.K.OA.1.5		K.OA.A.5	30
K.NBT.1	K.NBT.A.1	K.NBT.A.1	MAFS.K.NBT.1.1	Number and Operations in Base Ten	K.NBT.A.1	78
2.MD.9	2.MD.D.9	2.MD.D.9	MAFS.2.MD.4.9		2.MD.D.9	154
2.MD.10	2.MD.D.10	2.MD.D.10	MAFS.2.MD.4.10		2.MD.D.10	155
2.G.1	2.G.A.1	2.G.A.1	MAFS.2.G.1.1	Geometry	2.G.A.1	186
2.G.2	2.G.A.2	2.G.A.2	MAFS.2.G.1.2		2.G.A.2	187
2.G.3	2.G.A.3	2.G.A.3/2.G.A.4	MAFS.2.G.1.3		2.G.A.3	188

Uncorrelated or Differently Correlated Standard

Alaska: K.OA.6; K.MD4; K.MD.5 = 1.MD.B.3(CC); K.MD.6 = 2.MD.C.8(CC); 1.CC.1; 1.CC.2; 1.CC.3; 1.CC.4; 1.CC.6; 1.OA.9; 1.MD.4; 1.MD.5 = 2.MD.C.8(CC); 1.MD.6 = 2.MD.C.8(CC); 2.OA.5

Arkansas: K.CC.C.8; K.MD.C.4; K.MD.C.5 (Intro to 1.MD.B.3(CC)); K.MD.C.6 (Intro to 1.MD.B.4/5(CC)); 1.MD.B.4 = 2.MD.C.8(CC); 1.MD.B.5 = 2.MD.C.8(CC)

Florida: MAFS.K.MD.1.a = 1.MD.A.2(CC); MAFS.1.MD.1.a = 2.MD.A.1(CC); MAFS.1.MD.2.a; MAFS.2.OA.1.a

n/a = not present in or directly correlated to the Common Core

State-specific standards are organized by grade for easy reference.

Where a state has standards that are not present in CCSS-M, they are noted here.

The correlating Common Core Domain and Standard are listed next to each state's standards.

Some states' standards are less directly correlated to Common Core than others. In those cases, you can see a more dynamic cross-referencing and see where mathematical content is described a bit differently, shifts up or down a grade, or is not present in this book.

Mathematics Standards of Learning for Virginia Public Schools

Virginia Strand	Virginia Standard	Common Core Standard	Page(s)
Kindergarten			
Number and Number Sense	K.1a	K.CC.B.5	10
	K.1b	K.CC.A.3	7
	K.2a	K.CC.C.6	12
	K.2b	n/a	n/a
	K.3a	K.CC.A.1	5
	K.3b	n/a	n/a
	K.3c	n/a	n/a
	K.3d	K.CC.A.1	5
	K.4a	K.OA.A.3	28
	K.4b	K.OA.A.3	28
	K.5	1.G.A.3	182
Computation and Estimation	K.6	K.OA.A.2	27
Measurement and Geometry	K.7	2.MD.C.8	152
	K.8	n/a	n/a
	K.9	K.MD.A.2	125
	K.10a	K.G.A.2	169
	K.10b	K.G.B.4	172
	K.10c	K.G.A.1/K.G.A.2	168, 169
Probability and Statistics	K.11a	1.MD.C.4	138
	K.11b	1.MD.C.4/2.MD.D.10	138, 155
Patterns, Functions, and Algebra	K.12	K.MD.B.3	127
	K.13	n/a	n/a
First Grade			
Number and Number Sense	1.1a	1.NBT.A.1	83
	1.1b	1.NBT.A.1	83
	1.1c	2.NBT.A.2	102
	1.1d	2.NBT.A.2	102
	1.2a	1.NBT.B.2	85
	1.2b	1.NBT.B.3	88
	1.2c	n/a	n/a
	1.3	n/a	n/a
	1.4a	n/a	n/a
	1.4b	1.G.A.3	182

"n/a" is used to show standards that are not present in or do not have a direct correlation to the Common Core.

Virginia Strand	Virginia Standard	Common Core Standard	Page(s)
First Grade			
	1.5a	n/a	n/a
	1.5b	n/a	n/a
Computation and Estimation	1.6	1.OA.A.1	36
	1.7a	K.OA.A.3	28
	1.7b	1.OA.C.6	47
Measurement and Geometry	1.8	2.MD.C.8	152
	1.9a	1.MD.B.3	135
	1.9b	n/a	n/a
	1.10	1.MD.A.2	133
	1.11a	1.G.A.1	180
	1.11b	K.G.A.2	169
Probability and Statistics	1.12a	1.MD.C.4	138
	1.12b	1.MD.C.4	138
Patterns, Functions, and Algebra	1.13	K.MD.B.3	127
	1.14	3.OA.D.9/4.OA.C.5	24 and 42 in the 3–5 book
	1.15	1.OA.D.7	49
Second Grade			
Number and Number Sense	2.1a	2.NBT.A.1/2.NBT.A.3	99, 103
	2.1b	1.NBT.C.5/2.NBT.B.8	92, 112
	2.1c	1.NBT.B.3/2.NBT.A.4	88, 104
	2.1d	3.NBT.A.1	66 in the 3–5 book
	2.2a	2.NBT.A.2	102
	2.2b	n/a	n/a
	2.2c	2.OA.C.3	65
	2.3a	n/a	n/a
	2.3b	n/a	n/a
	2.4a	2.G.A.3/3.NF.A.1/3.NF.A.2	188 in this book, 115 and 118 in the 3–5 book
	2.4b	3.G.A.2/3.NF.A.1/3.NF.A.2	234, 115, and 118 in the 3–5 book
	2.4c	3.NF.A.2	118 in the 3–5 book
Computation and Estimation	2.5a	1.OA.A.1/1.OA.B.4	36, 42
	2.5b	2.OA.B.2	63
	2.6a	n/a	n/a
	2.6b	2.OA.A.1	59

Callouts indicate where further information can be found in another grade-level version of *Your Mathematics Standards Companion*.

Operations and Algebraic Thinking

Domain Overview

KINDERGARTEN

Students build upon their understanding of counting to develop meaning for addition and subtraction through modeling and representing problem situations, using concrete objects and pictorial representations. This domain comprises the major work of kindergarten and will be developed across the entire school year. Table 1 in the Resource section provides a detailed chart of addition and subtraction situations.

GRADE 1

As first graders continue to develop fluency with addition and subtraction, problem solving provides an opportunity for them to make sense of these operations using various situations and contexts. First graders extend their work from kindergarten by representing additional situations for addition and subtraction (Table 1). They also develop more sophisticated strategies for addition by counting on rather than starting with 1, for subtraction by counting back from a total (sum), and by composing and decomposing addends.

Note that in the early grades the term *total* is used rather than *sum* when referring to the answer in addition or the starting number in subtraction. This is intentional in order to avoid any confusion between *sum* and *some*, words that sound the same but have very different meanings.

GRADE 2

As students demonstrate understanding, skill, and ability to apply addition and subtraction to all problem situations, the range of numbers with which they work increases to 100. Problem situations include simple two-step problems for students to model and explore. Students extend their expertise with mental mathematics strategies (Table 2) initially using concrete materials and later as they continue to practice and become fluent with addition and subtraction facts including all facts through sums of 20.

This domain is not taught in isolation from the Number and Base Ten domain. Students work across domains to develop a deep understanding of addition and subtraction focusing on the instructional shifts of developing conceptual understanding, building skill and fluency, and applying addition and subtraction in problem contexts.

SUGGESTED MATERIALS FOR THIS DOMAIN			
K	**1**	**2**	
✓	✓	✓	Objects for counting such as beans, linking cubes, two-color counter chips, coins
✓			Five frames (Reproducible 1)
✓	✓	✓	Ten frames (Reproducible 2)
	✓	✓	Double ten frames (Reproducible 3)
✓	✓	✓	Hundreds chart (Reproducible 4)
✓	✓	✓	Dot cards (Reproducible 5)
✓			Numeral cards (Reproducible 6)
	✓	✓	Number line to 20 (Reproducible 7)
	✓	✓	Open number line (Reproducible 8)
✓	✓	✓	Part-Part-Whole chart (Reproducible 9)
✓	✓	✓	Place value chart (Reproducible 10)
✓	✓	✓	Various Dice (1–6, 1–10)
✓	✓	✓	Various Spinners (1–4, 1–5, 1–6, 1–10)

Key Vocabulary:
Vocabulary included in the domain, noting the grade levels at which that term is used.

Domain: General mathematical topic for this group of standards as described in the Common Core (CCSS-M). Consult the index to find your state standard that correlates.

Cluster: Statements that summarize related standards.

KEY VOCABULARY

K	1	2	
✓	✓	✓	**add** to combine or join together *related words: add, and, plus, join, put together, (+)*
	✓	✓	*** associative property of addition** an extension of the commutative property, to change the order and group 2 addends to find convenient sums (such as 10) in order to make the addition easier. Note that students do not use parenthesis at this level. The focus is on looking for sums of 10. $4 + 8 + 2 = 4 + 10 = 14$ or $6 + 8 + 4 = 6 + 4 + 8 = 18$
	✓	✓	*** commutative property of addition** reversing the order of the addends does not change the total (sum) $8 + 5 = 13$ and $5 + 8 = 13$; therefore, $8 + 5 = 5 + 8$
✓	✓	✓	**compare** to look for similarities or differences among numbers
	✓	✓	**compose** put a number together using other numbers $1 + 9$, $2 + 8$, $3 + 7$, $4 + 6$, $5 + 5$, $1 + 2 + 3 + 4$ are ways to compose 10
	✓	✓	**decompose** separate a number into parts using other numbers 8 can be decomposed into $4 + 4$, $3 + 5$, $2 + 2 + 2 + 2$
✓	✓	✓	**difference** the amount by which one number is greater or less than another number. The difference can be found by subtracting, comparing, or finding a missing addend.
✓	✓	✓	**equal (=)** same as in value or size
	✓	✓	**equation** a mathematical sentence in which one part is the same as, or equal to, the other part

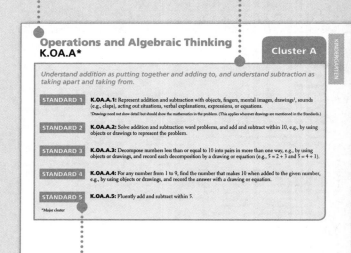

Operations and Algebraic Thinking
K.OA.A*

Cluster A

KINDERGARTEN

Understand addition as putting together and adding to, and understand subtraction as taking apart and taking from.

STANDARD 1   **K.OA.A.1:** Represent addition and subtraction with objects, fingers, mental images, drawings[1], sounds (e.g., claps), acting out situations, verbal explanations, expressions, or equations.
[1]Drawings need not show detail but should show the mathematics in the problem. (This applies wherever drawings are mentioned in the Standards.)

STANDARD 2   **K.OA.A.2:** Solve addition and subtraction word problems, and add and subtract within 10, e.g., by using objects or drawings to represent the problem.

STANDARD 3   **K.OA.A.3:** Decompose numbers less than or equal to 10 into pairs in more than one way, e.g., by using objects or drawings, and record each decomposition by a drawing or equation (e.g., $5 = 2 + 3$ and $5 = 4 + 1$).

STANDARD 4   **K.OA.A.4:** For any number from 1 to 9, find the number that makes 10 when added to the given number, e.g., by using objects or drawings, and record the answer with a drawing or equation.

STANDARD 5   **K.OA.A.5:** Fluently add and subtract within 5.

*Major cluster

Standards:
Mathematical statements that define what students should understand and be able to do.

Each cluster begins with a brief description of the mathematics in that cluster.

K = Grade
OA = Domain
A = Cluster

Standard: The standard as written in the Common Core is followed by an explanation of the meaning of the mathematics in that standard and what it looks like in the classroom.

What the TEACHER does: An overview of actions the teacher might take in introducing and teaching the standard. This is not meant to be all-inclusive but rather to give you an idea of what classroom instruction might look like. We include illustrations of how to use materials to teach a concept when using models and representations called for in the standard.

Operations and Algebraic Thinking K.OA.A

Cluster A: Understand addition as putting together and adding to, and understand subtraction as taking apart and taking from.
Kindergarten Overview
Students begin to explore addition and subtraction through solving problems first using concrete objects and then using pictures, eventually becoming familiar with expression (3 + 5) and equation (3 + 5 = 8) notation. The vocabulary of addition and subtraction actions emphasizes addition as joining two sets or adding on to a set. Taking items from a set or taking apart a set are subtraction situations that students experience by modeling (Table 1). These conceptual understandings are the basis for relating addition and subtraction; they also provide early strategies that lead to fact fluency. Note that the word *total* is used in place of *sum* at this level to avoid confusion with its homonym, *some*.

Standards for Mathematical Practice
SFMP 1. Make sense of problems and persevere in solving them.
SFMP 2. Use quantitative reasoning.
SFMP 3. Construct viable arguments and critique the reasoning of others.
SFMP 4. Model with mathematics.

In kindergarten, students begin to explore the operations of addition and subtraction by using a variety of concrete materials to model specific problem situations. As students develop understanding of numbers and their meaning, they should develop the habit of asking themselves if their answer makes sense. Within the classroom lesson, students should have many opportunities to explain and justify their thinking to the teacher, to a partner, to a small group, or to the class. They also learn to listen to the explanations of classmates.

Related Content Standards
1.OA.B.3   1.OA.B.4   1.OA.B.8   1.NBT.C.4   1.NBT.C   2.OA.A.1   2.OA.A.2

STANDARD 1 (K.OA.A.1)

Represent addition and subtraction with objects, fingers, mental images, drawings¹, sounds (e.g., claps), acting out situations, verbal explanations, expressions, or equations.

¹ Drawings need not show details, but should show the mathematics in the problem. (This applies wherever drawings are mentioned in the Standards.)

Students develop an understanding of the meaning of addition and subtraction by modeling how they can put together (compose) or take apart (decompose) up to 10 objects in different ways. It is critical for students to have a variety of experiences with concrete materials, progress to drawing pictures to express their thinking, and finally see written addition and subtraction expressions and equations. The teacher may write equations if students are not ready to do this on their own.

What the TEACHER does:
- Give students tasks in which they compose and decompose numbers up to 5 using concrete materials and counting.

chips

○ ○ ○ ○ ○

linking cubes

five frame

- Pose questions that ask students to explain their work using pictures and words.
- Introduce addition and subtraction terminology as students are ready.
  ○ Addition: add, put together, join, combine, plus, total
  ○ Subtraction: take away, minus, subtract, take apart, separate, compare, difference
- Continue with similar tasks using numbers from 6 to 10.
- Introduce students to numerical representations by writing equations that represent student work.

What the STUDENTS do:
- Use concrete materials to model how numbers up to 5 are composed (put together).
- Describe their models using pictures, words, and numbers with emphasis on appropriate addition and subtraction terminology.
- Extend their work to numbers from 6 to 10.
- Match their models with equations and expressions provided by the teacher.

Addressing Student Misconceptions and Common Errors

If students do not have time to draw pictures before working with numerical expressions and equations, they may be more likely to use finger counting and rote memorization in working with addition and subtraction—especially when learning basic facts.

Notes

Related Content Standards: Provides a list of standards connected to this topic in other grade levels, as well as standards in this grade level related to this topic. Consider the related standards as described by your state as you plan your instruction for each cluster.

Standards for Mathematical Practice: This section gives examples of how you might incorporate some of the practices into your instruction on this topic.

What the STUDENTS do: Some examples of what students might be doing as they explore and begin to understand the standard. Again, this is not intended to be directive but rather to frame what student actions might look like.

Addressing Student Misconceptions and Common Errors: Each standard concludes with a description of student misconceptions and common errors and suggested actions to address those misconceptions.

Sample Planning Page: We have provided a complete sample planning page for one individual standard at the end of each grade level. It is not meant to be a final lesson plan, but rather to identify the areas you should consider while planning your lessons for the standards.

Defines the purpose of the lesson and shows how it connects to previous (and future) ideas.

Identifies the mathematical practices that might be emphasized in this lesson.

Planning Page: A planning template is provided at the end of each cluster. This template is provided for your use as you consider instructional actions around a particular standard. You might want to make copies of this page and use them for each standard within the cluster. This is not intended to be an all-inclusive lesson plan. Rather, it gives you a place to record your thoughts about teaching a mathematical topic as you read the standard.

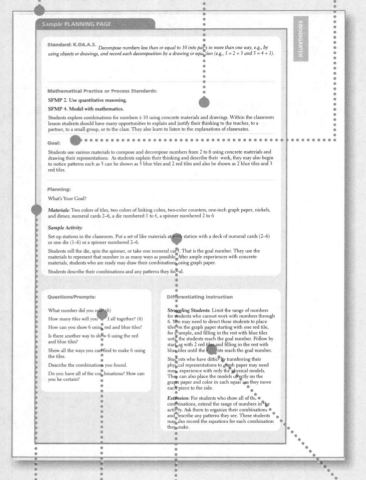

Sample PLANNING PAGE

Standard: K.OA.A.3. *Decompose numbers less than or equal to 10 into pairs in more than one way, e.g., by using objects or drawings, and record each decomposition by a drawing or equation (e.g., 5 = 2 + 3 and 5 = 4 + 1).*

Mathematical Practice or Process Standards:

SFMP 2. Use quantitative reasoning.
SFMP 4. Model with mathematics.

Students explore combinations for numbers ≤ 10 using concrete materials and drawings. Within the classroom lesson students should have many opportunities to explain and justify their thinking to the teacher, to a partner, to a small group, or to the class. They also learn to listen to the explanations of classmates.

Goal:

Students use various materials to compose and decompose numbers from 2 to 6 using concrete materials and drawing their representations. As students explain their thinking and describe their work, they may also begin to notice patterns such as 5 can be shown as 3 blue tiles and 2 red tiles and also shown as 2 blue tiles and 3 red tiles.

Planning:

What's Your Goal?

Materials: Two colors of tiles, two colors of linking cubes, two-color counters, one-inch graph paper, nickels, and dimes; numeral cards 2–6, a die numbered 1 to 6, a spinner numbered 2 to 6

Sample Activity:

Set up stations in the classroom. Put a set of like materials at each station with a deck of numeral cards (2–6) or one die (1–6) or a spinner numbered 2–6.

Students roll the die, spin the spinner, or take one numeral card. That is the goal number. They use the materials to represent that number in as many ways as possible. After ample experiences with concrete materials, students who are ready may draw their combinations using graph paper.

Students describe their combinations and any patterns they found.

Questions/Prompts:

What number did you roll? (6)
How many tiles will you build all together? (6)
How can you show 6 using red and blue tiles?
Is there another way to show 6 using the red and blue tiles?
Show all the ways you can find to make 6 using the tiles.
Describe the combinations you found.
Do you have all of the combinations? How can you be certain?

Differentiating Instruction

Struggling Students: Limit the range of numbers for students who cannot work with numbers through 6. You may need to direct these students to place tiles on the graph paper starting with one red tile, for example, and filling in the rest with blue tiles until the students reach the goal number. Follow by starting with 2 red tiles and filling in the rest with blue tiles until the students reach the goal number.

Students who have difficulty transferring their physical representations to graph paper may need more experience with only the physical models. They can also place the models directly on the graph paper and color in each square as they move each piece to the side.

Extension: For students who show all of the combinations, extend the range of numbers in the activity. Ask them to organize their combinations and describe any patterns they see. These students may also record the equations for each combination they make.

PLANNING PAGE

Standard:

Mathematical Practice or Process Standards:

Goal:

Planning:

Materials:

Sample Activity:

Questions/Prompts:

Differentiating Instruction:

Struggling Students:

Extension:

Lists the materials that will be used to teach this standard.

Includes directions for the task students will complete.

It is important to anticipate student thinking throughout the lesson. Think about the questions or prompts you might give to help build student understanding and encourage student thinking.

Provides an area where teachers can identify how they might adjust the lesson to (1) address the needs of students who are struggling and (2) extend the lesson for students who demonstrate understanding of the mathematics.

Resources: In the resources section you will find an overview of the Standards for Mathematical Practice and what each standard means for students, the effective teaching practices from NCTM's *Principles to Actions*, and an overview of each practice for teachers to consider and implement; Table 1 from the CCSS-M which provides problem-solving situations, Table 2 which provides strategic competencies for students, and Table 3 which scaffolds and includes modeling examples for the operations of addition and subtraction across Grades K–2; and reproducibles for some of the materials recommended for each grade level.

Various problem situations for addition and subtraction with suggested grade levels.

An example of a problem that exemplifies the situation.

Equation(s) that represent the situation.

SITUATION	PROBLEM	PHYSICAL MODEL	PART PART WHOLE	EQUATION(S)
Add to—result unknown Grades K, 1, 2	Frank had 5 pennies. Mark gave him 4 more. How many pennies does Frank have?	1¢ 1¢ 1¢ 1¢ 1¢ 1¢ 1¢ 1¢ 1¢	Whole [ ] Part Part 1¢ 1¢ 1¢ 1¢ 1¢ 1¢ 1¢ 1¢ 1¢	**5 + 4 = □**
Take from—result unknown Grades K, 1, 2	Frank had 9 pennies. He spent 5 pennies on a jawbreaker. How many pennies does he have left?	1¢ 1¢ 1¢ 1¢ 1¢ 1¢ 1¢ 1¢ 1¢	Whole 1¢ 1¢ 1¢ 1¢ 1¢ 1¢ 1¢ 1¢ 1¢ Part Part [ ] 1¢ 1¢ 1¢ 1¢ 1¢	**9 − 5 = □**
Put together take apart—total unknown Grades K, 1, 2	Anna has 8 pennies and 3 nickels. How many coins does she have?	1¢ 1¢ 1¢ 1¢ 1¢ 1¢ 1¢ 1¢ 5¢ 5¢ 5¢	Whole [ ] Part Part 1¢ 1¢ 1¢ 1¢ 1¢ 5¢ 5¢ 5¢ 1¢ 1¢ 1¢	**8 + 3 = □**
Put together take apart—addends unknown Grades K, 1, 2	Anna has 11 coins. Some are pennies and some are nickels. How many pennies and how many nickels could Anna have?	**Show table with different combinations of pennies and nickels that will total 11 (use illustrations of coins)** **Pennies** **Nickels** 1. 1¢ 10. 5¢ 5¢ 5¢ 5¢ 5¢ 5¢ 5¢ 5¢ 5¢ 5¢ 2. 1¢ 1¢ 9. 5¢ 5¢ 5¢ 5¢ 5¢ 5¢ 5¢ 5¢ 5¢ 3. 1¢ 1¢ 1¢ 8. 5¢ 5¢ 5¢ 5¢ 5¢ 5¢ 5¢ 5¢ 4. 1¢ 1¢ 1¢ 1¢ 7. 5¢ 5¢ 5¢ 5¢ 5¢ 5¢ 5¢ 5. 1¢ 1¢ 1¢ 1¢ 1¢ 6. 5¢ 5¢ 5¢ 5¢ 5¢ 5¢	Whole 1¢ 1¢ 1¢ 1¢ 1¢ 1¢ 5¢ 5¢ 5¢ 5¢ 5¢ Part Part [ ] [ ]	**1 + 10 = 11** **2 + 9 = 11** **3 + 8 = 11** **4 + 7 = 11** **5 + 6 = 11** **6 + 5 = 11** **7 + 4 = 11** **8 + 3 = 11** **9 + 2 = 11** **10 + 1 = 11**

A physical model that students might use to represent the situation.

An alternate model (part whole/bar model).

This table includes a scaffolded list of concepts and skills that students should develop in K–2.

A variety of reproducibles can also be downloaded from the companion website at **resources.corwin.com/ yourmathcompanionk-2** for student use.

Table 3 Scaffolding Addition and Subtraction

As you plan examples for addition, keep in mind how to scaffold examples with regrouping. Some students may need this broken into smaller concepts while others may be able to make generalizations. What is particularly important is to give students the opportunity to solve each type of example by making sense of the numbers and using various representations.

Grade Level	Description	Example
K 1 2	1 digit + 1 digit	9 + 7
1	2 digit + 1 digit; no regrouping	23 + 6
1	Add 2 digit number + a multiple of 10	33 + 50
1	2 digit + 2 digit; no regrouping	33 + 25
1 2	2 digit + 1 digit with regrouping	35 + 7
1 2	2 digit + 2 digit regrouping	25 + 26
2	3 digit + 1 and 2 digit; no regrouping	372 + 7
2	3 digit plus 1 digit; regroup ones to tens	345 + 8
2	3 digit plus 2 digit; regroup ones to tens	356 + 38
2	3 digit plus 2 digit; regroup tens to hundreds	428 + 26
2	3 digit plus 2 digit; regroup ones to tens and tens to hundreds	567 + 48
2	3 digit + 3 digit; no regrouping	256 + 121
2	3 digit plus 3 digit; regroup ones to tens	234 + 126
2	3 digit plus 3 digit; regroup tens to hundreds	154 + 162
2	3 digit plus 3 digit; regroup ones to tens and tens to hundreds	274 + 247

As you plan examples for subtraction, keep in mind how to scaffold examples with regrouping. Some students may need this broken into smaller concepts while others may be able to make generalizations. What is particularly important is to give students the opportunity to solve each type of example by making sense of the numbers and using various representations.

Grade Level	Description	Example
K 1 2	Subtraction facts in two forms subtract missing addend	5 − 2 = 3 2 + ___ = 5
1	Subtracting multiples of 10 from multiples of 10	50 − 20 20 + ___ = 50
2	Subtract 1 digit from 2 digits; no regrouping	27 − 4 4 + ___ 27
2	Subtract 2 digits from 2 digits; no regrouping	78 − 45

Reproducible 4. Hundreds Chart

1	2	3	4	5	6	7	8	9	10
11	12	13	14	15	16	17	18	19	20
21	22	23	24	25	26	27	28	29	30
31	32	33	34	35	36	37	38	39	40
41	42	43	44	45	46	47	48	49	50
51	52	53	54	55	56	57	58	59	60
61	62	63	64	65	66	67	68	69	70
71	72	73	74	75	76	77	78	79	80
81	82	83	84	85	86	87	88	89	90
91	92	93	94	95	96	97	98	99	100

Your Mathematics Standards Companion, Grades K–2

Your Mathematics Standards Companion, Grades K–2

What They Mean and How to Teach Them

Linda M. Gojak

Ruth Harbin Miles

Series Creator: Jim Burke

Mathematics Series Creator: Linda M. Gojak

Name: _____

Department: _____

Learning Team: _____

A JOINT PUBLICATION

NATIONAL COUNCIL OF TEACHERS OF MATHEMATICS

FOR INFORMATION:

Corwin

A SAGE Company

2455 Teller Road

Thousand Oaks, California 91320

(800) 233-9936

www.corwin.com

SAGE Publications Ltd.

1 Oliver's Yard

55 City Road

London EC1Y 1SP

United Kingdom

SAGE Publications India Pvt. Ltd.

B 1/I 1 Mohan Cooperative Industrial Area

Mathura Road, New Delhi 110 044

India

SAGE Publications Asia-Pacific Pte. Ltd.

3 Church Street

#10-04 Samsung Hub

Singapore 049483

Series Creator: Jim Burke

Mathematics Series Creator: Linda M. Gojak

State Standards Indexer: Tom Muchlinski

Acquisitions Editor: Erin Null

Editorial Development Manager: Julie Nemer

Editorial Assistant: Nicole Shade

Production Editors: Olivia Weber-Stenis and
                    Melanie Birdsall

Copy Editors: Patricia Sutton and Deanna Noga

Typesetter: C&M Digitals (P) Ltd.

Proofreaders: Theresa Kay and Alison Syring

Cover and Interior Designer: Scott Van Atta

Marketing Manager: Margaret O'Connor

Printed in the United States of America

Library of Congress Cataloging-in-Publication Data

Names: Gojak, Linda. | Miles, Ruth Harbin. | Burke, Jim

Title: Your mathematics standards companion, grades K–2 : what they mean and how to teach them / Linda M. Gojak, Ruth Harbin Miles ; series creator, Jim Burke.

Description: Thousand Oaks : Corwin, [2018] | Includes bibliographical references.

Identifiers: LCCN 2017016210 | ISBN 9781506382234 (pbk. : alk. paper)

Subjects: LCSH: Mathematics—Study and teaching (Elementary)—Standards—United States.

Classification: LCC QA135.6 .G639 2018 | DDC 372.7049—dc23
LC record available at https://lccn.loc.gov/2017016210

This book is printed on acid-free paper.

17 18 19 20 21 10 9 8 7 6 5 4 3 2 1

Contents

Part 3. Number and Operations in Base Ten

Part 4. Measurement and Data

Reproducibles

For downloadable versions of the Indexes Cross-Referencing Your State Standards, Reproducibles, and a Planning Page Template, visit the companion website at
resources.corwin.com/yourmathcompanionk-2

Indexes Cross-Referencing Your State Standards

online resources — Available for download at **resources.corwin.com/yourmathcompanionk-2**

Alaska Standards for Mathematics

Arizona's College and Career Ready Standards

Arkansas Mathematics Standards

Mathematics Florida Standards (MAFS)

Alaska	Arizona	Arkansas	Florida	Common Core Domain	Common Core Standard	Page(s)
Kindergarten						
K.CC.1	K.CC.A.1	K.CC.A.1	MAFS.K.CC.1.1	Counting and Cardinality	K.CC.A.1	5
K.CC.2	K.CC.A.2	K.CC.A.2	MAFS.K.CC.1.2		K.CC.A.2	6
K.CC.3	K.CC.A.3	K.CC.A.3	MAFS.K.CC.1.3		K.CC.A.3	7
K.CC.4	K.CC.B.4	K.CC.B.4	MAFS.K.CC.2.4		K.CC.B.4	9
K.CC.5	K.CC.B.5	K.CC.B.5	MAFS.K.CC.2.5		K.CC.B.5	10
K.CC.6	K.CC.C.6	K.CC.C.6	MAFS.K.CC.3.6		K.CC.C.6	12
K.CC.7	K.CC.C.7	K.CC.C.7	MAFS.K.CC.3.7		K.CC.C.7	14
K.OA.1	K.OA.A.1	K.OA.A.1	MAFS.K.OA.1.1	Operations and Algebraic Thinking	K.OA.A.1	26
K.OA.2	K.OA.A.2	K.OA.A.2	MAFS.K.OA.1.a/1.2		K.OA.A.2	27
K.OA.3	K.OA.A.3	K.OA.A.3	n/a		K.OA.A.3	28
K.OA.4	K.OA.A.4	K.OA.A.4	MAFS.K.OA.1.4		K.OA.A.4	29
K.OA.5	K.OA.A.5	K.OA.A.5	MAFS.K.OA.1.5		K.OA.A.5	30
K.NBT.1	K.NBT.A.1	K.NBT.A.1	MAFS.K.NBT.1.1	Number and Operations in Base Ten	K.NBT.A.1	78
K.MD.1	K.MD.A.1	K.MD.A.1	MAFS.K.MD.1.1	Measurement and Data	K.MD.A.1	124
K.MD.2	K.MD.A.2	K.MD.A.2	MAFS.K.MD.1.2		K.MD.A.2	125
K.MD.3	K.MD.B.3	K.MD.B.3	MAFS.K.MD.2.3		K.MD.B.3	127
K.G.1	K.G.A.1	K.G.A.1	MAFS.K.G.1.1	Geometry	K.G.A.1	168
K.G.2	K.G.A.2	K.G.A.2	MAFS.K.G.1.2		K.G.A.2	169
K.G.3	K.G.A.3	K.G.A.3	MAFS.K.G.1.3		K.G.A.3	170
K.G.4	K.G.B.4	K.G.B.4	MAFS.K.G.2.4		K.G.B.4	172
K.G.5	K.G.B.5	K.G.B.5	MAFS.K.G.2.5		K.G.B.5	173
K.G.6	K.G.B.6	K.G.B.6	MAFS.K.G.2.6		K.G.B.6	174

(Continued)

Alaska	Arizona	Arkansas	Florida	Common Core Domain	Common Core Standard	Page(s)
First Grade						
1.OA.1	1.OA.A.1	1.OA.A.1	MAFS.1.OA.1.1	Operations and Algebraic Thinking	1.OA.A.1	36
1.OA.2	1.OA.A.2	1.OA.A.2	MAFS.1.OA.1.2		1.OA.A.2	38
1.OA.3	1.OA.B.3	1.OA.B.3	MAFS.1.OA.2.3		1.OA.B.3	40
1.OA.4	1.OA.B.4	1.OA.B.4	MAFS.1.OA.2.4		1.OA.B.4	42
1.OA.5	1.OA.C.5	1.OA.C.5	MAFS.1.OA.3.5		1.OA.C.5	45
1.OA.6	1.OA.C.6	1.OA.C.6	MAFS.1.OA.3.6		1.OA.C.6	47
1.OA.7	1.OA.D.7	1.OA.D.7	MAFS.1.OA.4.7		1.OA.D.7	49
1.OA.8	1.OA.D.8	1.OA.D.8	MAFS.1.OA.4.8		1.OA.D.8	50
1.NBT.1	1.NBT.A.1	1.NBT.A.1	MAFS.1.NBT.1.1	Number and Operations in Base Ten	1.NBT.A.1	83
1.NBT.2	1.NBT.B.2	1.NBT.B.2	MAFS.1.NBT.2.2		1.NBT.B.2	85
1.NBT.3/1.CC.5	1.NBT.B.3	1.NBT.B.3	MAFS.1.NBT.2.3		1.NBT.B.3	88
1.NBT.4	1.NBT.C.4	1.NBT.C.4	MAFS.1.NBT.3.4		1.NBT.C.4	90
1.NBT.5	1.NBT.C.5	1.NBT.C.5	MAFS.1.NBT.3.5		1.NBT.C.5	92
1.NBT.6	1.NBT.C.6	1.NBT.C.6	MAFS.1.NBT.3.6		1.NBT.C.6	93
1.MD.1	1.MD.A.1	1.MD.A.1	MAFS.1.MD.1.1	Measurement and Data	1.MD.A.1	132
1.MD.2	1.MD.A.2	1.MD.A.2	n/a		1.MD.A.2	133
1.MD.3	1.MD.B.3	1.MD.B.3	MAFS.1.MD.2.3		1.MD.B.3	135
1.MD.7	1.MD.C.4	1.MD.C.6	MAFS.1.MD.3.4		1.MD.C.4	138
1.G.1	1.G.A.1	1.G.A.1	MAFS.1.G.1.1	Geometry	1.G.A.1	180
1.G.2	1.G.A.2	1.G.A.2	MAFS.1.G.1.2		1.G.A.2	181
1.G.3	1.G.A.3	1.G.A.3	MAFS.1.G.1.3		1.G.A.3	182
Second Grade						
2.OA.1	2.OA.A.1	2.OA.A.1	MAFS.2.OA.1.1	Operations and Algebraic Thinking	2.OA.A.1	59
2.OA.2	2.OA.B.2	2.OA.B.2	MAFS.2.OA.2.2		2.OA.B.2	63
2.OA.3	2.OA.C.3	2.OA.C.3	MAFS.2.OA.3.3		2.OA.C.3	65
2.OA.4	2.OA.C.4	2.OA.C.4	MAFS.2.OA.3.4		2.OA.C.4	66
2.NBT.1	2.NBT.A.1	2.NBT.A.1	MAFS.2.NBT.1.1	Number and Operations in Base Ten	2.NBT.A.1	99
2.NBT.2	2.NBT.A.2	2.NBT.A.2	MAFS.2.NBT.1.2		2.NBT.A.2	102
2.NBT.3	2.NBT.A.3	2.NBT.A.3	MAFS.2.NBT.1.3		2.NBT.A.3	103
2.NBT.4	2.NBT.A.4	2.NBT.A.4	MAFS.2.NBT.1.4		2.NBT.A.4	104
2.NBT.5	2.NBT.B.5	2.NBT.B.5	MAFS.2.NBT.2.5		2.NBT.B.5	106
2.NBT.6	2.NBT.B.6	2.NBT.B.6	MAFS.2.NBT.2.6		2.NBT.B.6	108

Alaska	Arizona	Arkansas	Florida	Common Core Domain	Common Core Standard	Page(s)
Second Grade						
2.NBT.7	2.NBT.B.7	2.NBT.B.7	MAFS.2.NBT.2.7		2.NBT.B.7	109
2.NBT.8	2.NBT.B.8	2.NBT.B.8	MAFS.2.NBT.2.8		2.NBT.B.8	112
2.NBT.9	2.NBT.B.9	2.NBT.B.9	MAFS.2.NBT.2.9		2.NBT.B.9	113
2.MD.1	2.MD.A.1	2.MD.A.1	MAFS.2.MD.1.1	Measurement and Data	2.MD.A.1	144
2.MD.2	2.MD.A.2	2.MD.A.2	MAFS.2.MD.1.2		2.MD.A.2	145
2.MD.3	2.MD.A.3	2.MD.A.3	MAFS.2.MD.1.3		2.MD.A.3	146
2.MD.4	2.MD.A.4	2.MD.A.4	MAFS.2.MD.1.4		2.MD.A.4	146
2.MD.5	2.MD.B.5	2.MD.B.5	MAFS.2.MD.2.5		2.MD.B.5	148
2.MD.6	2.MD.B.6	2.MD.B.6	MAFS.2.MD.2.6		2.MD.B.6	149
2.MD.7	2.MD.C.7	2.MD.C.7	MAFS.2.MD.3.7		2.MD.C.7	151
2.MD.8	2.MD.C.8	2.MD.C.8	MAFS.2.MD.3.8		2.MD.C.8	152
2.MD.9	2.MD.D.9	2.MD.D.9	MAFS.2.MD.4.9		2.MD.D.9	154
2.MD.10	2.MD.D.10	2.MD.D.10	MAFS.2.MD.4.10		2.MD.D.10	155
2.G.1	2.G.A.1	2.G.A.1	MAFS.2.G.1.1	Geometry	2.G.A.1	186
2.G.2	2.G.A.2	2.G.A.2	MAFS.2.G.1.2		2.G.A.2	187
2.G.3	2.G.A.3	2.G.A.3/2.G.A.4	MAFS.2.G.1.3		2.G.A.3	188

Uncorrelated or Differently Correlated Standard

Alaska: K.OA.6; K.MD4; K.MD.5 = 1.MD.B.3(CC); K.MD.6 = 2.MD.C.8(CC); 1.CC.1; 1.CC.2; 1.CC.3; 1.CC.4; 1.CC.6; 1.OA.9; 1.MD.4; 1.MD.5 = 2.MD.C.8(CC); 1.MD.6 = 2.MD.C.8(CC); 2.OA.5

Arkansas: K.CC.C.8; K.MD.C.4; K.MD.C.5 (Intro to 1.MD.B.3(CC)); K.MD.C.6 (Intro to 1.MD.B.4/5(CC)); 1.MD.B.4 = 2.MD.C.8(CC); 1.MD.B.5 = 2.MD.C.8(CC)

Florida: MAFS.K.MD.1.a = 1.MD.A.2(CC); MAFS.1.MD.1.a = 2.MD.A.1(CC); MAFS.1.MD.2.a; MAFS.2.OA.1.a

n/a = not present in or directly correlated to the Common Core

Georgia Standards of Excellence — Mathematics
Iowa Core Mathematics
Kansas College and Career Readiness Standards for Mathematics
Louisiana Student Standards for Mathematics

Georgia	Iowa	Kansas	Louisiana	Common Core Domain	Common Core Standard	Page(s)
Kindergarten						
MGSEK.CC.1	K.CC.A.1	K.CC.1	K.CC.A.1	Counting and Cardinality	K.CC.A.1	5
MGSEK.CC.2	K.CC.A.2	K.CC.2	K.CC.A.2		K.CC.A.2	6
MGSEK.CC.3	K.CC.A.3	K.CC.3	K.CC.A.3		K.CC.A.3	7
MGSEK.CC.4	K.CC.B.4	K.CC.4	K.CC.B.4		K.CC.B.4	9
MGSEK.CC.5	K.CC.B.5	K.CC.5	K.CC.B.5		K.CC.B.5	10
MGSEK.CC.6	K.CC.C.6	K.CC.6	K.CC.C.6		K.CC.C.6	12
MGSEK.CC.7	K.CC.C.7	K.CC.7	K.CC.C.7		K.CC.C.7	14
MGSEK.OA.1	K.OA.A.1	K.OA.1	K.OA.A.1	Operations and Algebraic Thinking	K.OA.A.1	26
MGSEK.OA.2	K.OA.A.2	K.OA.2	K.OA.A.2		K.OA.A.2	27
MGSEK.OA.3	K.OA.A.3	K.OA.3	K.OA.A.3		K.OA.A.3	28
MGSEK.OA.4	K.OA.A.4	K.OA.4	K.OA.A.4		K.OA.A.4	29
MGSEK.OA.5	K.OA.A.5	K.OA.5	K.OA.A.5		K.OA.A.5	30
MGSEK.NBT.1	K.NBT.A.1	K.NBT.1	K.NBT.A.1	Number and Operations in Base Ten	K.NBT.A.1	78
MGSEK.MD.1	K.MD.A.1	K.MD.1	K.MD.A.1	Measurement and Data	K.MD.A.1	124
MGSEK.MD.2	K.MD.A.2	K.MD.2	K.MD.A.2		K.MD.A.2	125
MGSEK.MD.3	K.MD.B.3	K.MD.3	K.MD.B.3		K.MD.B.3	127
MGSEK.G.1	K.G.A.1	K.G.1	K.G.A.1	Geometry	K.G.A.1	168
MGSEK.G.2	K.G.A.2	K.G.2	K.G.A.2		K.G.A.2	169
MGSEK.G.3	K.G.A.3	K.G.3	K.G.A.3		K.G.A.3	170
MGSEK.G.4	K.G.B.4	K.G.4	K.G.B.4		K.G.B.4	172
MGSEK.G.5	K.G.B.5	K.G.5	K.G.B.5		K.G.B.5	173
MGSEK.G.6	K.G.B.6	K.G.6	K.G.B.6		K.G.B.6	174
First Grade						
MGSE1.OA.1	1.OA.A.1	1.OA.1	1.OA.A.1	Operations and Algebraic Thinking	1.OA.A.1	36
MGSE1.OA.2	1.OA.A.2	1.OA.2	1.OA.A.2		1.OA.A.2	38
MGSE1.OA.3	1.OA.B.3	1.OA.3	1.OA.B.3		1.OA.B.3	40
MGSE1.OA.4	1.OA.B.4	1.OA.4	1.OA.B.4		1.OA.B.4	42
MGSE1.OA.5	1.OA.C.5	1.OA.5	1.OA.C.5		1.OA.C.5	45
MGSE1.OA.6	1.OA.C.6	1.OA.6	1.OA.C.6		1.OA.C.6	47

Georgia	Iowa	Kansas	Louisiana	Common Core Domain	Common Core Standard	Page(s)
First Grade						
MGSE1.OA.7	1.OA.D.7	1.OA.7	1.OA.D.7		1.OA.D.7	49
MGSE1.OA.8	1.OA.D.8	1.OA.8	1.OA.D.8		1.OA.D.8	50
MGSE1.NBT.1	1.NBT.A.1	1.NBT.1	1.NBT.A.1	Number and Operations in Base Ten	1.NBT.A.1	83
MGSE1.NBT.2	1.NBT.B.2	1.NBT.2	1.NBT.B.2		1.NBT.B.2	85
MGSE1.NBT.3	1.NBT.B.3	1.NBT.3	1.NBT.B.3		1.NBT.B.3	88
MGSE1.NBT.4	1.NBT.C.4	1.NBT.4	1.NBT.C.4		1.NBT.C.4	90
MGSE1.NBT.5	1.NBT.C.5	1.NBT.5	1.NBT.C.5		1.NBT.C.5	92
MGSE1.NBT.6	1.NBT.C.6	1.NBT.6	1.NBT.C.6		1.NBT.C.6	93
MGSE1.MD.1	1.MD.A.1	1.MD.1	1.MD.A.1	Measurement and Data	1.MD.A.1	132
MGSE1.MD.2	1.MD.A.2	1.MD.2	1.MD.A.2		1.MD.A.2	133
MGSE1.MD.3	1.MD.B.3	1.MD.3	1.MD.B.3		1.MD.B.3	135
MGSE1.MD.4	1.MD.C.4	1.MD.4	1.MD.C.4		1.MD.C.4	138
MGSE1.G.1	1.G.A.1	1.G.1	1.G.A.1	Geometry	1.G.A.1	180
MGSE1.G.2	1.G.A.2	1.G.2	1.G.A.2		1.G.A.2	181
MGSE1.G.3	1.G.A.3	1.G.3	1.G.A.3		1.G.A.3	182
Second Grade						
MGSE2.OA.1	2.OA.A.1	2.OA.1	2.OA.A.1	Operations and Algebraic Thinking	2.OA.A.1	59
MGSE2.OA.2	2.OA.B.2	2.OA.2	2.OA.B.2		2.OA.B.2	63
MGSE2.OA.3	2.OA.C.3	2.OA.3	2.OA.C.3		2.OA.C.3	65
MGSE2.OA.4	2.OA.C.4	2.OA.4	2.OA.C.4		2.OA.C.4	66
MGSE2.NBT.1	2.NBT.A.1	2.NBT.1	2.NBT.A.1	Number and Operations in Base Ten	2.NBT.A.1	99
MGSE2.NBT.2	2.NBT.A.2	2.NBT.2	2.NBT.A.2		2.NBT.A.2	102
MGSE2.NBT.3	2.NBT.A.3	2.NBT.3	2.NBT.A.3		2.NBT.A.3	103
MGSE2.NBT.4	2.NBT.A.4	2.NBT.4	2.NBT.A.4		2.NBT.A.4	104
MGSE2.NBT.5	2.NBT.B.5	2.NBT.5	2.NBT.B.5		2.NBT.B.5	106
MGSE2.NBT.6	2.NBT.B.6	2.NBT.6	2.NBT.B.6		2.NBT.B.6	108
MGSE2.NBT.7	2.NBT.B.7	2.NBT.7	2.NBT.B.7		2.NBT.B.7	109
MGSE2.NBT.8	2.NBT.B.8	2.NBT.8	2.NBT.B.8		2.NBT.B.8	112
MGSE2.NBT.9	2.NBT.B.9	2.NBT.9	2.NBT.B.9		2.NBT.B.9	113
MGSE2.MD.1	2.MD.A.1	2.MD.1	2.MD.A.1	Measurement and Data	2.MD.A.1	144
MGSE2.MD.2	2.MD.A.2	2.MD.2	2.MD.A.2		2.MD.A.2	145
MGSE2.MD.3	2.MD.A.3	2.MD.3	2.MD.A.3		2.MD.A.3	146
MGSE2.MD.4	2.MD.A.4	2.MD.4	2.MD.A.4		2.MD.A.4	146
MGSE2.MD.5	2.MD.B.5	2.MD.5	2.MD.B.5		2.MD.B.5	148

(Continued)

Georgia	Iowa	Kansas	Louisiana	Common Core Domain	Common Core Standard	Page(s)
Second Grade						
MGSE2.MD.6	2.MD.B.6	2.MD.6	2.MD.B.6		2.MD.B.6	149
MGSE2.MD.7	2.MD.C.7	2.MD.7	2.MD.C.7		2.MD.C.7	151
MGSE2.MD.8	2.MD.C.8	2.MD.8	2.MD.C.8		2.MD.C.8	152
MGSE2.MD.9	2.MD.D.9	2.MD.9	2.MD.D.9		2.MD.D.9	154
MGSE2.MD.10	2.MD.D.10	2.MD.10	2.MD.D.10		2.MD.D.10	155
MGSE2.G.1	2.G.A.1	2.G.1	2.G.A.1	Geometry	2.G.A.1	186
MGSE2.G.2	2.G.A.2	2.G.2	2.G.A.2		2.G.A.2	187
MGSE2.G.3	2.G.A.3	2.G.3	2.G.A.3		2.G.A.3	188

Uncorrelated or Differently Correlated Standard

Georgia: MGSE1.NBT.7

Louisiana: K.MD.C.4 (see 2.MD.C.8(CC)); 1.MD.D.5 (see 2.MD.C.8(CC))

Maryland's College and Career Ready Standards — Mathematics
Mississippi College and Career Readiness Standards for Mathematics
New Jersey Student Learning Standards for Mathematics
North Carolina Mathematics Standard Course of Study

Maryland	Mississippi	New Jersey	North Carolina	Common Core Domain	Common Core Standard	Page(s)
Kindergarten						
K.CC.A.1	K.CC.1	K.CC.A.1	K.CC.1	Counting and Cardinality	K.CC.A.1	5
K.CC.A.2	K.CC.2	K.CC.A.2	K.CC.2		K.CC.A.2	6
K.CC.A.3	K.CC.3	K.CC.A.3	K.CC.3		K.CC.A.3	7
K.CC.B.4a-c	K.CC.4	K.CC.B.4	K.CC.4		K.CC.B.4	9
K.CC.B.5	K.CC.5	K.CC.B.5	K.CC.5		K.CC.B.5	10
K.CC.C.6	K.CC.6	K.CC.C.6	K.CC.6		K.CC.C.6	12
K.CC.C.7	K.CC.7	K.CC.C.7	K.CC.7		K.CC.C.7	14
K.OA.A.1	K.OA.1	K.OA.A.1	K.OA.1	Operations and Algebraic Thinking	K.OA.A.1	26
K.OA.A.2	K.OA.2	K.OA.A.2	K.OA.2		K.OA.A.2	27
K.OA.A.3	K.OA.3	K.OA.A.3	K.OA.3		K.OA.A.3	28
K.OA.A.4	K.OA.4	K.OA.A.4	K.OA.4		K.OA.A.4	29
K.OA.A.5	K.OA.5	K.OA.A.5	K.OA.5		K.OA.A.5	30
K.NBT.A.1	K.NBT.1	K.NBT.A.1	K.NBT.1	Number and Operations in Base Ten	K.NBT.A.1	78
K.MD.A.1	K.MD.1	K.MD.A.1	K.MD.1	Measurement and Data	K.MD.A.1	124
K.MD.A.2	K.MD.2	K.MD.A.2	K.MD.2		K.MD.A.2	125
K.MD.B.3	K.MD.3	K.MD.B.3	K.MD.3		K.MD.B.3	127
K.G.A.1	K.G.1	K.G.A.1	K.G.1	Geometry	K.G.A.1	168
K.G.A.2	K.G.2	K.G.A.2	K.G.2		K.G.A.2	169
K.G.A.3	K.G.3	K.G.A.3	K.G.3		K.G.A.3	170
K.G.B.4	K.G.4	K.G.B.4	K.G.4		K.G.B.4	172
K.G.B.5	K.G.5	K.G.B.5	K.G.5		K.G.B.5	173
K.G.B.6	K.G.6	K.G.B.6	K.G.6		K.G.B.6	174
First Grade						
1.OA.A.1	1.OA.1	1.OA.A.1	1.OA.1	Operations and Algebraic Thinking	1.OA.A.1	36
1.OA.A.2	1.OA.2	1.OA.A.2	1.OA.2		1.OA.A.2	38
1.OA.B.3	1.OA.3	1.OA.B.3	1.OA.3		1.OA.B.3	40
1.OA.B.4	1.OA.4	1.OA.B.4	1.OA.4		1.OA.B.4	42
1.OA.C.5	1.OA.5	1.OA.C.5	1.OA.5		1.OA.C.5	45
1.OA.C.6	1.OA.6	1.OA.C.6	1.OA.6		1.OA.C.6	47
1.OA.D.7	1.OA.7	1.OA.D.7	1.OA.7		1.OA.D.7	49
1.OA.D.8	1.OA.8	1.OA.D.8	1.OA.8		1.OA.D.8	50
1.NBT.A.1	1.NBT.1	1.NBT.A.1	1.NBT.1	Number and Operations in Base Ten	1.NBT.A.1	83
1.NBT.B.2a-c	1.NBT.2	1.NBT.B.2	1.NBT.2		1.NBT.B.2	85

(Continued)

Maryland	Mississippi	New Jersey	North Carolina	Common Core Domain	Common Core Standard	Page(s)
First Grade						
1.NBT.B.3	1.NBT.3	1.NBT.B.3	1.NBT.3		1.NBT.B.3	88
1.NBT.C.4	1.NBT.4	1.NBT.C.4	1.NBT.4		1.NBT.C.4	90
1.NBT.C.5	1.NBT.5	1.NBT.C.5	1.NBT.5		1.NBT.C.5	92
1.NBT.C.6	1.NBT.6	1.NBT.C.6	1.NBT.6		1.NBT.C.6	93
1.MD.A.1	1.MD.1	1.MD.A.1	1.MD.1	Measurement and Data	1.MD.A.1	132
1.MD.A.2	1.MD.2	1.MD.A.2	1.MD.2		1.MD.A.2	133
1.MD.B.3	1.MD.3a	1.MD.B.3	1.MD.3a		1.MD.B.3	135
1.MD.C.4	1.MD.4	1.MD.C.4	1.MD.4		1.MD.C.4	138
1.G.A.1	1.G.1	1.G.A.1	1.G.1	Geometry	1.G.A.1	180
1.G.A.2	1.G.2	1.G.A.2	1.G.2		1.G.A.2	181
1.G.A.3	1.G.3	1.G.A.3	1.G.3		1.G.A.3	182
Second Grade						
2.OA.A.1	2.OA.1	2.OA.A.1	2.OA.1	Operations and Algebraic Thinking	2.OA.A.1	59
2.OA.B.2	2.OA.2	2.OA.B.2	2.OA.2		2.OA.B.2	63
2.OA.C.3	2.OA.3	2.OA.C.3	2.OA.3		2.OA.C.3	65
2.OA.C.4	2.OA.4	2.OA.C.4	2.OA.4		2.OA.C.4	66
2.NBT.A.1a-b	2.NBT.1	2.NBT.A.1	2.NBT.1	Number and Operations in Base Ten	2.NBT.A.1	99
2.NBT.A.2	2.NBT.2	2.NBT.A.2	2.NBT.2		2.NBT.A.2	102
2.NBT.A.3	2.NBT.3	2.NBT.A.3	2.NBT.3		2.NBT.A.3	103
2.NBT.A.4	2.NBT.4	2.NBT.A.4	2.NBT.4		2.NBT.A.4	104
2.NBT.B.5	2.NBT.5	2.NBT.B.5	2.NBT.5		2.NBT.B.5	106
2.NBT.B.6	2.NBT.6	2.NBT.B.6	2.NBT.6		2.NBT.B.6	108
2.NBT.B.7	2.NBT.7	2.NBT.B.7	2.NBT.7		2.NBT.B.7	109
2.NBT.B.8	2.NBT.8	2.NBT.B.8	2.NBT.8		2.NBT.B.8	112
2.NBT.B.9	2.NBT.9	2.NBT.B.9	2.NBT.9		2.NBT.B.9	113
2.MD.A.1	2.MD.1	2.MD.A.1	2.MD.1	Measurement and Data	2.MD.A.1	144
2.MD.A.2	2.MD.2	2.MD.A.2	2.MD.2		2.MD.A.2	145
2.MD.A.3	2.MD.3	2.MD.A.3	2.MD.3		2.MD.A.3	146
2.MD.A.4	2.MD.4	2.MD.A.4	2.MD.4		2.MD.A.4	146
2.MD.B.5	2.MD.5	2.MD.B.5	2.MD.5		2.MD.B.5	148
2.MD.B.6	2.MD.6	2.MD.B.6	2.MD.6		2.MD.B.6	149
2.MD.C.7	2.MD.7	2.MD.C.7	2.MD.7		2.MD.C.7	151
2.MD.C.8	2.MD.8a	2.MD.C.8	2.MD.8a		2.MD.C.8	152
2.MD.D.9	2.MD.9	2.MD.D.9	2.MD.9		2.MD.D.9	154
2.MD.D.10	2.MD.10	2.MD.D.10	2.MD.10		2.MD.D.10	155
2.G.A.1	2.G.1	2.G.A.1	2.G.1	Geometry	2.G.A.1	186
2.G.A.2	2.G.2	2.G.A.2	2.G.2		2.G.A.2	187
2.G.A.3	2.G.3	2.G.A.3	2.G.3		2.G.A.3	188

Uncorrelated or Differently Correlated Standard

Mississippi: 1.MD.3b; 1.MD.5a–d (see 2.MD.C.8(CC)); 2.MD.8b

South Carolina College and Career Ready Standards for Mathematics
Tennessee's State Mathematics Standards
Utah Core State Standards for Mathematics
Next Generation (NxG) West Virginia Content Standards and Objectives for Mathematics

South Carolina	Tennessee	Utah	West Virginia	Common Core Domain	Common Core Standard	Page(s)
Kindergarten						
K.NS.1	CC 1	K.CC.1	M.K.CC.1	Counting and Cardinality	K.CC.A.1	5
K.NS.2	CC 2	K.CC.2	M.K.CC.2		K.CC.A.2	6
K.NS.3	CC 3	K.CC.3	M.K.CC.3		K.CC.A.3	7
K.NS.4	CC 4	K.CC.4	M.K.CC.4		K.CC.B.4	9
K.NS.5	CC 5	K.CC.5	M.K.CC.5		K.CC.B.5	10
K.NS.7	CC 6	K.CC.6	M.K.CC.6		K.CC.C.6	12
K.NS.8	CC 7	K.CC.7	M.K.CC.7		K.CC.C.7	14
K.ATO.1	OAT 1	K.OA.1	M.K.OA.1	Operations and Algebraic Thinking	K.OA.A.1	26
K.ATO.2	OAT 2	K.OA.2	M.K.OA.2		K.OA.A.2	27
K.ATO.3	OAT 3	K.OA.3	M.K.OA.3		K.OA.A.3	28
K.ATO.4	OAT 4	K.OA.4	M.K.OA.4		K.OA.A.4	29
K.ATO.5	OAT 5	K.OA.5	M.K.OA.5		K.OA.A.5	30
K.NSBT.1	NOBT 1	K.NBT.1	M.K.NBT.1	Number and Operations in Base Ten	K.NBT.A.1	78
K.MDA.1	MD 1	K.MD.1	M.K.MD.1	Measurement and Data	K.MD.A.1	124
K.MDA.2	MD 2	K.MD.2	M.K.MD.2		K.MD.A.2	125
K.MDA.3	MD 3	K.MD.3	M.K.MD.3		K.MD.B.3	127
K.G.1	G 1	K.G.1	M.K.G.1	Geometry	K.G.A.1	168
K.G.2	G 2	K.G.2	M.K.G.2		K.G.A.2	169
K.G.3	G 3	K.G.3	M.K.G.3		K.G.A.3	170
K.G.4	G 4	K.G.4	M.K.G.4		K.G.B.4	172
K.G.5	G 5	K.G.5	M.K.G.5		K.G.B.5	173
	G 6	K.G.6	M.K.G.6		K.G.B.6	174
First Grade						
1.ATO.1	OAT 1	1.OA.1	M.1.OA.1	Operations and Algebraic Thinking	1.OA.A.1	36
1.ATO.2	OAT 2	1.OA.2	M.1.OA.2		1.OA.A.2	38
1.ATO.3	OAT 3	1.OA.3	M.1.OA.3		1.OA.B.3	40
1.ATO.4	OAT 4	1.OA.4	M.1.OA.4		1.OA.B.4	42
1.ATO.5	OAT 5	1.OA.5	M.1.OA.5		1.OA.C.5	45

(Continued)

South Carolina	Tennessee	Utah	West Virginia	Common Core Domain	Common Core Standard	Page(s)
First Grade						
1.ATO.6	OAT 6	1.OA.6	M.1.OA.6		1.OA.C.6	47
1.ATO.7	OAT 7	1.OA.7	M.1.OA.7		1.OA.D.7	49
1.ATO.8	OAT 8	1.OA.8	M.1.OA.8		1.OA.D.8	50
1.NSBT.1	NOBT 1	1.NBT.1	M.1.NBT.1	Number and Operations in Base Ten	1.NBT.A.1	83
1.NSBT.2	NOBT 2	1.NBT.2	M.1.NBT.2		1.NBT.B.2	85
1.NSBT.3	NOBT 3	1.NBT.3	M.1.NBT.3		1.NBT.B.3	88
1.NSBT.4	NOBT 4	1.NBT.4	M.1.NBT.4		1.NBT.C.4	90
1.NSBT.5	NOBT 5	1.NBT.5	M.1.NBT.5		1.NBT.C.5	92
1.NSBT.6	NOBT 6	1.NBT.6	M.1.NBT.6		1.NBT.C.6	93
1.MDA.1	MD 1	1.MD.1	M.1.MD.1	Measurement and Data	1.MD.A.1	132
1.MDA.2	MD 2	1.MD.2	M.1.MD.2		1.MD.A.2	133
1.MDA.3	MD 3	1.MD.3	M.1.MD.3		1.MD.B.3	135
1.MDA.4/ 1.MDA.5	MD 4	1.MD.4	M.1.MD.4		1.MD.C.4	138
1.G.1	G 1	1.G.1	M.1.G.1	Geometry	1.G.A.1	180
1.G.2	G 2	1.G.2	M.1.G.2		1.G.A.2	181
1.G.3	G 3	1.G.3	M.1.G.3		1.G.A.3	182
Second Grade						
2.AOT.1	OAT 1	2.OA.1	M.2.OA.1	Operations and Algebraic Thinking	2.OA.A.1	59
2.AOT.2	OAT 2	2.OA.2	M.2.OA.2		2.OA.B.2	63
2.AOT.3	OAT 3	2.OA.3	M.2.OA.3		2.OA.C.3	65
2.AOT.4	OAT 4	2.OA.4	M.2.OA.4		2.OA.C.4	66
2.NSBT.1	NOBT 1	2.NBT.1	M.2.NBT.1	Number and Operations in Base Ten	2.NBT.A.1	99
2.NSBT.2	NOBT 2	2.NBT.2	M.2.NBT.2		2.NBT.A.2	102
2.NSBT.3	NOBT 3	2.NBT.3	M.2.NBT.3		2.NBT.A.3	103
2.NSBT.4	NOBT 4	2.NBT.4	M.2.NBT.4		2.NBT.A.4	104
2.NSBT.5	NOBT 5	2.NBT.5	M.2.NBT.5		2.NBT.B.5	106
2.NSBT.6	NOBT 6	2.NBT.6	M.2.NBT.6		2.NBT.B.6	108
2.NSBT.7	NOBT 7	2.NBT.7	M.2.NBT.7		2.NBT.B.7	109
2.NSBT.8	NOBT 8	2.NBT.8	M.2.NBT.8		2.NBT.B.8	112
	NOBT 9	2.NBT.9	M.2.NBT.9		2.NBT.B.9	113
2.MDA.1	MD 1	2.MD.1	M.2.MD.1	Measurement and Data	2.MD.A.1	144
2.MDA.2	MD 2	2.MD.2	M.2.MD.2		2.MD.A.2	145
2.MDA.3	MD 3	2.MD.3	M.2.MD.3		2.MD.A.3	146
2.MDA.4	MD 4	2.MD.4	M.2.MD.4		2.MD.A.4	146

South Carolina	Tennessee	Utah	West Virginia	Common Core Domain	Common Core Standard	Page(s)
Second Grade						
	MD 5	2.MD.5	M.2.MD.5		2.MD.B.5	148
2.MDA.5	MD 6	2.MD.6	M.2.MD.6		2.MD.B.6	149
2.MDA.6	MD 7	2.MD.7	M.2.MD.7		2.MD.C.7	151
2.MDA.7	MD 8	2.MD.8	M.2.MD.8		2.MD.C.8	152
2.MDA.8	MD 9	2.MD.9	M.2.MD.9		2.MD.D.9	154
2.MDA.9/ 2.MDA.10	MD 10	2.MD.10	M.2.MD.10		2.MD.D.10	155
2.G.1	G 1	2.G.1	M.2.G.1	Geometry	2.G.A.1	186
2.G.2	G 2	2.G.2	M.2.G.2		2.G.A.2	187
2.G.3	G 3	2.G.3	M.2.G.3		2.G.A.3	188
Uncorrelated or Differently Correlated Standard						

Utah: 1.MD.5 (see 2.MD.C.8(CC))

Indiana Academic Standards for Mathematics

Indiana Strand	Indiana Standard	Common Core Standard	Page(s)
Kindergarten			
Number Sense	MA.K.NS.1	K.CC.A.1/K.CC.A.2	5, 6
	MA.K.NS.2	K.CC.A.3	7
	MA.K.NS.3	n/a	n/a
	MA.K.NS.4	K.CC.B.4	9
	MA.K.NS.5	K.CC.B.5	10
	MA.K.NS.6	n/a	n/a
	MA.K.NS.7	K.CC.C.6	12
	MA.K.NS.8	K.CC.C.7	14
	MA.K.NS.9	n/a	n/a
	MA.K.NS.10	n/a	n/a
	MA.K.NS.11	K.NBT.A.1	78
Computation and Algabraic Thinking	MA.K.CA.1	K.OA.A.1	26
	MA.K.CA.2	K.OA.A.2/K.OA.A.5	27, 30
	MA.K.CA.3	K.OA.A.3	28
	MA.K.CA.4	K.OA.A.4	29
	MA.K.CA.5	n/a	n/a
Geometry	MA.K.G.1	K.G.A.1	168
	MA.K.G.2	K.G.A.3/K.G.B.4	170, 172
	MA.K.G.3	K.G.B.5	173
	MA.K.G.4	K.G.B.6	174
Measurement	MA.K.M.1	K.MD.A.1/K.MD.A.2	124, 125
	MA.K.M.2	n/a	n/a
Data Analysis	MA.K.DA.1	K.MD.B.3	127
First Grade			
Number Sense	MA.1.NS.1	1.NBT.A.1	83
	MA.1.NS.2	1.NBT.B.2	85
	MA.1.NS.3	n/a	n/a
	MA.1.NS.4	1.NBT.B.3	88
	MA.1.NS.5	1.NBT.C.5/1.NBT.C.6	92, 93
	MA.1.NS.6	1.NBT.B.2	85
Computation and Algabraic Thinking	MA.1.CA.1	1.OA.B.4/1.OA.C.6	42, 47
	MA.1.CA.2	1.OA.A.1/1.OA.C.5	36, 45
	MA.1.CA.3	n/a	n/a
	MA.1.CA.4	1.OA.A.2/1.OA.D.8	38, 50
	MA.1.CA.5	1.NBT.C.4	90
	MA.1.CA.6	1.OA.D.7	49

Indiana Strand	Indiana Standard	Common Core Standard	Page(s)
First Grade			
	MA.1.CA.7	n/a	n/a
Geometry	MA.1.G.1	K.G.A.3/K.G.B.4	170, 172
	MA.1.G.2	1.G.A.1	180
	MA.1.G.3	1.G.A.2	181
	MA.1.G.4	1.G.A.3	182
Measurement	MA.1.M.1	1.MD.A.1/1.MD.A.2	132, 133
	MA.1.M.2	1.MD.B.3	135
	MA.1.M.3	2.MD.C.8	152
Data Analysis	MA.1.DA.1	1.MD.C.4	138
Second Grade			
Number Sense	MA.2.NS.1	2.NBT.A.2	102
	MA.2.NS.2	2.NBT.A.3	103
	MA.2.NS.3	2.MD.B.6	149
	MA.2.NS.4	n/a	n/a
	MA.2.NS.5	2.OA.C.3	65
	MA.2.NS.6	2.NBT.A.1	99
	MA.2.NS.7	2.NBT.A.4	104
Computation and Algabraic Thinking	MA.2.CA.1	2.OA.B.2/2.NBT.B.5	63, 106
	MA.2.CA.2	2.OA.A.1	59
	MA.2.CA.3	2.MD.B.5	148
	MA.2.CA.4	2.NBT.B.6/2.NBT.B.7/2.NBT.B.8	108, 109, 112
	MA.2.CA.5	2.OA.C.4	66
	MA.2.CA.6	1.OA.C.3/2.NBT.B.9	65, 113
	MA.2.CA.7	n/a	n/a
Geometry	MA.2.G.1	2.G.A.1	186
	MA.2.G.2	n/a	n/a
	MA.2.G.3	2.G.A.2	187
	MA.2.G.4	3.MD.C.6/3.MD.C.7	187 in the 3–5 book
	MA.2.G.5	2.G.A.3	188
Measurement	MA.2.M.1	4.MD.A.1	200 in the 3–5 book
	MA.2.M.2	2.MD.A.1/2.MD.A.3/2.MD.D.9	144, 146, 154
	MA.2.M.3	2.MD.A.2	145
	MA.2.M.4	2.MD.C.7	151
	MA.2.M.5	2.MD.C.7	151
	MA.2.M.6	n/a	n/a
	MA.2.M.7	2.MD.C.8	152
Data Analysis	MA.2.DA.1	2.MD.D.10	155

n/a = not present in or directly correlated to the Common Core

Minnesota Academic Standards in Mathematics

Minnesota Strand	Minnesota Standard	Common Core Standard	Page(s)
Kindergarten			
Number and Operation	K.1.1.1	K.CC.B.4	9
	K.1.1.2	K.CC.A.3	7
	K.1.1.3	K.CC.A.2	6
	K.1.1.4	n/a	n/a
	K.1.1.5	K.CC.C.7	14
	K.1.2.1	K.OA.A.1	26
	K.1.2.2	K.OA.A.3	28
Algebra	K.2.1.1	n/a	n/a
Geometry and Measurement	K.3.1.1	K.G.A.2	169
	K.3.1.2	K.MD.B.3	127
	K.3.1.3	K.G.B.5	173
	K.3.2.1	K.MD.A.2	125
	K.3.2.2	1.MD.A.1	132
First Grade			
Number and Operation	1.1.1.1	1.NBT.B.2	85
	1.1.1.2	1.NBT.A.1	83
	1.1.1.3	1.NBT.A.1	83
	1.1.1.4	1.NBT.C.5	92
	1.1.1.5	1.NBT.B.3	88
	1.1.1.6	K.CC.C.6/1.NBT.B.3	12, 88
	1.1.1.7	2.MD.D.10	155
	1.1.2.1	1.OA.A.1	36
	1.1.2.2	1.OA.C.6	47
	1.1.2.3	1.OA.C.5	45
Algebra	1.2.1.1	n/a	n/a
	1.2.2.1	K.OA.A.1	26
	1.2.2.2	1.OA.D.7	49
	1.2.2.3	1.OA.D.8	50
	1.2.2.4	K.OA.A.1	26
Geometry and Measurement	1.3.1.1	K.G.B.4	172
	1.3.1.2	1.G.A.2	181
	1.3.2.1	1.MD.A.2	133
	1.3.2.2	1.MD.B.3	135
	1.3.2.3	2.MD.C.8	152

Minnesota Strand	Minnesota Standard	Common Core Standard	Page(s)
Second Grade			
Number and Operation	2.1.1.1	2.NBT.A.3	103
	2.1.1.2	2.NBT.A.1	99
	2.1.1.3	2.NBT.B.8	112
	2.1.1.4	3.NBT.A.1	66 in the 3–5 book
	2.1.1.5	2.NBT.A.4	104
	2.1.2.1	2.NBT.B.5/2.NBT.B.7	106, 109
	2.1.2.2	2.OA.B.2/2.NBT.B.5/3.NBT.A.2	63 and 106 in this book, 68 in the 3–5 book
	2.1.2.3	3.OA.D.8	23 in the 3–5 book
	2.1.2.4	2.OA.A.1/2.NBT.B.5	59, 106
	2.1.2.5	2.OA.A.1	59
	2.1.2.6	2.MD.D.10/3.MD.B.3	155 in this book, 184 in the 3–5 book
Algebra	2.2.1.1	3.OA.D.9	24 in the 3–5 book
	2.2.2.1	2.OA.A.1/3.OA.D.8	59 in this book, 23 in the 3–5 book
	2.2.2.2	2.OA.A.1	59
Geometry and Measurement	2.3.1.1	K.G.B.4	172
	2.3.1.2	K.G.A.2/2.G.A.1	169, 186
	2.3.2.1	1.MD.A.2	133
	2.3.2.2	2.MD.A.1	144
	2.3.3.1	1.MD.B.3/2.MD.C.7	135, 151
	2.3.3.2	2.MD.C.8	152

n/a = not present in or directly correlated to the Common Core

Missouri Learning Standards — Mathematics Grade-Level Expectations

Missouri Strand		Missouri Standard	Common Core Standard	Page(s)
Kindergarten				
Number Sense		K.NS.A.1	K.CC.A.1	5
		K.NS.A.2	K.CC.A.2	6
		K.NS.A.3	n/a	n/a
		K.NS.A.4	K.CC.A.3	7
		K.NS.B.5	K.CC.B.4	9
		K.NS.B.6	K.CC.B.4	9
		K.NS.B.7	K.CC.B.4	9
		K.NS.B.8	n/a	n/a
		K.NS.B.9	K.CC.B.5	10
		K.NS.C.10	K.CC.C.6	12
		K.NS.C.11	K.CC.C.7	14
Number Sense and Operations in Base Ten		K.NBT.A.1	K.NBT.A.1	78
Relationships and Algebraic Thinking		K.RA.A.1	K.OA.A.1/K.OA.A.2	26, 27
		K.RA.A.2	K.OA.A.5	30
		K.RA.A.3	K.OA.A.3	28
		K.RA.A.4	K.OA.A.4	29
Geometry and Measurement		K.GM.A.1	K.MD.A.1	124
		K.GM.A.2	K.MD.A.2	125
		K.GM.B.3	n/a	n/a
		K.GM.B.4	n/a	n/a
		K.GM.B.5	2.MD.C.8	152
		K.GM.C.6	K.G.A.1/K.G.A.2	168, 169
		K.GM.C.7	K.G.A.1	168
		K.GM.C.8	K.G.A.3/K.G.B.4	170, 172
		K.GM.C.9	K.G.B.5	173
		K.GM.C.10	K.G.B.6	174
Data and Statistics		K.DS.A.1	K.MD.B.3	127
		K.DS.A.2	K.MD.B.3	127
First Grade				
Number Sense		1.NS.A.1	1.NBT.A.1	83
		1.NS.A.2	1.NBT.A.1	83
		1.NS.A.3	n/a	n/a
		1.NS.A.4	n/a	n/a

Missouri Strand	Missouri Standard	Common Core Standard	Page(s)
First Grade			
Number Sense and Operations in Base Ten	1.NBT.A.1	1.NBT.B.2	85
	1.NBT.A.2	1.NBT.B.2	85
	1.NBT.A.3	1.NBT.B.3	88
	1.NBT.A.4	n/a	n/a
	1.NBT.B.5	1.NBT.C.4	90
	1.NBT.B.6	1.NBT.C.5	92
	1.NBT.B.7	1.NBT.C.6	93
Relationships and Algebraic Thinking	1.RA.A.1	1.OA.A.1	36
	1.RA.A.2	1.OA.A.2	38
	1.RA.A.3	1.OA.D.7	49
	1.RA.A.4	1.OA.D.8	50
	1.RA.B.5	1.OA.B.3/1.OA.C.5	40, 45
	1.RA.B.6	1.OA.B.4	42
	1.RA.C.7	1.OA.C.6	47
	1.RA.C.8	1.OA.C.6	47
Geometry and Measurement	1.GM.A.1	1.G.A.1	180
	1.GM.A.2	1.G.A.2	181
	1.GM.A.3	n/a	n/a
	1.GM.A.4	1.G.A.3	182
	1.GM.B.5	1.MD.A.1	132
	1.GM.B.6	1.MD.A.1	132
	1.GM.B.7	1.MD.A.2	133
	1.GM.C.8	1.MD.B.3	135
	1.GM.C.9	2.MD.C.8	152
Data and Statistics	1.DS.A.1	1.MD.C.4	138
	1.DS.A.2	1.MD.C.4	138
Second Grade			
Number Sense and Operations in Base Ten	2.NBT.A.1	2.NBT.A.1	99
	2.NBT.A.2	2.NBT.A.1	99
	2.NBT.A.3	2.NBT.A.2	102
	2.NBT.A.4	2.NBT.A.3	103
	2.NBT.A.5	2.NBT.A.4	104
	2.NBT.B.6	2.NBT.B.5/2.NBT.B.9	106, 113
	2.NBT.B.7	2.NBT.B.6	108

(Continued)

Missouri Strand	Missouri Standard	Common Core Standard	Page(s)
Second Grade			
	2.NBT.B.8	2.NBT.B.7	109
	2.NBT.B.9	2.NBT.B.7	109
	2.NBT.B.10	2.NBT.B.8	112
	2.NBT.C.11	2.OA.A.1	59
Relationships and Algebraic Thinking	2.RA.A.1	2.OA.B.2	63
	2.RA.B.2	2.OA.C.3	65
	2.RA.B.3	2.OA.C.4	66
Geometry and Measurement	2.GM.A.1	2.G.A.1	186
	2.GM.A.2	2.G.A.2	187
	2.GM.A.3	2.G.A.3	188
	2.GM.B.4	2.MD.A.1	144
	2.GM.B.5	2.MD.A.2	145
	2.GM.B.6	2.MD.A.3	146
	2.GM.B.7	2.MD.A.4	146
	2.GM.C.8	2.MD.B.5	148
	2.GM.C.9	2.MD.B.6	149
	2.GM.D.10	2.MD.C.7	151
	2.GM.D.11	n/a	n/a
	2.GM.D.12	2.MD.C.8	152
	2.GM.D.13	2.MD.C.8	152
Data and Statistics	2.DS.A.1	2.MD.D.9	154
	2.DS.A.2	2.MD.D.9	154
	2.DS.A.3	2.MD.D.10	155
	2.DS.A.4	2.MD.D.10	155
	2.DS.A.5	2.MD.D.10	155

n/a = not present in or directly correlated to the Common Core

Nebraska Strand	Nebraska Standard	Common Core Standard	Page(s)
Kindergarten			
Number	MA 0.1.1.a	K.CC.A.1	5
	MA 0.1.1.b	K.CC.B.4	9
	MA 0.1.1.c	K.CC.B.4	9
	MA 0.1.1.d	K.CC.B.4	9
	MA 0.1.1.e	K.CC.B.5	10
	MA 0.1.1.f	K.CC.A.3	7
	MA 0.1.1.g	K.NBT.A.1	78
	MA 0.1.1.h	K.CC.C.6	12
	MA 0.1.1.i	K.CC.C.7	14
	MA 0.1.2.a	K.OA.A.5	30
Algebra	MA 0.2.1.a	K.OA.A.3	28
	MA 0.2.1.b	K.OA.A.4	29
	MA 0.2.3.a	K.OA.A.2	27
Geometry	MA 0.3.1.a	K.G.A.2	169
	MA 0.3.1.b	K.G.A.3	170
	MA 0.3.1.c	K.G.B.4	172
	MA 0.3.1.d	K.G.B.5	173
	MA 0.3.1.e	K.G.B.6	174
	MA 0.3.2.a	K.G.A.1	168
	MA 0.3.3.a	K.MD.A.1	124
	MA 0.3.3.b	K.MD.A.2	125
Data	MA 0.4.2.a	K.MD.B.3	127
First Grade			
Number	MA 1.1.1.a	1.NBT.A.1	83
	MA 1.1.1.b	1.NBT.A.1	83
	MA 1.1.1.c	K.NBT.A.1	78
	MA 1.1.1.d	1.NBT.B.2	85
	MA 1.1.1.e	1.NBT.B.2	85
	MA 1.1.1.f	1.NBT.B.3	88
	MA 1.1.2.a	1.OA.C.6	47
	MA 1.1.2.b	1.OA.C.6	47
	MA 1.1.2.c	1.NBT.C.6	93
	MA 1.1.2.d	1.NBT.C.5	92

(Continued)

Nebraska Strand	Nebraska Standard	Common Core Standard	Page(s)
First Grade			
	MA 1.1.2.e	1.NBT.C.4	90
Algebra	MA 1.2.1.a	1.OA.D.7	49
	MA 1.2.1.b	1.OA.B.4	42
	MA 1.2.1.c	1.OA.C.5	45
	MA 1.2.1.d	1.OA.D.8	50
	MA 1.2.2.a	1.OA.B.3/1.OA.C.6	40, 47
	MA 1.2.3.a	1.OA.A.1	36
	MA 1.2.3.b	1.OA.A.2	38
	MA 1.2.3.c	n/a	n/a
Geometry	MA 1.3.1.a	1.G.A.1	180
	MA 1.3.1.b	1.G.A.3	182
	MA 1.3.1.c	1.G.A.2	181
	MA 1.3.3.a	2.MD.C.8	152
	MA 1.3.3.b	1.MD.B.3	135
	MA 1.3.3.c	1.MD.A.2	133
	MA 1.3.3.d	1.MD.A.1	132
Data	MA 1.4.1.a	1.MD.C.4	138
	MA 1.4.2.a	1.MD.C.4	138
Second Grade			
Number	MA 2.1.1.a	2.NBT.A.2	102
	MA 2.1.1.b	2.NBT.A.3	103
	MA 2.1.1.c	2.NBT.A.1	99
	MA 2.1.1.d	2.NBT.A.1	99
	MA 2.1.1.e	2.NBT.A.4	104
	MA 2.1.2.a	2.OA.B.2	63
	MA 2.1.2.b	2.NBT.B.5	106
	MA 2.1.2.c	2.NBT.B.8	112
	MA 2.1.2.d	2.NBT.B.6	108
	MA 2.1.2.e	2.NBT.B.7	109
	MA 2.1.2.f	2.OA.C.4	66
Algebra	MA 2.2.1.a	2.OA.C.3	65
	MA 2.2.3.a	2.OA.A.1	59
	MA 2.2.3.b	n/a	n/a
Geometry	MA 2.3.1.a	2.G.A.1	186
	MA 2.3.1.b	2.G.A.2	187

Nebraska Strand	Nebraska Standard	Common Core Standard	Page(s)
Second Grade			
	MA 2.3.1.c	2.G.A.3	188
	MA 2.3.1.d	2.G.A.3	188
	MA 2.3.3.a	2.MD.C.8	152
	MA 2.3.3.b	2.MD.C.7	151
	MA 2.3.3.c	2.MD.A.1	144
	MA 2.3.3.d	2.MD.A.2	145
	MA 2.3.3.e	2.MD.A.3	146
	MA 2.3.3.f	2.MD.A.4	146
	MA 2.3.3.g	2.MD.B.6	149
	MA 2.3.3.h	2.MD.B.5	148
Data	MA 2.4.1.a	2.MD.D.10	155
	MA 2.4.1.b	2.MD.D.9	154
	MA 2.4.2.a	2.MD.D.10	155

n/a = not present in or directly correlated to the Common Core

Oklahoma Academic Standards for Mathematics

Oklahoma Strand	Oklahoma Standard	Common Core Standard	Page(s)
Kindergarten			
Number and Operations	K.N.1.1	K.CC.A.1	5
	K.N.1.2	K.CC.A.3	7
	K.N.1.3	n/a	n/a
	K.N.1.4	n/a	n/a
	K.N.1.5	K.CC.A.2	6
	K.N.1.6	K.CC.A.3	7
	K.N.1.7	n/a	n/a
	K.N.1.8	K.CC.C.6/K.CC.C.7	12, 14
	K.N.2.1	K.OA.A.3/K.OA.A.4	28, 29
	K.N.3.1	n/a	n/a
	K.N.4.1	2.MD.C.8	152
Algebraic Reasoning and Algebra	K.A.1.1	K.MD.B.3	127
	K.A.1.2	n/a	n/a
Geometry and Measurement	K.GM.1.1	K.G.A.2	169
	K.GM.1.2	K.MD.B.3	127
	K.GM.1.3	K.G.B.4	172
	K.GM.1.4	K.G.B.6	174
	K.GM.1.5	K.G.B.5	173
	K.GM.1.6	K.G.B.5	173
	K.GM.2.1	K.MD.A.1/K.MD.A.2/ K.G.A.1/K.G.B.4	124, 125, 168, 172
	K.GM.2.2	K.MD.A.2	125
	K.GM.2.3	K.MD.B.3	127
	K.GM.2.4	K.MD.A.2	125
	K.GM.3.1	n/a	n/a
Data and Probability	K.D.1.1	K.MD.B.3	127
	K.D.1.2	n/a	n/a
	K.D.1.3	n/a	n/a
First Grade			
Number and Operations	1.N.1.1	n/a	n/a
	1.N.1.2	1.NBT.B.2	85
	1.N.1.3	1.NBT.A.1	83
	1.N.1.4	1.NBT.A.1/2.NBT.A.2	83, 102
	1.N.1.5	1.NBT.C.5	92

Oklahoma Strand	Oklahoma Standard	Common Core Standard	Page(s)
First Grade			
	1.N.1.6	1.NBT.B.3	88
	1.N.1.7	2.MD.B.6	149
	1.N.1.8	1.NBT.B.3	88
	1.N.2.1	K.OA.A.1/ K.OA.A.2/ 1.OA.A.1/ 1.OA.A.2	26, 27, 36, 38
	1.N.2.2	1.OA.D.7	49
	1.N.2.3	1.OA.C.6	47
	1.N.3.1	1.G.A.3	182
	1.N.3.2	1.G.A.3	182
	1.N.4.1	2.MD.C.8	152
	1.N.4.2	2.MD.C.8	152
	1.N.4.3	2.MD.C.8	152
Algebraic Reasoning and Algebra	1.A.1.1	n/a	n/a
Geometry and Measurement	1.GM.1.1	K.G.A.2	169
	1.GM.1.2	1.G.A.2	181
	1.GM.1.3	1.G.A.2	181
	1.GM.1.4	K.G.A.2	169
	1.GM.2.1	1.MD.A.1	132
	1.GM.2.2	1.MD.A.1	132
	1.GM.2.3	2.MD.A.2	145
	1.GM.2.4	1.MD.A.1	132
	1.GM.2.5	3.MD.A.2	182 in the 3–5 book
	1.GM.3.1	1.MD.B.3	135
Data and Probability	1.D.1.1	1.MD.C.4	138
	1.D.1.2	1.MD.C.4	138
	1.D.1.3	1.MD.C.4	138
Second Grade			
Number and Operations	2.N.1.1	2.NBT.A.2/2.NBT.A.3	102, 103
	2.N.1.2	2.MD.B.6	149
	2.N.1.3	2.NBT.A.1	99
	2.N.1.4	2.NBT.A.2/2.NBT.B.8	102, 112
	2.N.1.5	3.NBT.A.1	66 in the 3–5 book
	2.N.1.6	2.NBT.A.4	104
	2.N.2.1	1.OA.B.4/2.OA.B.2	42, 63
	2.N.2.2	2.OA.B.2/2.NBT.B.5	63, 106

(Continued)

Oklahoma Strand	Oklahoma Standard	Common Core Standard	Page(s)
Second Grade			
	2.N.2.3	n/a	n/a
	2.N.2.4	2.OA.A.1/2.NBT.B.6/2.NBT.B.7	59, 108, 109
	2.N.2.5	2.OA.A.1/2.MD.B.5	59, 148
	2.N.2.6	2.OA.C.4	66
	2.N.3.1	2.G.A.3	188
	2.N.3.2	2.G.A.2/2.G.A.3	187, 188
	2.N.4.1	2.MD.C.8	152
	2.N.4.2	2.MD.C.8	152
Algebraic Reasoning and Algebra	2.A.1.1	n/a	n/a
	2.A.1.2	n/a	n/a
	2.A.2.1	K.OA.A.1/1.OA.A.1/2.MD.B.5/2.MD.B.6	26, 36, 148, 149
	2.A.2.2	n/a	n/a
	2.A.2.3	1.OA.B.3	40
Geometry and Measurement	2.GM.1.1	K.G.A.2/2.G.A.1	169, 186
	2.GM.1.2	K.G.B.4/2.MD.A.4/2.G.A.2	172, 146, 187
	2.GM.1.3	1.G.A.2	181
	2.GM.1.4	4.G.A.1/4.G.A.2	238, 239 in the 3–5 book
	2.GM.2.1	1.MD.A.1	132
	2.GM.2.2	2.MD.A.1/2.MD.A.3	144, 146
	2.GM.2.3	n/a	n/a
	2.GM.3.1	2.MD.C.7	151
Data and Probability	2.D.1.1	n/a	n/a
	2.D.1.2	2.MD.D.10	155
	2.D.1.3	2.MD.D.10	155
	2.D.1.4	2.MD.D.10	155

n/a = not present in or directly correlated to the Common Core

Pennsylvania Strand	Pennsylvania Standard	Common Core Standard	Page(s)
Kindergarten			
Number and Operations	CC.2.1.K.A.1	K.CC.A.1/K.CC.A.2/K.CC.A.3	5, 6, 7
	CC.2.1.K.A.2	K.CC.B.4/K.CC.B.5	9, 10
	CC.2.1.K.A.3	K.CC.C.6/K.CC.C.7	12, 14
	CC.2.1.K.B.1	K.NBT.A.1	78
Algebraic Concepts	CC.2.2.K.A.1	K.OA.A.1/K.OA.A.2/K.OA.A.3/K.OA.A.4/K.OA.A.5	26, 27, 28, 29, 30
Geometry	CC.2.3.K.A.1	K.G.A.1/K.G.A.2/K.G.A.3	168, 169, 170
	CC.2.3.K.A.2	K.G.B.4/K.G.B.5/K.G.B.6	172, 173, 174
Measurement, Data, and Probability	CC.2.4.K.A.1	K.MD.A.1/K.MD.A.2	124, 125
	CC.2.4.K.A.4	K.MD.B.3	127
First Grade			
Number and Operations	CC.2.1.1.B.1	1.NBT.A.1	83
	CC.2.1.1.B.2	1.NBT.B.2/1.NBT.B.3	85, 88
	CC.2.1.1.B.3	1.NBT.C.4/1.NBT.C.5/1.NBT.C.6	90, 92, 93
Algebraic Concepts	CC.2.2.1.A.1	1.OA.A.1/1.OA.A.2/1.OA.C.5/1.OA.C.6	36, 38, 45, 47
	CC.2.2.1.A.2	1.OA.B.3/1.OA.B.4/1.OA.D.7/1.OA.D.8	40, 42, 49, 50
Geometry	CC.2.3.1.A.1	1.G.A.1/1.G.A.2	180, 181
	CC.2.3.1.A.2	1.G.A.3	182
Measurement, Data, and Probability	CC.2.4.1.A.1	1.MD.A.1/1.MD.A.2	132, 133
	CC.2.4.1.A.2	1.MD.B.3	135
	CC.2.4.1.A.4	1.MD.C.4	138
Second Grade			
Number and Operations	CC.2.1.2.B.1	2.NBT.A.1	99
	CC.2.1.2.B.2	2.NBT.A.2/2.NBT.A.3	102, 103
	CC.2.1.2.B.3	2.NBT.B.5/2.NBT.B.6/2.NBT.B.7/2.NBT.B.8/2.NBT.B.9	106, 108, 109, 112, 113
Algebraic Concepts	CC.2.2.2.A.1	2.OA.A.1	59
	CC.2.2.2.A.2	2.OA.A.1/2.OA.B.2	59, 63
	CC.2.2.2.A.3	2.OA.C.3/2.OA.C.4	65, 66
Geometry	CC.2.3.2.A.1	2.G.A.1/2.G.A.2	186, 187
	CC.2.3.2.A.2	2.G.A.3	188
Measurement, Data, and Probability	CC.2.4.2.A.1	2.MD.A.1/2.MD.A.2/2.MD.A.3/2.MD.A.4	144, 145, 146
	CC.2.4.2.A.2	2.MD.C.7	151
	CC.2.4.2.A.3	2.MD.C.8	152
	CC.2.4.2.A.4	2.MD.D.9	154
	CC.2.4.2.A.6	2.MD.B.5/2.MD.B.6	148, 149

n/a = not present in or directly correlated to the Common Core

Mathematics Standards of Learning for Virginia Public Schools

Virginia Strand	Virginia Standard	Common Core Standard	Page(s)
Kindergarten			
Number and Number Sense	K.1a	K.CC.B.5	10
	K.1b	K.CC.A.3	7
	K.2a	K.CC.C.6	12
	K.2b	n/a	n/a
	K.3a	K.CC.A.1	5
	K.3b	n/a	n/a
	K.3c	n/a	n/a
	K.3d	K.CC.A.1	5
	K.4a	K.OA.A.3	28
	K.4b	K.OA.A.3	28
	K.5	1.G.A.3	182
Computation and Estimation	K.6	K.OA.A.2	27
Measurement and Geometry	K.7	2.MD.C.8	152
	K.8	n/a	n/a
	K.9	K.MD.A.2	125
	K.10a	K.G.A.2	169
	K.10b	K.G.B.4	172
	K.10c	K.G.A.1/K.G.A.2	168, 169
Probability and Statistics	K.11a	1.MD.C.4	138
	K.11b	1.MD.C.4/2.MD.D.10	138, 155
Patterns, Functions, and Algebra	K.12	K.MD.B.3	127
	K.13	n/a	n/a
First Grade			
Number and Number Sense	1.1a	1.NBT.A.1	83
	1.1b	1.NBT.A.1	83
	1.1c	2.NBT.A.2	102
	1.1d	2.NBT.A.2	102
	1.2a	1.NBT.B.2	85
	1.2b	1.NBT.B.3	88
	1.2c	n/a	n/a
	1.3	n/a	n/a
	1.4a	n/a	n/a
	1.4b	1.G.A.3	182

Virginia Strand	Virginia Standard	Common Core Standard	Page(s)
First Grade			
	1.5a	n/a	n/a
	1.5b	n/a	n/a
Computation and Estimation	1.6	1.OA.A.1	36
	1.7a	K.OA.A.3	28
	1.7b	1.OA.C.6	47
Measurement and Geometry	1.8	2.MD.C.8	152
	1.9a	1.MD.B.3	135
	1.9b	n/a	n/a
	1.10	1.MD.A.2	133
	1.11a	1.G.A.1	180
	1.11b	K.G.A.2	169
Probability and Statistics	1.12a	1.MD.C.4	138
	1.12b	1.MD.C.4	138
Patterns, Functions, and Algebra	1.13	K.MD.B.3	127
	1.14	3.OA.D.9/4.OA.C.5	24 and 42 in the 3–5 book
	1.15	1.OA.D.7	49
Second Grade			
Number and Number Sense	2.1a	2.NBT.A.1/2.NBT.A.3	99, 103
	2.1b	1.NBT.C.5/2.NBT.B.8	92, 112
	2.1c	1.NBT.B.3/2.NBT.A.4	88, 104
	2.1d	3.NBT.A.1	66 in the 3–5 book
	2.2a	2.NBT.A.2	102
	2.2b	n/a	n/a
	2.2c	2.OA.C.3	65
	2.3a	n/a	n/a
	2.3b	n/a	n/a
	2.4a	2.G.A.3/3.NF.A.1/3.NF.A.2	188 in this book, 115 and 118 in the 3–5 book
	2.4b	3.G.A.2/3.NF.A.1/3.NF.A.2	234, 115, and 118 in the 3–5 book
	2.4c	3.NF.A.2	118 in the 3–5 book
Computation and Estimation	2.5a	1.OA.A.1/1.OA.B.4	36, 42
	2.5b	2.OA.B.2	63
	2.6a	n/a	n/a
	2.6b	2.OA.A.1	59

(Continued)

Virginia Strand	Virginia Standard	Common Core Standard	Page(s)
Second Grade			
	2.6c	2.OA.A.1	59
Measurement and Geometry	2.7a	2.MD.C.8	152
	2.7b	2.MD.C.8	152
	2.8a	2.MD.A.1/2.MD.A.3	144, 146
	2.8b	n/a	n/a
	2.9	2.MD.C.7	151
	2.10a	n/a	n/a
	2.10b	n/a	n/a
	2.11	n/a	n/a
	2.12a	4.G.A.3	240 in the 3–5 book
	2.12b	4.G.A.3	240 in the 3–5 book
	2.13	K.G.A.2/K.G.A.3/K.G.B.4	169, 170, 172
Probability and Statistics	2.14	n/a	n/a
	2.15a	2.MD.D.10	155
	2.15b	2.MD.D.10	155
Patterns, Functions, and Algebra	2.16	3.OA.D.9/4.OA.C.5	24, 42 in the 3–5 book
	2.17	1.OA.D.7	49

n/a = not present in or directly correlated to the Common Core

Quick Reference Guide

KINDERGARTEN

Counting and Cardinality — K.CC

A. Know number names and the count sequence.

1. Count to 100 by ones and by tens.

2. Count forward beginning from a given number within the known sequence.

3. Write numbers from 0 to 20. Represent a number of objects with a written numeral 0-20.

B. Count to tell the number of objects.

4. Understand the relationship between numbers and quantities; connect counting to cardinality.

   a. When counting objects, say the number names in the standard order, pairing each object with one and only one number name and each number name with one and only one object.

   b. Understand that the last number name said tells the number of objects counted. The number of objects is the same regardless of their arrangement or the order in which they were counted.

   c. Understand that each successive number name refers to a quantity that is one larger.

5. Count to answer "how many?" questions about as many as 20 things arranged in a line, a rectangular array, or a circle, or as many as 10 things in a scattered configuration; given a number from 1–20, count out that many objects.

C. Compare numbers.

6. Identify whether the number of objects in one group is greater than, less than, or equal to the number of objects in another group, e.g., by using matching and counting strategies.

7. Compare two numbers between 1 and 10 presented as written numerals.

Operations and Algebraic Thinking — K.OA

A. Understand addition as putting together and adding to, and understand subtraction as taking apart and taking from.

1. Represent addition and subtraction with objects, fingers, mental images, drawings,[1] sounds, acting out situations, verbal explanations, expressions, or equations.

2. Solve addition and subtraction word problems, and add and subtract within 10, e.g., by using objects or drawings to represent the problem.

3. Decompose numbers less than or equal to 10 into pairs in more than one way, e.g., by using objects or drawings, and record each decomposition by a drawing or equation.

4. For any number from 1 to 9, find the number that makes 10 when added to the given number.

5. Fluently add and subtract within 5.

1. Drawings need not show details, but should show the mathematics in the problem. (This applies wherever drawings are mentioned in the Standards.)

Number and Operations in Base Ten — K.NBT

A. Work with numbers 11–19 to gain foundations for place value.

1. Compose and decompose numbers from 11 to 19 into ten ones and some further ones, e.g., by using objects or drawings, and record each composition or decomposition by a drawing or equation; understand that these numbers are composed of ten ones and one, two, three, four, five, six, seven, eight, or nine ones.

Measurement and Data — K.MD

A. Describe and compare measurable attributes.

1. Describe measurable attributes of objects, such as length or weight. Describe several measurable attributes of a single object.

2. Directly compare two objects with a measurable attribute in common, to see which object has "more of"/"less of" the attribute, and describe the difference.

B. Classify objects and count the number of objects in each category.

3. Classify objects into given categories; count the numbers of objects in each category and sort the categories by count.

Geometry — K.G

A. Identify and describe shapes (squares, circles, triangles, rectangles, hexagons, cubes, cones, cylinders, and spheres).

1. Describe objects in the environment using names of shapes, and describe the relative positions of these objects using terms such as *above, below, beside, in front of, behind,* and *next to.*

2. Correctly name shapes regardless of their orientations or overall size.

3. Identify shapes as two-dimensional or three-dimensional.

B. Analyze, compare, create, and compose shapes.

4. Analyze and compare two- and three-dimensional shapes, in different sizes and orientations, using informal language to describe their similarities, differences, parts and other attributes.

5. Model shapes in the world by building shapes from components and drawing shapes.

6. Compose simple shapes to form larger shapes.

Note: More detail and examples from individual standards can be found in the complete standards document available at www.corestandards.org

GRADE 1

Operations and Algebraic Thinking   1.OA

A. Represent and solve problems involving addition and subtraction.

1. Use addition and subtraction within 20 to solve word problems involving situations of adding to, taking from, putting together, taking apart, and comparing, with unknowns in all positions, e.g., by using objects, drawings, and equations with a symbol for the unknown number to represent the problem (Table 1).

2. Solve word problems that call for addition of three whole numbers whose sum is less than or equal to 20, e.g., by using objects, drawings, and equations with a symbol for the unknown number to represent the problem.

B. Understand and apply properties of operations and the relationship between addition and subtraction.

3. Apply properties of operations as strategies to add and subtract.

4. Understand subtraction as an unknown-addend problem.

C. Add and subtract within 20.

5. Relate counting to addition and subtraction.

6. Add and subtract within 20, demonstrating fluency for addition and subtraction within 10. Use strategies such as counting on; making ten; decomposing a number leading to a ten; using the relationship between addition and subtraction; and creating equivalent but easier or known sums.

D. Work with addition and subtraction equations.

7. Understand the meaning of the equal sign, and determine if equations involving addition and subtraction are true or false.

8. Determine the unknown whole number in an addition or subtraction equation relating three whole numbers.

Number and Operations in Base Ten   1.NBT

A. Extend the counting sequence.

1. Count to 120, starting at any number less than 120. In this range, read and write numerals and represent a number of objects with a written numeral.

B. Understand place value.

2. Understand that the two digits of a two-digit number represent amounts of tens and ones. Understand the following as special cases:

   a. 10 can be thought of as a bundle of ten ones—called a "ten."

   b. The numbers from 11 to 19 are composed of a ten and one, two, three, four, five, six, seven, eight, or nine ones.

   c. The numbers 10, 20, 30, 40, 50, 60, 70, 80, 90 refer to one, two, three, four, five, six, seven, eight, or nine tens (and 0 ones).

3. Compare two two-digit numbers based on meanings of the tens and ones digits, recording the results of comparisons with the symbols >, =, and <.

C. Use place value understanding and properties of operations to add and subtract.

4. Add within 100, including adding a two-digit number and a one-digit number, and adding a two-digit number and a multiple of 10, using concrete models or drawings and strategies based on place value, properties of operations, and/or the relationship between addition and subtraction; relate the strategy to a written method and explain the reasoning used. Understand that in adding two-digit numbers, one adds tens and tens, ones and ones; and sometimes it is necessary to compose a ten.

5. Given a two-digit number, mentally find 10 more or 10 less than the number, without having to count; explain the reasoning used.

6. Subtract multiples of 10 in the range 10–90 from multiples of 10 in the range 10–90 (positive or zero differences), using concrete models or drawings and strategies based on place value, properties of operations, and/or the relationship between addition and subtraction; relate the strategy to a written method and explain the reasoning used.

Measurement and Data   1.MD

A. Measure lengths indirectly and by iterating length units.

1. Order three objects by length; compare the lengths of two objects indirectly by using a third object.

2. Express the length of an object as a whole number of length units, by laying multiple copies of a shorter object (the length unit) end to end; understand that the length measurement of an object is the number of same-size length units that span it with no gaps or overlaps.

B. Tell and write time.

3. Tell and write time in hours and half-hours using analog and digital clocks.

C. Represent and interpret data.

4. Organize, represent, and interpret data with up to three categories; ask and answer questions about the total number of data points, how many in each category, and how many more or less are in one category than in another.

Geometry   1.G

A. Reason with shapes and their attributes.

1. Distinguish between defining attributes versus non-defining attributes; build and draw shapes to possess defining attributes.

2. Compose two-dimensional shapes or three-dimensional shapes to create a composite shape, and compose new shapes from the composite shape.[1]

3. Partition circles and rectangles into two and four equal shares, describe the shares using the words *halves*, *fourths*, and *quarters*, and use the phrases *half of*, *fourth of*, and *quarter of*. Describe the whole as two of, or four of the shares. Understand for these examples that decomposing into more equal shares creates smaller shares.

1. Students do not need to learn formal names such as "right rectangular prism."

GRADE 2

Operations and Algebraic Thinking	2.OA

A. Represent and solve problems involving addition and subtraction.

1. Use addition and subtraction within 100 to solve one- and two-step word problems involving situations of adding to, taking from, putting together, taking apart, and comparing, with unknowns in all positions.

B. Add and subtract within 20.

2. Fluently add and subtract within 20 using mental strategies. By end of Grade 2, know from memory all sums of two one-digit numbers.

C. Work with equal groups of objects to gain foundations for multiplication.

3. Determine whether a group of objects (up to 20) has an odd or even number of members, e.g., by pairing objects or counting them by 2s; write an equation to express an even number as a sum of two equal addends.

4. Use addition to find the total number of objects arranged in rectangular arrays with up to 5 rows and up to 5 columns; write an equation to express the total as a sum of equal addends.

Number and Operations in Base Ten	2.NBT

A. Understand place value.

1. Understand that the three digits of a three-digit number represent amounts of hundreds, tens, and ones; e.g., 706 equals 7 hundreds, 0 tens, and 6 ones. Understand the following as special cases:

   a. 100 can be thought of as a bundle of ten tens—called a "hundred."

   b. The numbers 100, 200, 300, 400, 500, 600, 700, 800, 900 refer to one, two, three, four, five, six, seven, eight, or nine hundreds (and 0 tens and 0 ones).

2. Count within 1000; skip-count by 5s, 10s, and 100s.

3. Read and write numbers to 1000 using base-ten numerals, number names, and expanded form.

4. Compare two three-digit numbers based on meanings of the hundreds, tens, and ones digits, using >, =, and < symbols to record the results of comparisons.

B. Use place value understanding and properties of operations to add and subtract.

5. Fluently add and subtract within 100 using strategies based on place value, properties of operations, and/or the relationship between addition and subtraction.

6. Add up to four two-digit numbers using strategies based on place value and properties of operations.

7. Add and subtract within 1000, using concrete models or drawings and strategies based on place value, properties of operations, and/or the relationship between addition and subtraction; relate the strategy to a written method. Understand that in adding or subtracting three-digit numbers, one adds or subtracts hundreds and hundreds, tens and tens, ones and ones; and sometimes it is necessary to compose or decompose tens or hundreds.

8. Mentally add 10 or 100 to a given number 100–900, and mentally subtract 10 or 100 from a given number 100–900.

9. Explain why addition and subtraction strategies work, using place value and the properties of operations.

Measurement and Data	2.MD

A. Measure and estimate lengths in standard units.

1. Measure the length of an object by selecting and using appropriate tools such as rulers, yardsticks, meter sticks, and measuring tapes.

2. Measure the length of an object twice, using length units of different lengths for the two measurements; describe how the two measurements relate to the size of the unit chosen.

3. Estimate lengths using units of inches, feet, centimeters, and meters.

4. Measure to determine how much longer one object is than another, expressing the length difference in terms of a standard length unit.

B. Relate addition and subtraction to length.

5. Use addition and subtraction within 100 to solve word problems involving lengths that are given in the same units, and equations with a symbol for the unknown number to represent the problem.

6. Represent whole numbers as lengths from 0 on a number line diagram with equally spaced points corresponding to the numbers 0, 1, 2, . . . , and represent whole-number sums and differences within 100 on a number line diagram.

C. Work with time and money.

7. Tell and write time from analog and digital clocks to the nearest five minutes, using a.m. and p.m.

8. Solve word problems involving dollar bills, quarters, dimes, nickels, and pennies, using $ and ¢ symbols appropriately.

D. Represent and interpret data.

9. Generate measurement data by measuring lengths of several objects to the nearest whole unit, or by making repeated measurements of the same object. Show the measurements by making a line plot, where the horizontal scale is marked off in whole-number units.

10. Draw a picture graph and a bar graph (with single-unit scale) to represent a data set with up to four categories. Solve simple put-together, take-apart, and compare problems[1] using information presented in a bar graph.

1. Sizes are compared directly or visually, not compared by measuring.

Geometry   2.G

A. Reason with shapes and their attributes.

1. Recognize and draw shapes having specified attributes, such as a given number of angles or a given number of equal faces.[1] Identify triangles, quadrilaterals, pentagons, hexagons, and cubes.

2. Partition a rectangle into rows and columns of same-size squares and count to find the total number of them.

3. Partition circles and rectangles into two, three, or four equal shares, describe the shares using the words halves, thirds, half of, a third of, etc., and describe the whole as two halves, three thirds, four fourths. Recognize that equal shares of identical wholes need not have the same shape.

1. Sizes are compared directly or visually, not compared by measuring.

Standards for Mathematical Practice (K–2)

1. Make sense of problems and persevere in solving them.

2. Reason abstractly and quantitatively.

3. Construct viable arguments and critique the reasoning of others.

4. Model with mathematics.

5. Use appropriate tools strategically.

6. Attend to precision.

7. Look for and make use of structure.

8. Look for and express regularity in repeated reasoning.

Acknowledgments

Thank you to all who have influenced my work as a K–8 mathematics teacher: Dr. James Heddens, my graduate advisor; Dr. Johnny Hill, who always pushed my thinking; Kay Gilliland, my mentor and friend; and the many colleagues with whom I have worked and learned throughout my teaching career. Finally, thank you to all of my students who, through their work and questions, helped me to think more deeply about my own understanding of mathematics and to realize how lucky I am to have spent my time doing something I love!

—Linda M. Gojak

A very special thanks is due to the best teacher I have ever known, my incredible father, Dr. Calvin E. Harbin, who taught me to value my education and at the age of 99 is still modeling lifelong learning. Acknowledgment and thanks must also be given to my extraordinary mentors, Dr. Ramona Anshutz and Dr. Shirley A. Hill, who both inspired me to become a mathematics education leader. Their influence and guidance completely changed my life's work. Words could never express the thanks and credit I owe to my dear colleagues, Dr. Ted H. Hull and Dr. Don S. Balka, who are simply the best partners and team I have had the privilege to work with. Most importantly I thank my loving husband, Sam Miles, for *always* being there for me.

—Ruth Harbin Miles

Special publisher's acknowledgment: Thank you to Tom Muchlinski for the focused thought and keen insight that went into creating the Indexes Cross-Referencing Your State Standards and for ensuring that all states were represented.

Letter to Grades K–2 Teachers

Dear Teachers of Grades K–2,

We believe that the key to successful mathematics teaching is to start with the standards. We also believe that looking more deeply at your own state standards and what they mean has the potential to change mathematics instruction and ensure student success. This is significant since content standards help ensure that students understand the mathematics they are expected to know at a given point in their education. Content standards are the foundation for developing a rigorous, relevant, and coherent mathematics curriculum for every student and will help ensure all students are ready to enter college or the workforce.

This is why we have created *Your Mathematics Standards Companion, Grades K–2: What They Mean and How to Teach Them*, and we hope it will support you as you help your students learn mathematics in meaningful ways. While state standards may vary, most are more similar than they are different regarding the mathematics they address. As we like to say, "math is math." To highlight these similarities and help you more deeply understand what a standard means and what it looks like in classroom instruction, we have cross-referenced your state standards to those in other states and those found in the Common Core. A brief overview for each content standard along with effective teaching practices, vocabulary, models, manipulatives, representations, common misconceptions, and differentiation ideas are included to provide you with instructional support that will help you teach each mathematics topic to build student understanding as well as skill.

Although the structure for individual state standards may vary, the major mathematical areas or domains for Grades K–2 mathematics are similar, and although they may be described using different terminology, they all include the big ideas of Counting and Cardinality, Operations and Algebraic Thinking, Number and Operations in Base Ten, Measurement and Data, and Geometry. The individual standards describe the specific conceptual understanding and procedural skills that every student should know and be able to do by the end of that grade level.

The Standards for Mathematical Practice, or process standards, describe what a mathematically proficient student does. Although they may differ in wording across the states, the core ideas in the Standards for Mathematical Practice are inherent in every set of process standards. They are

1. Make sense of problems and persevere in solving them.
2. Reason abstractly and quantitatively.
3. Construct viable arguments and critique the reasoning of others.
4. Model with mathematics.
5. Use appropriate tools strategically.
6. Attend to precision.
7. Look for and make use of structure.
8. Look for and express regularity in repeated reasoning.

When students are actively involved in using these practices, they are doing meaningful, high-quality mathematics.

We suggest that you work with your grade-level colleagues to use this book as you study your standards to help you decide on sequencing and clustering of standards as well as selecting appropriate instructional resources. Be sure to study the content for the grade before and after the one you teach to better understand what students learned previously and what they will be learning next. Keep in mind that implementation of the standards and practices is a process that will take time to do well.

Sincerely,

Linda M. Gojak

Ruth Harbin Miles

Letter to Elementary School Principals

Dear Principal,

An instructional leader must support and help teachers understand that student success and achievement is the goal for implementing mathematics content standards and the Standards for Mathematical Practice (process standards). The role of a leader is to not only promote standards but also ensure the mathematics content standards are taught and the Standards for Mathematical Practice are achieved in every classroom. As an instructional leader, a principal must help teachers engage in professional learning to study both content standards and the practice standards they will be teaching. Teachers will need guidance to understand the depth and sequencing of each standard as well as the content before and after their grade levels. Leaders must help teachers understand that their state's mathematics standards help students reach the goal of being college and career ready and have the prospect of ensuring equity and access to high-quality mathematics for every student.

Each state's mathematics standards define what students should understand and be able to do in Grades K–2. Implemented properly, these standards will lay the foundation for concepts and skills students will be expected to know later in Grades 3–12. Although the structure for individual state standards may vary, and the major mathematical areas or domains for Grades K–2 mathematics may be described using different terminology, they all include the big ideas of Counting and Cardinality, Operations and Algebraic Thinking, Number and Operations in Base Ten, Measurement and Data, and Geometry. The standards describe the conceptual understanding and procedural skills that every student should know and be able to do by the end of a particular grade level.

Also important are the Standards for Mathematical Practice, also referred to as process standards. Again, the terminology may differ from state to state, but the big ideas of these standards are fundamentally the same. These standards describe the habits of mind our students should develop as they learn with deep understanding. The practices included are

1. Make sense of problems and persevere in solving them.

2. Reason abstractly and quantitatively.

3. Construct viable arguments and critique the reasoning of others.

4. Model with mathematics.

5. Use appropriate tools strategically.

6. Attend to precision.

7. Look for and make use of structure.

8. Look for and express regularity in repeated reasoning.

When students are actively involved in doing these practices, they are learning meaningful, high-quality mathematics.

Your Mathematics Standards Companion, Grades K–2: What They Mean and How to Teach Them will help you support teachers in their understanding and implementation of your state's mathematics standards. It will be your guide as you lead teachers in collaborating to improve mathematics instruction so that all students will be successful in learning and doing mathematics.

Sincerely,

Linda M. Gojak

Ruth Harbin Miles

Introduction

A Brief History of Current State Standards

Contrary to popular belief, academic standards are not new. In fact, they have been around for more than 25 years. The first set of curriculum-specific standards, *The Curriculum and Evaluation Standards for School Mathematics*, was released by the National Council of Teachers of Mathematics in 1989, followed by an updated set of standards, *Principles and Standards for School Mathematics*, in 2001. Both these documents provided a vision for K–12 mathematics by grade-level band. They also formed the foundation for most states' grade-level standards.

In April 2009, the National Governor's Association and the Council of Chief State School Officers met to discuss the creation of the Common Core State Standards Initiative. The purpose of such an initiative was to develop a set of common standards across states to balance the quality of mathematics instruction and learning. Following that meeting, the process of writing the Common Core Standards began. The Standards Development team, led by William McCallum, Phil Daro, and Jason Zimba, included mathematicians, mathematics educators, mathematics education researchers, and classroom teachers. The process included an open invitation for feedback, not only from mathematics educators and associations including the National Council of Teachers of Mathematics but also from the general public. This feedback was considered, and much of it was incorporated into the final document, which was released in June 2010. Following the release of the standards, individual states went through their own processes for reviewing, adopting, and, if necessary, ratifying the adoption of the Common Core State Standards.

Since the release of the Common Core State Standards, most of the states that adopted these standards have made some minor revisions by clarifying a standard, moving a standard to a different grade level, combining standards, and in relatively few cases adding or deleting a standard. A few states have totally revised their standards, and the few states that did not adopt the Common Core State Standards for Mathematics (CCSS-M) continue to work with the standards adopted by their state. Even so, the mathematical content remains similar across states. That is good news because it means that the relevancy, rigor, and notion of shared standards have not been lost.

College and Career Ready Standards for Mathematics

The Common Core State Standards (2010) were originally designed to be a clear set of shared goals and expectations for the conceptual knowledge and skills students need in mathematics at each grade level so they can be prepared to succeed in college, career, and life. Keep in mind that most states have maintained the core standards from the original document, while at the same time some states have clarified, combined, or moved some of the standards to a different grade level. In fewer cases, standards have been added or deleted. In this book, we have designed a tool for teachers—the index in the front of this book—to find their state standards, see how they relate to the Common Core standard, and then find the relevant content in this book that will help them better understand what instruction around any mathematical content might look and sound like in the classroom.

The CCSS-M, updated state standards, revised state standards, and rewritten state standards all have a few things in common. They included two critical components of learning mathematics: the content standards and the Standards for Mathematical Practice, sometimes referred to as process standards.

The first group of standards—the content standards—explicitly outline the mathematics we want students to know and be able to do at each grade level. In all cases, the content standards are fewer in number than most previous state standards, and the expectation is that students will develop deeper understanding of that content so less time is spent on re-teaching from year to year. Additionally the standards have been constructed to show connections among ideas at a grade level as well as vertical progressions across grades. For example, you will find that the standards in Grade 1 develop from the mathematical work that students have completed in kindergarten. Similarly, the standards in Grade 2 develop from work completed in kindergarten and first grade. Thus it is important for teachers to be knowledgeable of the standards not only at the level they are teaching but also at the preceding grade level and the next grade level. This continuity is present across all states' standards.

The second group—the Standards for Mathematical Practice, referred to as process standards in some states—describes the habits of mind that students should develop as they do mathematics. Some states have maintained the National Council of Teachers of Mathematics' (NCTM) original nomenclature of process standards, but the underlying principles are the same. These standards remain the same across all grade levels, K–12. As teachers plan mathematics lessons they should consider how students will use the practices in learning and doing mathematics.

True across all states is that the standards *are not* intended to serve as a curriculum. Decisions about mathematics programs, textbooks and materials, sequencing topics and units, and instructional frameworks are left for local and state school districts to make. They do not tell teachers how to teach. It is important to remember that they describe what students need to know and be able to do. Schools and teachers know best how to help students reach both the content and the practice standards.

Further, there is no universal body that dictates specific assessments. Some states use assessments developed by SBAC (Smarter Balanced Assessment Consortium) or PARRC (Partnership for Assessment of Readiness for College and Careers). Others have developed and are using their own assessments. Other facts and information can be found at http://www.corestandards.org or on your state department of education website.

Instructional Shifts

While the standards do not call for a particular instructional model or philosophy, they are based on the best of existing standards. What is different is that they call for specific instructional shifts: focus, coherence, and rigor.

The content standards call for greater *focus* on fewer topics. An examination of the mathematics standards of high-performing countries indicate that fewer, more focused topics at a grade level allow students to deepen their understanding of the mathematics and gain a stronger foundation for ongoing study of mathematics. Within the standards, the major mathematical work of each grade level has been identified (www.corestandards.org). That means that not all the content within a grade is emphasized equally among the content standards. The list of content standards for a grade is neither linear, nor is it a checklist. Some clusters require greater emphasis than others. They take more time for students to master with depth of understanding. The major work of Grades K–2 includes place value, building conceptual understanding, skills, and problem solving with addition and subtraction of whole numbers. This means the majority of instructional time in Grades K–2 (65%–85%) should be spent on these mathematical topics. This does not mean that other standards should be skipped. Rather, supporting standards should be taught to connect mathematical ideas to the essential standards. The additional standards provide students with experiences that will be foundational to work in future grades. Neglecting material will leave gaps in student skill and understanding.

Many of us learned mathematics as a set of disconnected topics, with much of our skill based on tricks ("Ours is not to reason why, just invert and multiply") or mnemonic devices (Please Excuse My Dear Aunt Sally). In reality, mathematics is a coherent body of knowledge made up of topics that are connected and build on each other. The call for *coherence* in the content standards ensures that there are carefully constructed progressions from grade to grade so students build new understandings on the foundations built in previous years. Each standard is not a new topic, but an extension of previous learning. In addition to the progressions across grade levels, the standards incorporate specific connections within a grade level. For example, as students develop conceptual understanding of multiplication and division, the relationship of these operations to each other is consistently reinforced through building conceptual understanding, procedural skills, and applying these understanding and skills to various contexts.

The final instructional shift, *rigor*, refers to how we support students in developing deep understanding of each standard. Understanding does not develop by assigning more worksheets or more difficult examples and problems. Rather, it calls for instructional practice that balances conceptual understanding, procedural skills, and applying mathematical ideas to a variety of contexts.

The following descriptions of each component of rigor come from the standards document, which can be found at www.core standards.org.

Conceptual understanding: The standards call for conceptual understanding of key concepts, such as place value. Students must be able to access concepts from a number of perspectives to see mathematics as more than a set of rules or procedures.

Procedural skills and fluency: The standards call for speed and accuracy in calculation. Students must practice core skills, such as basic facts and addition/subtraction computation, to have access to more complex concepts and procedures. Fluency is built on conceptual understanding and, with young children, through the development of ideas through representations using concrete materials, pictures, numbers, and words.

Application: The standards call for students to use mathematics in situations that require mathematical knowledge. Correctly applying mathematical knowledge depends on students having a solid conceptual understanding and procedural fluency.

Terminology Used in This Book

The language of the Common Core and other standards differs from traditional standards. Familiarity with the structure, descriptive terminology, and functions of each section will help you make the best use of your standards. While what follows describes the Common Core Standards' structure, most states have utilized the same description in their updated standards. You will need to check your individual state standards to find any changes to these descriptors. Numbering and identification systems for your state standards may also be slightly different; the index in the front of this book will help you correlate your standards with the original numbering system of the Common Core Standards.

Standards define what students should understand and be able to do.

Clusters summarize groups of related Standards. Note that Standards from different clusters may sometimes be closely related, because mathematics is a connected subject.

Domains are larger groups of related Standards. Standards from different domains may sometimes be closely related.

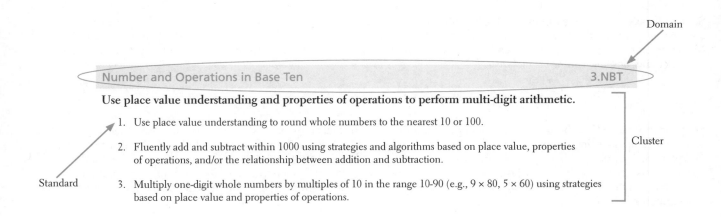

Source: Common Core State Standards for Mathematics (www.corestandards.org)

As districts develop units of study for a grade level, careful consideration should be given to the order and connection among topics and standards. For example, as kindergarten students are learning to rote count within a range of numbers (20 to 40) K.CC.A.1, they might be counting objects to develop an understanding of number within a different range (1 to 10) K.CC.B.4a at the same time.

The Standards for Mathematical Practice (Processes) describe the habits of mind teachers must incorporate into classroom instruction to develop depth of understanding of critical mathematical concepts in their students. The mathematical practices are not intended to be taught in isolation but should be integrated into daily lessons. Some lessons may focus on developing one or two of these standards; others may incorporate seven or all eight standards. Note that you do not "teach" these standards. Rather, they are the type of mathematical thinking and doing that we want students to practice as they are developing mathematical understanding.

Throughout the following chapters, we have included examples of mathematical practice that can be used in each cluster. These are not meant to limit lessons to using only the practices. They are examples of key practices that should be included in lessons around that particular cluster. It is likely that you will use all the practices throughout the cluster and domain.

These practices, briefly explained on the next page, are essential for student success. If students are actively engaged in using the eight practices, they are learning rigorous, meaningful mathematics. Keep in mind that your state may have combined some of these or reverted to the five processes from NCTM's Principles and Standards for School Mathematics (2000). Whether you are dealing with the practice standards or the process standards, you will find the foundational practices (problem solving, communication, connections, representations, and reasoning and proof) to be very similar across all these standards.

SFMP 1. Make sense of problems and persevere in solving them.

Students work to understand the information given in a problem and the question that is asked. They plan a solution path by choosing a strategy they can use to find a solution and check to make sure their answer makes sense. As students in Grades K–2 work to understand place value, addition, and subtraction using materials to solve problems helps them develop conceptual understanding, which leads to procedural fluency (see Table 1).

SFMP 2. Reason abstractly and quantitatively.

Students make sense of quantities and their relationships in problem situations. They develop operational sense by associating contexts to numbers (thinking about 4 + 3 as having four items and adding on 3 more items to find the total number of items). Modeling problem situations with concrete materials will help students understand the meaning of multiplication and division and build a foundation for work with fractions.

SFMP 3. Construct viable arguments and critique the reasoning of others.

Students in Grades K–2 should have many opportunities to explain their thinking, justify, and communicate their conclusions both orally and in writing. Students at this level are just beginning to develop a mathematical vocabulary and use that vocabulary to explain their thinking. This takes time and needs to be carefully developed with young learners. Listening to others and finding how their strategies are similar may take prompting questions from the teacher such as: "Why do you think that works?" or "How is your method the same as . . . ?" Mathematical discussions should be a common expectation in mathematics lessons. Explaining one's thinking helps develop deeper conceptual understanding.

SFMP 4. Model with mathematics.

Students use various representations, models, and symbols to connect conceptual understanding to skills and applications. As students work with the big ideas of Grades K–2, they represent mathematics situations using objects, pictures, numbers, and words. Problem-solving strategies such as draw a picture, make a list, find a pattern, and write an equation have explicit connections to representations and models and can be introduced over time. It is important not to rush this process with young children.

SFMP 5. Use appropriate tools strategically.

Students consider the available tools when solving a mathematics problem. Representations for adding, joining, taking away, finding missing addends, and comparison situations are crucial to support students who are working to make sense of the various structures of addition and subtraction (see Table 1). A variety of concrete materials such as counters, tiles, straws and rubber bands, and physical number lines will support students in representing their thinking.

SFMP 6. Attend to precision.

Students communicate precisely with others. Students in Grades K–2 begin to think about explaining their thinking using appropriate mathematical vocabulary. Students expand their knowledge of mathematical symbols that should explicitly connect to vocabulary development. In the early grades, it is important to support students as they work to share their thinking through the questions we ask and the models they are using.

SFMP 7. Look for and make use of structure.

Students look closely to find patterns and structure in their mathematics work. For example, students begin work with addition by composing and decomposing numbers. Through many explorations, they begin to make connections and develop strategies for becoming fluent with basic facts. The emphasis on looking for structure through the use of physical models rather than an algorithm will help students see and talk about the structure of place value and its place in regrouping in addition and subtraction.

SFMP 8. Look for and express regularity in repeated reasoning.

Students notice if calculations are repeated and begin to make generalizations. By recognizing that ten ones bundled together now presents us with a new unit, a ten, and enables one to be more efficient in computation. Later, students extend that understanding to bundling ten 10s to make a new unit, a hundred. If this is appropriately developed across K–2, the expectation is that by Grade 3 students can apply this to bundling ten 100s to make a new unit, a thousand. Although this standard mentions shortcuts, it should be noted that shortcuts are only appropriate when students discover them through making generalizations and understand why they work.

Effective Teaching Practices

Quality mathematics teaching is a critical key for student success. In *Principles to Actions* (2014), the National Council of Teachers of Mathematics outlines eight valuable teaching practices every teacher should incorporate to guarantee student achievement. These eight research-informed practices, briefly explained below, provide a foundation for effective Common Core Mathematics teaching and student learning.

1. Establish mathematics goals to focus learning.

Establishing learning goals sets the stage and helps guide instructional decisions. Teachers must keep in mind what is to be learned, why the goal is important, and where students need to go (the trajectory), as well as how learning can be extended. Students must clearly understand the purpose of each lesson beyond simply repeating the standard.

2. Implement tasks that promote reasoning and problem solving.

Implementing tasks that promote reasoning and problem solving provides opportunities for students to engage in exploration and encourages students to use procedures in ways that are connected to conceptual understanding. The tasks teachers choose should be built on current student understandings and have various entry points with multiple ways for the problems to be solved.

3. Use and connect mathematical representations.

Using and connecting representations leads students to deeper understanding. Different representations including concrete models, pictures, words, and numbers should be introduced, discussed, and connected to support students in explaining their thinking and reasoning.

4. Facilitate meaningful mathematical discourse.

Facilitating meaningful student mathematical conversations provides students with opportunities to share ideas, clarify their understanding, and develop convincing arguments. Talking and sharing aloud can advance the mathematical thinking of the whole class.

5. Pose purposeful questions.

Posing purposeful questions reveals students' current understanding of a concept and encourages students to explain, elaborate, and clarify thinking. Asking good questions makes the learning of mathematics more visible and accessible for student examination.

6. Build procedural fluency from conceptual understanding.

Building procedural fluency from conceptual understanding based on experiences with concrete representations allows students to flexibly choose from a variety of methods to solve problems.

7. Support productive struggle in learning mathematics.

Supporting productive struggle in learning mathematics is significant and essential to learning mathematics with understanding. Productive struggle allows students to grapple with ideas and relationships. Giving young students ample time to work with and make sense out of new ideas is critical to their learning with understanding.

8. Elicit and use evidence of student thinking.

Eliciting and using evidence of student thinking helps teachers access learning progress and can be used to make instructional decisions during the lessons as well as help prepare what will occur in the next lesson. Formative assessment through student written and oral ideas are excellent artifacts to assess student thinking and understanding.

The purpose of this book is to help teachers more deeply understand the mathematical meaning of each cluster and standard within the five domains of Grades K–2. We want this book to be your toolkit for teaching the mathematics standards, and we have left ample space for you to take notes and add ideas and other resources you have found to be helpful.

You will find that each section is made up of one Domain and begins with an overview of how the domain progresses across kindergarten, first, and second grade. A list of helpful materials, black line masters (BLM), and key vocabulary from the domain is included in the overview as well.

We track each domain across kindergarten, first, and second grade with a page for each cluster and the standards within that cluster. A description of the cluster and how the Standards for Mathematical Practice can be incorporated into your teaching of the cluster concepts follows. Since the standards are intentionally designed to connect within and across domains and grade levels, a list of related standards is included in the cluster overview. We suggest that as you prepare work on a cluster you look at these standards to have a better idea of the mathematics students learned in previous grades and where they are going in future grades. A list of all the standards is found inside the front and back covers.

Each standard within a cluster is explained with an example of what the teacher does to work with that standard in the classroom followed by what the students do. It is important to note that most standards will take several days, and it is likely that you will be connecting across standards and domains as you teach for understanding.

Addressing student misconceptions and common errors in developing student understanding of a concept concludes the contents for each standard.

Each cluster ends with a template for what to consider when planning instruction for that cluster. A black line master of the template guide is included in the resource section for duplication and use with additional standards. This is also downloadable from **resources.corwin.com/yourmathcompanionk-2**. A sample planning page for each domain at each grade level has been included as the last page in each grade-level domain.

In the Resources section, you will find Table 1, which is fundamental to the Operations and Algebraic Thinking and Number and Operations in Base Ten domains. You will also find BLM for key materials that you can photocopy or download from **resources .corwin.com/yourmathcompanionk-2**. These are designed to be samples, and we encourage you to use them or redesign them to best meet the needs of your students. A list of our favorite resource books and high-quality online resources that are particularly useful to developing mathematical ideas in Grades K–2 are also included in the Resources section.

Most important, we have aligned all these materials with the updated standards from most states not identified as a Common Core State Standard. If you teach in a state that is not using the Common Core Standards, you can find the standards listed for your state and your grade in the beginning of this book. Read across the table to see how any given standard relates to the original Common Core version and to see where to find the guidance in this book to help you more deeply understand how a mathematical concept or skill should be developed with your students. You'll note that in some cases there are uncorrelated or differently correlated standards, and in some cases the standards have been moved up or down a grade and the relevant information may be found in *Your Mathematics Standards Companion* for Grades 3–5.

We believe that this can become your mathematics standards bible! Read it and mark it with questions, comments, and ideas. We hope that it will help you use these standards and good teaching practice to lay the essential foundation that will ensure your students success in your grade and in all of their future study of mathematics.

Reflection Questions

1. What instructional shifts have you seen in your own state standards, and how do they differ from your current instructional practice?

2. The Standards for Mathematical Practice describe the habits of mind that students need for thinking about and doing mathematics. While not every standard will be in every lesson, select one standard at your grade level and consider some ways you can incorporate these practices in a lesson for that standard. How will these practices provide you with information about student understanding? How will this help you to better assess students? How will this information help you in planning lessons?

3. The Effective Teaching Practices from *Principles to Actions* (2014; NCTM) describe specific actions that teachers must consider in planning and implementing lessons and assessing student performance. How are these practices connected? Work with colleagues to plan a lesson that employs all of these practices. What needs to be considered as you consider goals for the lesson? How can you modify a traditional task so that it promotes reasoning and problem solving? What representations will help students more deeply understand the concept? What questions will you ask students? How will you connect the conceptual understanding to build procedural fluency? What questions will support students who are working to make sense of a new idea? What kind of information will you look for to help inform your instruction? (For more information on the Effective Teaching Practices, go to www.nctm.org.)

Part 1

Counting and Cardinality

Counting and Cardinality

Domain Overview

KINDERGARTEN

Students enter kindergarten with a broad range of experiences with numbers. Some will be able to count by rote from 1 to 100 (or a subset of that range). Others may have limited experience with counting to 10. Keep in mind that the content standards identify what students should know and be able to do by the end of kindergarten.

Therefore, you will need to scaffold individual standards to meet the needs of students. For example, it is likely that you will begin the school year focusing on rote counting (sequencing number names) to 20 and at the same time work only on counting physical objects to 5. By the end of the year, students should be able to successfully complete all of these standards.

SUGGESTED MATERIALS FOR THIS DOMAIN

K

✓	Objects for counting such as beans, linking cubes, counter chips, coins
✓	Five frames (Reproducible 1)
✓	Ten frames (Reproducible 2)
✓	Double ten frames (Reproducible 3)
✓	Hundreds chart (Reproducible 4)
✓	Dot cards (Reproducible 5)
✓	Numeral cards (Reproducible 6)

KEY VOCABULARY   Vocabulary should be explored with kindergarten students using pictures and visual representations.

K

✓	**add** to combine or join together *related words: add, and, plus, join, put together, (+)*
✓	**compare** to look for similarities or differences among numbers or their size
✓	**count** to say numbers in order; to assign a value to a group of items based on one-to-one correspondence
✓	**difference** the amount by which one number is greater or less than another number. The difference can be found by subtracting, comparing, or finding a missing addend.
✓	**equal (=)** same as in value or size
✓	**fewer than** less than
✓	**five frame** a graphic representation that is useful to help students to count, see number relationships, and learn basic facts (Reproducible 1)
✓	**greater than** more than
✓	**hundreds chart** a 10-by-10 grid with the counting numbers from 1 to 100 listed; used to develop and demonstrate patterns and strategies for counting, addition, subtraction, and place value
✓	*** numeral** a symbol that represents a number; 3 is the numeral that represents a count of 3 objects
✓	**number** a count or measurement
✓	**subtract** to take one number away from another; to find the difference between two numbers *related words: subtract, minus, take from, take apart (–)*
✓	**ten frame** a graphic representation that is useful to help students to count, see number relationships, and learn basic facts (Reproducible 2)
✓	**total (sum)** the result when two or more numbers are added together

*Students are not responsible for these vocabulary words; however, they should understand the mathematical concept.

Counting and Cardinality
K.CC.A*

Know number names and the count sequence.

STANDARD 1   **K.CC.A.1:** Count to 100 by ones and by tens.

STANDARD 2   **K.CC.A.2:** Count forward beginning from a given number within the known sequence (instead of having to begin at 1).

STANDARD 3   **K.CC.A.3:** Write numbers from 0 to 20. Represent a number of objects with a written numeral 0–20 (with 0 representing a count of no objects).

*Major cluster

Counting and Cardinality K.CC.A

Cluster A: Know number names and the count sequence.
Kindergarten Overview

This cluster is about rote counting. Students do not need to have an understanding of what the numbers mean or of place value within this cluster. They will work with those concepts in the Order and Algebraic Thinking (OA) and Number and Operations in Base Ten (NBT) domains. Once students can count, they begin to connect number words with counting quantities. This should be accomplished in small increments.

Standards for Mathematical Practice
SFMP 6. Attend to precision

Students are learning numbers by rote counting. Vocabulary development, especially for students who have not had previous experience, includes counting as well as learning number names as they count by ones and by tens.

Related Content Standards

1.NBT.A.1   2.NBT.A.2

Notes

STANDARD 1 (K.CC.A.1)

Count to 100 by ones and by tens.

Students work over the course of the year to count from 1 to 100. They begin counting by ones, and as the range of numbers grows, they also count by tens. Although this standard includes recognizing numerals, it does not include reading or writing numerals.

What the TEACHER does:

- Provide many opportunities for students to count. Begin with a small range of numbers, such as 1 to 10, and increase the range depending on student needs. As students begin to rote count fluently, introduce the numeral representations for each number name. Give students a variety of opportunities to match the numeral with the number name.
- Use a variety of nursery rhymes, children's books, and songs to help students associate number sequence with situations that are already familiar to them.
- Once students can count to a given number, use a section of the hundreds chart to help them recognize the numerals that represent these numbers. Use matching games and activities to help students connect the number name with the numeral. The goal for this standard is for kindergarten students to count to 100 by the end of the year. This should develop over time depending on the readiness of students.
- As students become fluent in rote counting by ones, introduce counting by tens (10, 20, 30). Using a hundreds chart, ask them to identify any visual patterns they see in the numerals, such as they all end in 0 or the first digit goes in order.

What the STUDENTS do:

- Students begin by sequentially counting by ones. They start with a limited range of numbers and increase the range until they can count to 100.
- They begin to match the number name with the numeral. They play games and complete activities using numeral cards and portions of the hundreds chart to connect numerals with number names.
- Students count to 100 by tens. As they learn the numerals for the digits 0 to 9, they begin to recognize patterns in the written numerals.
- Motion with fingers on both hands to count by tens.
- Use dimes to count by tens; this is a good way to introduce coins to students when they are ready to understand that one dime can represent ten cents.

Addressing Student Misconceptions and Common Errors

Students who confuse the sequence of numbers (ex. 1, 4, 7, 3, 9, 2), skip numbers (ex. 1, 2, 3, 5, 6, 7, 9 . . .), or repeat numbers (1, 2, 3, 4, 2, 3, 4) need more experience counting within a smaller range of numbers. Students should be fluent within a range before increasing the range.

Words for the teen numbers may be confusing since they do not follow the pattern of other decade numbers (ex. fourteen vs. twenty-four). Provide more practice with reciting teen numbers and connecting the number name with the written numeral.

Focus on oral patterns such as the sequence of the ones place digits in the twenties is the same as the sequence of the ones place digits in the thirties.

20, 21, 22, 23, 24, 25, 26, 27, 28, 29

30, 31, 32, 33, 34, 35, 36, 37, 38, 39

Notes

Count forward beginning from a given number within the known sequence (instead of having to begin at 1).

Once students are fluent at counting beginning with 1, they begin to work on counting forward from a number other than 1 within a given range. This is a prerequisite skill for counting on as students begin to work with addition. This standard does not include writing numerals, which will follow at a later time.

What the TEACHER does:

- Give the students a start number greater than 1 and ask the students to count on to that number within a range of numbers. For example, give a starting number of 5 and ask the students to count to 10. As in the previous standard, this is rote counting using number names. Understanding *number* as a count of objects is not necessary within this standard.
- While students are increasing the range of numbers to which they are counting, they are beginning to work on the standards within K.OA and K.NBT domains using lesser numbers.

What the STUDENTS do:

- Students begin to rote count from a number other than 1 (counting on) without having to go back and start at 1.
- Given the number 3, the student should be able to continue the count (4, 5, 6) without starting from 1. Complete similar examples within a given range of numbers. Although recognition of written numerals may help students to count on, it is not essential. The expectation for this standard is rote counting.

Addressing Student Misconceptions and Common Errors

Students who struggle with developing this standard, particularly with numbers greater than 10, should master counting within a sequence before counting forward from a number in that sequence. For example, students should be able to rote count to 20 before they are expected to count on from 8. Begin with smaller numbers and progress to greater numbers. Limit how far you want students to count and then increase the range.

Notes

STANDARD 3 (K.CC.A.3)

Write numbers from 0 to 20. Represent a number of objects with a written numeral 0–20 (with 0 representing a count of no objects).

Students recognize and write the numerals 0 to 20. Begin with the single-digit numerals and represent the number of items in a set with the appropriate numeral. Additionally, given a numeral, students can represent that number of items in a set.

What the TEACHER does:

- Provide students with a variety of opportunities to recognize written numerals from 0 to 9. This can be accomplished with numeral cards, a deck of cards with both the numeral and a picture of the count of that many objects (Reproducible 6).
- Begin with a small range of numbers (0, 1, 2, 3). As students recognize those numerals with ease, add more cards to the range.

- Show students a collection of items and have them match the appropriate numeral card with the set.
- As students begin to recognize numerals, provide practice writing the numerals, using various modes including writing the numerals in the air as you model, writing numerals on large chart paper with a paint brush, writing in sand or shaving cream, or tracing the numerals on paper. Student readiness will vary with the development of eye-hand coordination and small motor skills.
- Teach this standard together with K.CC.B.2 so that as students count objects, they match the number of objects in a set with the numeral. Focus on activities that connect the concept of a specific quantity of objects and how they are represented by a number. The numeral is the written representation for that number.
- Start with a small range of numbers and continue with counting to 20, using a variety of objects to count including five frames, ten frames, and double ten frames. Include opportunities to count throughout the day such as counting steps, counting the number of students buying lunch, or counting the number of students who walk to school. Ask students to recognize and write numerals for the numbers they use throughout the day.

What the STUDENTS do:

- Recognize numerals from 1 to 20.
- Match a collection of items with the appropriate numeral.
- Over time, write numerals from 1 to 20. Readiness to write the numerals will vary with the development of eye-hand coordination and small motor skills.
- Represent sets of objects with numerals after they have had experience with CC. Cluster B: Count to tell the number of objects.
- Use a variety of modalities to trace numerals in the air, in sand, on paper.

Addressing Student Misconceptions and Common Errors

It is common for kindergarten students to invert or reverse numerals. With additional experience, most children will self-correct. Give children opportunities to have a variety of kinesthetic experiences to form numerals (write numerals in sand, rice, etc.) before they use paper and pencil.

Counting and Cardinality
K.CC.B*

Count to tell the number of objects.

STANDARD 4   **K.CC.B.4:** Understand the relationship between numbers and quantities; connect counting to cardinality.

   a. When counting objects, say the number names in the standard order, pairing each object with one and only one number name and each number name with one and only one object.

   b. Understand that the last number name said tells the number of objects counted. The number of objects is the same regardless of their arrangement or the order in which they were counted.

   c. Understand that each successive number name refers to a quantity that is one larger.

STANDARD 5   **K.CC.B.5:** Count to answer "how many?" questions about as many as 20 things arranged in a line, a rectangular array, or a circle, or as many as 10 things in a scattered configuration; given a number from 1 to 20, count out that many objects.

*Major cluster

Counting and Cardinality K.CC.B

Cluster B: Count to tell the number of objects.
Kindergarten Overview

Students move from rote counting to finding the number of objects in a set. Cardinality refers to the actual count or number of items in a set. This cluster connects to the previous cluster. As students show proficiency rote counting within a range of numbers, for example, 1 to 10, they can begin to find the number of objects in a set within that range. While working within clusters A and B, it is important for students to connect the physical objects (3 counters) with the oral number word (*three*) and the numeral (3). Students should begin with counting physical objects, progress to pictures, and then connect the physical representations to the numeral.

Standards for Mathematical Practice
SFMP 4. Model with mathematics.
SFMP 6. Attend to precision.

Students continue to develop counting skills extending rote counting to actually counting concrete objects. They begin to develop the idea of one-to-one correspondence as they realize one number name goes with each item. Counting sequentially, starting with 1 and later counting by adding one to the number of items in a collection, helps students to know number names and the correct order of numbers as they match each count with one item.

Related Content Standards

K.CC.C.6   K.CC.C.7   1.NBT.A.1   2.NBT.A.3

Notes

STANDARD 4 (K.CC.B.4)

Understand the relationship between numbers and quantities; connect counting to cardinality.

a. *When counting objects, say the number names in the standard order, pairing each object with one and only one number name and each number name with one and only one object.*

b. *Understand that the last number name said tells the number of objects counted. The number of objects is the same regardless of their arrangement or the order in which they were counted.*

c. *Understand that each successive number name refers to a quantity that is one larger.*

What the TEACHER does:

- Provide opportunities for students to count using a variety of objects such as buttons, counters, shells, coins, and dot cards.
- Ask student to count objects, beginning with a smaller range of items and increasing as students count accurately.
- After students have counted items placed in organized arrangements (straight line, circle), arrange objects randomly.
- Use five frames to model linear representations of object and to help students begin to see patterns that make 5 (Reproducible 1).

Show representations of 4 items

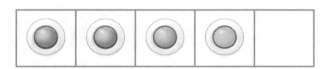

- Ask, "How many are there?" to reinforce that the last number name tells the count of items rather than the counting process itself.
- Use formative assessment protocols to be sure that students understand the last number said tells the number of items in a collection.
- Have students count 5 cubes. Add one more cube to the set and ask how many now? (6). Progress to a similar setup but do not add the cube . . . ask "How many will there be if I add one more cube?" This helps students to visualize the process.
- After many experiences, ask, "If you had 5 cubes and added one more, how many would there be?" without using materials. Begin with numbers 1–5 and then increase the range of numbers to 10. It will take time for students to develop this conceptual understanding, so this standard should be developed over several months.
- As students are ready, extend this work to 10 using ten frames (Reproducible 2).

What the STUDENTS do:

- Say the number name in consecutive order as they point to each object. Some students may find it helpful to move the objects as they count.
- Start by counting objects that are in a straight line and then move to organized representations (ex. arrays, circles) and finally randomly arranged objects.
- Indicate by counting that the last number said tells the number of items.
- Count on to the original number of items in a set, first by adding one item and later by mentally counting up one.

Addressing Student Misconceptions and Common Errors

Watch for students who find it confusing to say one number name with one object as they count (one-to-one correspondence). Begin with a smaller number of objects and model saying the number name as you physically move the object. Have students do the same.

Watch for students who double count an object. Physically moving the object and saying one number name for each object will help to reinforce one-to-one correspondence; that is, one object goes with one number name. Students may see 5 items spread out as different from 5 items close together. Students should physically move the objects matching one item from one set with one item from the other set to understand that the count of 5 remains the same no matter how the objects are organized.

Count to answer "how many?" questions about as many as 20 things arranged in a line, a rectangular array, or a circle, or as many as 10 things in a scattered configuration; given a number from 1–20, count out that many objects.

This standard builds on the previous standards in this cluster. Students continue to count items in a set, using physical and pictorial representations. In addition, given a number, students count out that quantity of items. Numeral recognition is developed throughout this cluster, so students should also recognize a written numeral and count a number of counters given the number orally or given the written numeral. Provide a variety of concrete experiences before students draw pictures.

What the TEACHER does:

- Provide students with a bag, box, or bucket of objects and ask them to count out a certain number of objects. For example, say, "Show me 5 buttons." Begin with numbers to 5 and extend the range to 10, 15, and 20 as students show skill counting out objects.
- Ask students to match numerals with the number of items in the set they have counted.
- Give students a numeral card and ask them to read the number. Students then count out that many items to represent the number.
- Give a drawing of countable items, such as flowers, teddy bears, or cars, then ask students to circle a number of items and write the numeral.

What the STUDENTS do:

- Count out a number of items using a variety of concrete objects.
- Match a numeral card with the number of items in a set.
- Given a written numeral, count that number of items from a collection of items.
- Given a drawing of items such as flowers, teddy bears, or cars, circle a number of items and write the numeral.
- Draw a given number of items.

Addressing Student Misconceptions and Common Errors

Some students may be able to match a quantity with a number (or numeral) but cannot produce that number of objects when given materials or asked to draw a picture. Looking for a specific quantity when given a choice of collections has a lower level cognitive demand (is easier) than having to produce a set of objects given a number. This standard will take time to develop.

| How many peanuts? | Versus | Show me 5 peanuts |

Notes

Counting and Cardinality
K.CC.C*

Compare numbers.

STANDARD 6 **K.CC.C.6:** Identify whether the number of objects in one group is greater than, less than, or equal to the number of objects in another group, e.g, by using matching and counting strategies.[1]

[1]Include groups with up to 10 objects.

STANDARD 7 **K.CC.C.7:** Compare two numbers between 1 and 10 presented as written numerals.

*Major cluster

Counting and Cardinality K.CC.C

Cluster C: Compare numbers.
Kindergarten Overview

Students build on the work of the previous clusters to develop strategies to compare two concrete quantities and later connect that idea to comparing two number words and two numerals. The language of more than (greater than) and less than (fewer than) can extend to "how many more?". . . and "how many less?," which begins the concept of additive thinking (one more than, two more than, one less than, etc.). Developing this language and giving students a variety of experiences will lay a solid foundation for future work with addition and subtraction.

Standards for Mathematical Practice
SFMP 4. Model with mathematics.
SFMP 6. Attend to precision.

This will be students' first experience with comparing quantities. Precision with language is critical in this cluster. Scaffolding experiences that start by using concrete materials with obvious comparisons and honing in on quantities that get closer in size will provide students with the time needed to understand the concepts.

Related Content Standards

K.MD.A.2   1.NBT.B.3   2.NBT.A.4

Notes

STANDARD 6 (K.CC.C.6)

Identify whether the number of objects in one group is greater than, less than, or equal to the number of objects in another group, e.g., by using matching and counting strategies.[1]

[1]Include groups with up to 10 objects.

Students begin to work with two sets of objects to compare the number in each set. Note the scaffolding of tasks in the descriptions that follow.

What the TEACHER does:

- Provide activities for students to compare quantities to determine which has more and which has less. Make the two groups very obvious so counting isn't needed to determine which has more. The focus is on developing appropriate vocabulary including greater than and less than. For example, show students a large bag of popcorn and a small bag of popcorn and develop the concept and language of more and less. "The big bag has *more than* the little bag." "The little bag has *less than* the big bag."
- Show two bags that are the same size and begin to work with the idea of equal using the language of *same as*.
- Once comparison vocabulary has been developed, students compare the number of items in two sets of objects and determine which has more and which has less. It is helpful to compare two different types of items (blue chips and red chips, circles and triangles), so there is no confusion when students begin to compare. There is a hierarchy of strategies involved when comparing. Students should use the strategy that makes the most sense to them.

- o *Matching*: Line up the items in each set using one-to-one correspondence. Which set has more? (triangles). Which set has less? (circles). Asking questions like "how do you know?" starts to develop reasoning and mathematical arguments called for in the Standards for Mathematical Practice.

- o *Observation*: I see there are more triangles than circles. When students use this strategy, it is important for them to explain how they "see" more triangles than circles. While an acceptable strategy, it is often difficult for them to explain how they know.
- o *Take away or fair share*: Each time I take a circle, you take a triangle. When all of the circles are gone, there will still be some triangles. Follow up with questions such as "Are there more triangles or circles? How do you know? Are there fewer triangles or circles? How do you know? Which shape has more? Which shape has fewer?"
- o *Compare counts*: Students count the number in each group and compare the counts. For example, there are 3 circles and 5 triangles, so there are fewer circles than triangles because 3 is less than 5.

- Transition to situations in which students are comparing the number of like items. For example, compare 5 peanuts with 7 peanuts.
- Once students recognize sets that are greater than or less than, give them situations in which they identify how much more than or how much less than one set is compared to another set (with differences of 1, 2, and 3).
- Provide situations where students identify equivalent sets. This may be their first experience with equality. Using the term *same as* may be more meaningful than *equal to* in describing equivalent sets.

What the STUDENTS do:

- Develop vocabulary of greater than (more than) and less than (fewer than) to compare the number of items in two sets.
- Use various strategies that make sense to compare items in two sets, including matching, observation, take away/fair share, counting.
- Explain their reasoning to show that one set has more or less than another.
- Identify how many more or how many fewer items one set has than another.
- Recognize two sets that have the same number of items using the description *same as*.

Addressing Student Misconceptions and Common Errors

Students who have trouble with the vocabulary of comparison need more opportunities to compare obvious amounts and practice the different ways to describe the comparison. For example, there are more teddy bear counters than chips. There are fewer chips than teddy bear counters.

The strategies above are listed in order of development. Students who are struggling to compare the size of two sets of items should line them up with one-to-one correspondence. If they are unable to keep the objects lined up, provide a sheet of one-inch graph paper and keep the items small enough so one item can fit in each square. Ask questions such as, Which row has more? How do you know? Which row has fewer (less)? How do you know?

Keep the number of objects in each set within the range of student success and then build to using greater numbers of items. Continue giving students opportunities to describe their thinking and to use comparison vocabulary.

Notes

STANDARD 7 (K.CC.C.7)

Compare two numbers between 1 and 10 presented as written numerals.

This is the culminating standard of the Counting and Cardinality domain because it requires students to synthesize all of the previous standards. Students must be able to count items in a group, recognize number words and numeral representations, compare two groups of objects to identify which is greater or less, and associate numbers with each set to begin understanding the abstract nature of comparing numbers given only the numerals.

What the TEACHER does:

- Once students show proficiency with comparing sets of objects (up to 10), repeat the same activities with different materials or pictorial representations. Have students place the numeral card for each set next to the items.
- Ask students to describe the comparison. There are more triangles than circles, so 5 is more than 3. As with the previous standards in this domain, students should have a variety of experiences with concrete and pictorial representations and then make explicit connections to the number names and numerals. Include situations so all of the comparison vocabulary is developed.

What the STUDENTS do:

- Given two sets of concrete materials, students label each set with the appropriate numeral.
- Students compare the number of items in each set using comparison vocabulary and then connect the comparison of physical objects to the number names in describing the comparison.

Addressing Student Misconceptions and Common Errors

Since this standard requires facility with all of the previous standards in this cluster, students who cannot accurately compare the number of physical objects are likely to struggle with comparing the numbers written as numerals. These students need additional practice comparing sets of objects and describing their reasoning before working with the numerals. Modeling the transition between the vocabulary of comparing the count of physical objects and using the same vocabulary with the number of items will help students to practice the vocabulary of greater than (more than), less than (fewer than), and same as.

Notes

Standard: K.CC.B.5. *Count to answer "how many" questions about as many as 20 things arranged in a line, a rectangular array, or a circle, or as many as 10 things in a scattered configuration; given a number from 1 to 20, count out that many objects.*

Mathematical Practice or Process Standards:

SFMP 4. Model with mathematics. Student uses a variety of concrete objects to show a given count.

SFMP 6. Attend to precision. Students will use correct number names and written numerals to accurately sequence numbers as they count out the number of items in the set.

Goal:

As students show proficiency with rote counting, for example, from 1 to 10, they can begin to find the number of objects in a set within that range (cardinality). It is important for students to connect the physical objects, with the number word and the numeral. Students should begin with counting physical objects, progress to pictures, and then connect the numeral to the physical representations.

Planning:

Materials: Counters including chips, buttons, shells, and the like; five and ten frames; numeral cards.

Sample Activity:

- Model counting the number of objects in a set of 3 chips. Count orally as you move the items.
- Provide each table with a collection of items to count (less than 6 to start). Let students take turns counting items.
- As students show accuracy with counting, increase the number of objects.
- Have students match the numeral card with the correct count.
- Students who can write numerals can label each collection by writing the numeral.

Questions/Prompts:

Show me 10 counters.

How can you prove there are 10?

Match the numeral for 10 with the items you counted.

If a student double counts an item, prompt him to say one number with each item he moves.

Write the number to show how many you have counted.

Differentiating Instruction:

Struggling Students: Begin with numbers less than 6. Have students move objects as they count. Be sure they are moving one item with each number. Next, have students point to each item as they count. Do not have students write numerals until they can count accurately.

Extension: Give the students the number and ask them to show that many items and, later, draw that many items. Let students model numbers with ten frames and double ten frames explaining different strategies to know the number. For example, I know there are 15 because 5 spots are empty.

Standard:

Mathematical Practice or Process Standards:

Goal:

Planning:

Materials:

Sample Activity:

Questions/Prompts:

Differentiating Instruction:

Struggling Students:

Extension:

Standard:

Mathematical Practice or Process Standards:

Goal:

Planning:

Materials:

Sample Activity:

Questions/Prompts:

Differentiating Instruction:

Struggling Students:

Extension:

Standard:

Mathematical Practice or Process Standards:

Goal:

Planning:

Materials:

Sample Activity:

Questions/Prompts:

Differentiating Instruction:

Struggling Students:

Extension:

Reflection Questions: Counting and Cardinality

The order of these standards is not meant to be linear—in other words, you do not teach one standard and then move to the next. Rather, they connect within a cluster, across clusters, and across domains.

1. Look at the standards in Cluster A: Know number names and the count sequence. How are these standards related? Discuss how to organize these standards to help meet the individual needs of your students.

2. Cluster B: Counting to tell the number of objects addresses students' ability to count objects. How does this cluster build from Cluster A? How can you assess student needs to determine the range of numbers to work with, beginning with the standards in Cluster A and then moving to Cluster B? For example, some students may need to work on counting to 5; others may be ready to count to 10 or even 20.

3. The standards in Cluster C talk about early comparison of two quantities. What are some grade-level-appropriate activities that kindergarten students can do to begin to understand the meaning of greater than (more than), less than (fewer than), and same as (equal)?

Part 2

Operations and Algebraic Thinking

Operations and Algebraic Thinking

Domain Overview

KINDERGARTEN

Students build upon their understanding of counting to develop meaning for addition and subtraction through modeling and representing problem situations, using concrete objects and pictorial representations. This domain comprises the major work of kindergarten and will be developed across the entire school year. Table 1 in the Resource section provides a detailed chart of addition and subtraction situations.

GRADE 1

As first graders continue to develop fluency with addition and subtraction, problem solving provides an opportunity for them to make sense of these operations using various situations and contexts. First graders extend their work from kindergarten by representing additional situations for addition and subtraction (Table 1). They also develop more sophisticated strategies for addition by counting on rather than starting with 1, for subtraction by counting back from a total (sum), and by composing and decomposing addends.

Note that in the early grades the term *total* is used rather than *sum* when referring to the answer in addition or the starting number in subtraction. This is intentional in order to avoid any confusion between *sum* and *some*, words that sound the same but have very different meanings.

GRADE 2

As students demonstrate understanding, skill, and ability to apply addition and subtraction to all problem situations, the range of numbers with which they work increases to 100. Problem situations include simple two-step problems for students to model and explore. Students extend their expertise with mental mathematics strategies (Table 2) initially using concrete materials and later as they continue to practice and become fluent with addition and subtraction facts including all facts through sums of 20.

This domain is not taught in isolation from the Number and Base Ten domain. Students work across domains to develop a deep understanding of addition and subtraction focusing on the instructional shifts of developing conceptual understanding, building skill and fluency, and applying addition and subtraction in problem contexts.

SUGGESTED MATERIALS FOR THIS DOMAIN

K	1	2	
✓	✓	✓	Objects for counting such as beans, linking cubes, two-color counter chips, coins
✓			Five frames (Reproducible 1)
✓	✓	✓	Ten frames (Reproducible 2)
	✓	✓	Double ten frames (Reproducible 3)
✓	✓	✓	Hundreds chart (Reproducible 4)
✓	✓	✓	Dot cards (Reproducible 5)
✓	✓		Numeral cards (Reproducible 6)
	✓	✓	Number line to 20 (Reproducible 7)
	✓	✓	Open number line (Reproducible 8)
✓	✓	✓	Part-Part-Whole chart (Reproducible 9)
✓	✓	✓	Place value chart (Reproducible 10)
✓	✓	✓	Various Dice (1–6, 1–10)
✓	✓	✓	Various Spinners (1–4, 1–5, 1–6, 1–10)

KEY VOCABULARY

K	1	2	
✓	✓	✓	**add** to combine or join together *related words: add, and, plus, join, put together, (+)*
	✓	✓	*** associative property of addition** an extension of the commutative property, to change the order and group 2 addends to find convenient sums (such as 10) in order to make the addition easier. Note that students do not use parenthesis at this level. The focus is on looking for sums of 10. $4 + 8 + 2 = 4 + 10 = 14$ or $6 + 8 + 4 = 6 + 4 + 8 = 18$
	✓	✓	*** commutative property of addition** reversing the order of the addends does not change the total (sum) $8 + 5 = 13$ and $5 + 8 = 13$; therefore, $8 + 5 = 5 + 8$
✓	✓	✓	**compare** to look for similarities or differences among numbers
	✓	✓	**compose** put a number together using other numbers $1 + 9$, $2 + 8$, $3 + 7$, $4 + 6$, $5 + 5$, $1 + 2 + 3 + 4$ are ways to compose 10

(Continued)

KEY VOCABULARY

K	1	2	
	✓	✓	**decompose** separate a number into parts using other numbers 8 can be decomposed into 4 + 4, 3 + 5, 2 + 2 + 2 + 2
✓	✓	✓	**difference** the amount by which one number is greater or less than another number. The difference can be found by subtracting, comparing, or finding a missing addend.
✓	✓	✓	**equal (=)** same as in value or size
	✓	✓	**equation** a mathematical sentence in which one part is the same as, or equal to, the other part 3 + 5 = 8 12 − 7 = 5 11 = 8 + 3 6 = 9 − 3
	✓	✓	**fact family** a set of related mathematics facts, such as 3 + 5 = 8 5 + 3 = 8 8 − 5 = 3 8 − 3 = 5
✓	✓	✓	**fewer** less than
✓	✓	✓	**greater** more than
✓	✓	✓	**hundreds chart** a 10 by 10 grid with the counting numbers from 1 to 100 listed; used to develop and demonstrate patterns and strategies for addition, subtraction, and place value
	✓	✓	*** identity property of addition** any number plus 0 equals the number 12 + 0 = 12 or 0 + 12 = 12
	✓	✓	*** identity property of subtraction** any number minus 0 equals the number. 15 − 0 = 15 or 15 = 15 − 0
✓	✓	✓	**missing addend** given an equation in which the total (sum) and one addend is known, the unknown addend 5 + ? = 8 In this equation, ? has a value of 3. It is the missing addend.
	✓	✓	**number line** a horizontal line used to show the position of a number in relation to other numbers (Reproducible 7)
	✓	✓	**open number line (empty number line)** a number line with no numbers or markers used as a visual representation for recording and sharing strategies for adding or subtracting numbers (Reproducible 8)
	✓	✓	**part-part-whole model** a visual model for showing the relationship among numbers in addition and subtraction situations (Reproducible 9)
	✓	✓	**place value** the value of a digit is determined by its place in a number (Reproducible 10) In 23, the 2 is in the tens place and has a value of 20; the 3 is in the ones place and has a value of 3.
✓	✓	✓	**subtract** to take one quantity away from another; to find the difference between two numbers *related words: subtract, minus, take from, take apart (−)*
✓	✓	✓	**ten frame** a graphic representation that is useful to help students to count, see number relationships, and learn basic facts (Reproducible 2)
✓	✓	✓	**total (sum)** the result when two or more numbers are added together

*Students are not responsible for these vocabulary words; however, they should understand the mathematical concepts.

Operations and Algebraic Thinking
K.OA.A*

Cluster A

Understand addition as putting together and adding to, and understand subtraction as taking apart and taking from.

STANDARD 1   **K.OA.A.1:** Represent addition and subtraction with objects, fingers, mental images, drawings[1], sounds (e.g., claps), acting out situations, verbal explanations, expressions, or equations.

[1]Drawings need not show detail but should show the mathematics in the problem. (This applies wherever drawings are mentioned in the Standards.)

STANDARD 2   **K.OA.A.2:** Solve addition and subtraction word problems, and add and subtract within 10, e.g., by using objects or drawings to represent the problem.

STANDARD 3   **K.OA.A.3:** Decompose numbers less than or equal to 10 into pairs in more than one way, e.g., by using objects or drawings, and record each decomposition by a drawing or equation (e.g., $5 = 2 + 3$ and $5 = 4 + 1$).

STANDARD 4   **K.OA.A.4:** For any number from 1 to 9, find the number that makes 10 when added to the given number, e.g., by using objects or drawings, and record the answer with a drawing or equation.

STANDARD 5   **K.OA.A.5:** Fluently add and subtract within 5.

*Major cluster

Operations and Algebraic Thinking K.OA.A

Cluster A: Understand addition as putting together and adding to, and understand subtraction as taking apart and taking from.
Kindergarten Overview

Students begin to explore addition and subtraction through solving problems first using concrete objects and then using pictures, eventually becoming familiar with expression $(3 + 5)$ and equation $(3 + 5 = 8)$ notation. The vocabulary of addition and subtraction actions emphasizes addition as joining two sets or adding on to a set. Taking items from a set or taking apart a set are subtraction situations that students experience by modeling (Table 1). These conceptual understandings are the basis for relating addition and subtraction; they also provide early strategies that lead to fact fluency. Note that the word *total* is used in place of *sum* at this level to avoid confusion with its homonym, *some*.

Standards for Mathematical Practice
SFMP 1. Make sense of problems and persevere in solving them.
SFMP 2. Use quantitative reasoning.
SFMP 3. Construct viable arguments and critique the reasoning of others.
SFMP 4. Model with mathematics.

In kindergarten, students begin to explore the operations of addition and subtraction by using a variety of concrete materials to model specific problem situations. As students develop understanding of numbers and their meaning, they should develop the habit of asking themselves if their answer makes sense. Within the classroom lesson, students should have many opportunities to explain and justify their thinking to the teacher, to a partner, to a small group, or to the class. They also learn to listen to the explanations of classmates.

Related Content Standards
1.OA.B.3   1.OA.B.4   1.OA.B.8   1.NBT.C.4   1.NBT.C   2.OA.A.1   2.OA.A.2

Represent addition and subtraction with objects, fingers, mental images, drawings[1], sounds (e.g., claps), acting out situations, verbal explanations, expressions, or equations.

[1] Drawings need not show details, but should show the mathematics in the problem. (This applies wherever drawings are mentioned in the Standards.)

Students develop an understanding of the meaning of addition and subtraction by modeling how they can put together (compose) or take apart (decompose) up to 10 objects in different ways. It is critical for students to have a variety of experiences with concrete materials, progress to drawing pictures to express their thinking, and finally see written addition and subtraction expressions and equations. The teacher may write equations if students are not ready to do this on their own.

What the TEACHER does:

- Give students tasks in which they compose and decompose numbers up to 5 using concrete materials and counting.

chips

● ● ● ○ ○

linking cubes

five frame

- Pose questions that ask students to explain their work using pictures and words.
- Introduce addition and subtraction terminology as students are ready.

  o Addition: add, put together, join, combine, plus, total
  o Subtraction: take away, minus, subtract, take apart, separate, compare, difference

- Continue with similar tasks using numbers from 6 to 10.
- Introduce students to numerical representations by writing equations that represent student work.

What the STUDENTS do:

- Use concrete materials to model how numbers up to 5 are composed (put together).
- Describe their models using pictures, words, and numbers with emphasis on appropriate addition and subtraction terminology.
- Extend their work to numbers from 6 to 10.
- Match their models with equations and expressions provided by the teacher.

Addressing Student Misconceptions and Common Errors

If students do not have time to draw pictures before working with numerical expressions and equations, they may be more likely to use finger counting and rote memorization in working with addition and subtraction—especially when learning basic facts.

Notes

STANDARD 2 (K.OA.A.2)

Solve addition and subtraction word problems, and add and subtract within 10, e.g., by using objects or drawings to represent the problem.

Students connect their work from K.OA.A.1 to applying addition and subtraction to various word problem situations.

Teachers should move back and forth between this standard and the previous standard as students work with larger addends (with the total being 10 or less). Students should first use concrete objects and later use drawings to represent what is happening in the problem. Table 1 shows all of the possible situations for addition and subtraction word problems. The situations for kindergarten are

- *Add to—result unknown (8 add some more equals a result: 8 + 3 = ☐)*
- *Take from—result unknown (7 take away some equals a result: 7 − 2 = ☐)*
- *Put together—total known (put together 8 and 3 and get a total: 8 + 3 = ☐)*
- *Take apart—total unknown (take 8 apart to make 2 groups: 8 = ☐ + ◯)*

Students should have multiple experiences with each situation but do not need to identify the situation by name.

What the TEACHER does:

- Provide addition and subtraction problems in story contexts with numbers up to 5 and extend to 10 for students to solve using objects or drawings. Limit problems to the situations identified for kindergarten in Table 1.
- Pose questions that have students explain their thinking and make connections to their previous work with addition and subtraction meanings (K.OA.A.1).

What the STUDENTS do:

- Solve problems using objects and drawings.
- Explain their thinking using appropriate addition and subtraction vocabulary.

Addressing Student Misconceptions and Common Errors

Students may develop the misconception that certain vocabulary always represents a particular operation. For example, they may perceive that the word *more* indicates addition, whereas later when working with comparisons, a situation with *more* may actually call for subtraction. It is critical that students connect what to do with the actions or problem situation and use models rather than to look for clue words.

Notes

Decompose numbers less than or equal to 10 into pairs in more than one way, e.g., by using objects or drawings, and record each decomposition by a drawing or equation (e.g., 5 = 2 + 3 and 5 = 4 + 1).

Understanding that numbers can be put together and taken apart in different ways is foundational to many future mathematics concepts including and beyond addition and subtraction. Students should have many opportunities to take apart numbers up to 10 in different ways using concrete materials and to explain their thinking and patterns that they have found. Spend ample time with numbers up to 5 to help students develop fluency with sums to 5.

What the TEACHER does:

- Use problem situations to give students many opportunities to model ways numbers can be decomposed.
  Provide a variety of materials for students to use in showing their thinking such as linking cubes, square tiles, five and ten frames, and two-color counters. For example, Bob has 5 marbles. Some are red and some are blue. Use blue and red cubes to show how many of each color Bob could have.
- Have students represent their concrete models using drawings.
- As students demonstrate expertise with concrete models and drawings, begin to make connections between the models and mathematical expressions and equations. At this point, the teacher writes the equations and poses questions to help students relate the models to the mathematical symbols.

What the STUDENTS do:

- Use concrete objects to show different ways that a given number can be broken into two sets in multiple ways.

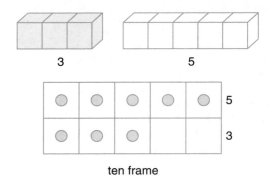

ten frame

- Describe their reasoning in solving problems.
- Connect physical representations to drawings.
- Make connections from concrete and pictorial representation to expressions and equations provided by the teacher.
- Recognize mathematical symbols for addition (+), subtraction (−), and equal to, or same as (=) as well as the terms *total* and *difference*.

Addressing Student Misconceptions and Common Errors

Although it is appropriate for kindergartners to use their fingers in initial counting and exploration experiences, focus on concrete and pictorial representations to develop an understanding that numbers can be put together and taken apart in a variety of ways. Students need many opportunities with different materials to explore this concept and to explain their thinking with numbers to 5 and later extending to 10. This forms the foundation for future work with place value and helps students to form mental images and strategies as they start to work with number facts.

Notes

STANDARD 4 (K.OA.A.4)

For any number from 1 to 9, find the number that makes 10 when added to the given number, e.g., by using objects or drawings, and record the answer with a drawing or equation.

Ten is one of the most important numbers in our number system. Once students have experienced decomposing 10 in a variety of ways, they begin to recognize number pairs that add to 10. Given any number less than 10, students should use materials such as ten frames and linking cubes to find the missing addend that will make a total of 10.

What the TEACHER does:

- Provide situations that require students to break 10 into various combinations using models such as ten frames, linking cubes, two-color counters, and sticky dots and later drawing pictures to represent the number pairs that make 10.

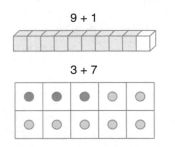

- Use situations appropriate for kindergarten students. Children's literature can offer many contexts for problems.
- Ask students to describe their models and explain their thinking.
- Write expressions and equations that represent student work.

What the STUDENTS do:

- Use physical models and later drawings to represent ways that 10 can be decomposed.
- Explain their thinking as they describe their models.
- Match representations to expressions and equations provided by the teacher.

Addressing Student Misconceptions and Common Errors

Watch for students who miscount the total number in their representation and actually decompose a number other than 10. Students who are struggling with counting strategies need more experience modeling how smaller numbers can be decomposed and justifying by counting before working with 10.

Notes

STANDARD 5 (K.OA.A.5)

Fluently add and subtract within 5.

By the end of kindergarten, students should know addition and subtraction facts with sums to 5 from memory. Students who are successfully meeting this standard have had a variety of experiences, using concrete materials and drawings to show these combinations. They also demonstrate understanding what it means to add and subtract. In order to be fluent, students should be able to give a sum or difference in about 3 seconds without resorting to counting.

What the TEACHER does:

- Provide students with a variety of experiences with sums to 5 using objects such as counters, dot cards, five frames, and linking cubes, as well as drawings, throughout the school year.
- Use five frames (Reproducible 1) with counters to develop and reinforce sums to 5.
- Give students opportunities to explain their thinking and any patterns they notice while using models.
- As students learn to write numerals, teachers should provide written addition and subtraction expressions that students read and complete with the total or difference.

What the STUDENTS do:

- Use a variety of materials to represent facts with sums to 5.
- Solve problems involving sums to 5 (both addition and subtraction) through concrete models and drawings.
- Recognize facts through sums to 5 written by the teacher as expressions or equations. Complete the expressions with a correct sum or difference either orally or in writing.

Addressing Student Misconceptions and Common Errors

Students who cannot give a correct response in a reasonable amount of time (3–4 seconds) or are depending on counting on their fingers have not developed fluency with these facts. An important prerequisite of adding and subtracting is being able to count. Students who continue to count from 1 or struggle with counting on need practice with rote counting as well as more experience with concrete materials and drawings. Only when they are ready should they work with making explicit connections to expressions and equations and basic facts. Begin with strategies such as counting on 1 or 2. Help students to see the pattern of what happens when they add zero. Explore with doubles facts (1 + 1, 2 + 2). The sums to 5 present opportunities to think about decomposing an addend to make the sum 2 + 2 + 1. Subtraction facts are usually more difficult for students to master and require more concrete experiences with subtraction problem situations and concrete connections to related addition facts.

Notes

Standard: K.OA.A.3. *Decompose numbers less than or equal to 10 into pairs in more than one way, e.g., by using objects or drawings, and record each decomposition by a drawing or equation (e.g., 5 = 2 + 3 and 5 = 4 + 1).*

Mathematical Practice or Process Standards:

SFMP 2. Use quantitative reasoning.

SFMP 4. Model with mathematics.

Students explore combinations for numbers ≤ 10 using concrete materials and drawings. Within the classroom lesson students should have many opportunities to explain and justify their thinking to the teacher, to a partner, to a small group, or to the class. They also learn to listen to the explanations of classmates.

Goal:

Students use various materials to compose and decompose numbers from 2 to 6 using concrete materials and drawing their representations. As students explain their thinking and describe their work, they may also begin to notice patterns such as 5 can be shown as 3 blue tiles and 2 red tiles and also be shown as 2 blue tiles and 3 red tiles.

Planning:

What's Your Goal?

Materials: Two colors of tiles, two colors of linking cubes, two-color counters, one-inch graph paper, nickels, and dimes; numeral cards 2–6, a die numbered 1 to 6, a spinner numbered 2 to 6

Sample Activity:

Set up stations in the classroom. Put a set of like materials at each station with a deck of numeral cards (2–6) or one die (1–6) or a spinner numbered 2–6.

Students roll the die, spin the spinner, or take one numeral card. That is the goal number. They use the materials to represent that number in as many ways as possible. After ample experiences with concrete materials, students who are ready may draw their combinations using graph paper.

Students describe their combinations and any patterns they found.

(Continued)

Questions/Prompts:

What number did you roll? (6)

How many tiles will you need all together? (6)

How can you show 6 using red and blue tiles?

Is there another way to show 6 using the red and blue tiles?

Show all the ways you can find to make 6 using the tiles.

Describe the combinations you found.

Do you have all of the combinations? How can you be certain?

Differentiating Instruction

Struggling Students: Limit the range of numbers for students who cannot work with numbers through 6. You may need to direct these students to place tiles on the graph paper starting with one red tile, for example, and filling in the rest with blue tiles until the students reach the goal number. Follow by starting with 2 red tiles and filling in the rest with blue tiles until the students reach the goal number.

Students who have difficulty transferring their physical representations to graph paper may need more experience with only the physical models. They can also place the models directly on the graph paper and color in each square as they move each piece to the side.

Extension: For students who show all of the combinations, extend the range of numbers in the activity. Ask them to organize their combinations and describe any patterns they see. These students may also record the equations for each combination they make.

Notes

Standard:

Mathematical Practice or Process Standards:

Goal:

Planning:

Materials:

Sample Activity:

Questions/Prompts:

Differentiating Instruction:

Struggling Students:

Extension:

Operations and Algebraic Thinking 1.OA.A.*

Represent and solve problems involving addition and subtraction.

STANDARD 1 **1.OA.A.1:** Use addition and subtraction within 20 to solve word problems involving situations of adding to, taking from, putting together, taking apart, and comparing, with unknowns in all positions, e.g., by using objects, drawings, and equations with a symbol for the unknown number to represent the problem (Table 1).

STANDARD 2 **1.OA.A.2:** Solve word problems that call for addition of three whole numbers whose sum is less than or equal to 20, e.g., by using objects, drawings, and equations with a symbol for the unknown number to represent the problem.

*Major cluster

Operations and Algebraic Thinking 1.OA.A

Cluster A: Represent and solve problems involving addition and subtraction.
Grade 1 Overview

Students use models including physical objects, part-part-whole charts, and number lines to develop strategies for adding and subtracting whole numbers, building on their previous work with smaller numbers. In kindergarten, they worked with *add to, take from, put together, and take apart* problem situations (Table 1) in which the answer (total or difference) was unknown. In first grade, students continue to work with problems that exemplify these situations using numbers to 20. In doing so, strategies for adding and subtracting become more sophisticated—developing beyond counting.

Students also begin to work with new situations developing strategies in which the starting number or amount of change is unknown. Finally, students begin to work with comparison problems that are different from previous situations in that they do not imply an action such as putting together or taking apart. Table 1 provides sample representations appropriate for each situation.

Developing an understanding of each situation takes time and should not be rushed. Using concrete models and pictures helps students to consider the actions or meaning of the problem and relate that meaning to mathematical operations. Careful planning across the year to introduce the situations in Table 1 allows students time to model the situation with materials and eventually move to writing equations.

Teaching key words does not help students to develop an understanding of these situations. Rather, by using concrete models and drawing pictures, students can relate their actions to whether the situation calls for addition or subtraction. In missing addend cases, students will determine what operation (addition or subtraction) makes the most sense to them, as either will result in a correct solution.

Standards for Mathematical Practice
SFMP 1. Make sense of problems and persevere in solving them.
SFMP 2. Use quantitative reasoning.
SFMP 3. Construct viable arguments and critique the reasoning of others.
SFMP 4. Model with mathematics.

First graders continue to work to understand the operations of addition and subtraction through experiences with a variety of problem-solving situations. Making models and connecting those models to pictures, number lines, and other representations help students make sense of problems and eventually link that understanding to mathematical notation (equations). As they relate what is happening in the problems to addition or subtraction, they begin to use quantitative reasoning by representing what is happening in the problem with mathematical symbols (decontextualize). Students should consistently ask themselves if their answer makes sense.

As problems become more complex, for example, situations with three addends, students will begin to experience the importance of perseverance. Guiding questions from the teacher support students in considering additional strategies or solutions paths if a chosen strategy is not leading to a reasonable solution.

Within the classroom lesson, students should have many opportunities to explain and justify their thinking to the teacher, to a partner, to a small group, or to the class. They also learn to listen to the explanations of classmates and begin to make comparisons of how their thinking is similar to or different from that of their peers.

Notice the use of concrete objects as the introduction to reasoning with addition and subtraction. This is critical to developing understanding of the meaning of these operations in a variety of situations. Students will be using models throughout their mathematics education. Linking concrete models to more abstract models (such as number lines) and to writing equations is a natural transition.

Related Content Standards

K.OA.A.1   K.OA.A.2   1.OA.B.3   1.OA.B.4   1.OA.B.8   1.NBT.C.4   1.NBT.C.5   2.OA.A.1   2.OA.A.2

Notes

Use addition and subtraction within 20 to solve word problems involving situations of adding to, taking from, putting together, taking apart, and comparing, with unknowns in all positions, e.g., by using objects, drawings, and equations with a symbol for the unknown number to represent the problem (Table 1).

Students explore solutions to problems using materials such as counters and five and ten frames to model various situations. They develop understanding of each problem situation (Table 1) over time. Problems should include addition and subtraction examples in which the numbers range up to a total (sum) of 20.

What the TEACHER does:

- Review situations taught in kindergarten extending numbers from 5 to 20. Since students are just beginning to read, the teacher presents problems in written form on chart paper or projecting them onto a screen or whiteboard, using pictures as necessary, and reads the problems to the students. As students become independent readers, they can begin to read the problems to themselves.
- Ask students to put the information in the problem into their own words.
- Have a variety of materials available for students to model the problems. Start by extending situations students used in kindergarten (Table 1). If students are ready, use numbers greater than 5.

  - Add to result unknown
  - Take from result unknown
  - Put together/take apart total unknown
  - Put together/take apart addends unknown

- After students have had a variety of experiences to model with concrete objects, provide additional situations for students to represent their thinking through drawings and using number lines.
- Ask students to describe their work using terms such as "I put together," "I took apart," or "I took away."
- Model writing equations that describe student actions with the expectation that when appropriate they will begin to use symbols to show their work mathematically.
- Over time, introduce these additional situations for students to model—starting with concrete materials; and as students are ready—working with drawings, part-part-whole tables, and number lines (Table 1). Students do not need to know the situation names.

  - Add to—change unknown
  - Add—start unknown
  - Take from—change unknown
  - Take from—start unknown
  - Put together/take apart—addend unknown

- Facilitate classroom discussions in which students explain their thinking with models and representations. Ask questions such as "How did you know? What does ____ represent? What operation did you use? What was your answer? Does it make sense? How can you convince me you are correct?"
- As students show proficiency with models and drawings, begin to demonstrate how to represent the actions using equations. Give students opportunities to say the equation orally and then in writing.

- When students demonstrate understanding of the above situations, begin to work with comparison situations. As with previous situations, students begin by modeling the example with concrete materials and progress to drawing pictures. Examples of models and representations are included in Table 1. Use a variety of contexts and materials including chips, linking cubes, coins, and other manipulative materials. Emphasize the difference between more than and fewer than situations as the language can be confusing to students (see Table 1). Students do not need to know the situation names.

  - Compare—difference unknown
  - Compare—bigger unknown
  - Compare—smaller unknown

What the STUDENTS do:

- Describe what is happening in the problem.
- Represent each problem situation using concrete materials.
- Identify what they are looking for in each problem situation. (Ex. The number of rabbits)
- Explain their reasoning to partners, in small groups, and to the class.
- Compare and discuss what is similar and what is different in various problems.
- Represent their thinking using objects, pictures, number lines, hundreds chart, words, and numbers.
- Develop appropriate vocabulary to describe less than, fewer than, and more than situations.
- Use and explain meaningful strategies to add the numbers in the problem including counting on, counting back, making groups of 10, and finding missing addends.
- Begin to write equations to represent their work.

The vocabulary of comparison situations can cause confusion for students. While the words *more than* implies addition and *fewer than* implies subtraction, in comparison situations, that is not always the case. Look at this example:

> **Patty has 16 tickets for the raffle. She has 8 fewer than Marcos. How many tickets does Marcos have?**

Although the problem includes the word *fewer,* a student would actually add 16 + 8 to find the solution. Modeling with concrete objects to use the information by showing Patty's tickets and 8 more will help students realize that this is actually an addition problem.

Notes

Solve word problems that call for addition of three whole numbers whose sum is less than or equal to 20, e.g., by using objects, drawings, and equations with a symbol for the unknown number to represent the problem.

What the TEACHER does:

- Build on the previous standards by providing students with problems that involve three addends beginning with *add to* and *put together* resulting in unknown situations (Table 1).

  ○ Anna had 4 daisies. Maria gave her 3 daisies. Sue Lin gave her 6 daisies. How many daisies does Anna have now?
  ○ Linda has 7 blue markers, 8 red markers, and 3 green markers. How many markers does Linda have?

- Scaffold instruction so that students begin with concrete models, pictures, number lines, words, and writing equations in that order.
- Facilitate classroom discussions that allow students to explain their thinking by sharing models and strategies they used to solve problems.
- Ask students to show and explain how they solved the problem using pictures, numbers, and words both orally and in writing.
- Model and encourage students to use various strategies to find the total (sum) of the three addends including making groups of 10, using open number lines, and counting up on the hundreds chart.

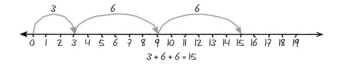

$$3 + 6 + 6 = 15$$

- Make explicit connections to properties of addition (Standard 1.OA.B.3) to help students develop strategies for adding examples with three addends.

What the STUDENTS do:

- Ask themselves what is happening in the problem and represent each problem situation using concrete models, number lines, and pictures.
- Identify what they are looking for in each problem situation.
- Use and explain meaningful strategies to add the numbers in the problem including counting on, counting back, and making groups of 10 to find the total or missing addends.
- Explain their reasoning to partners, in small groups, and to the class.
- Compare and discuss what is similar and what is different in various situations.
- Represent their thinking using pictures, words, and numbers.

Addressing Student Misconceptions and Common Errors

Some students think it is not possible to add more than two numbers. Although they may be familiar with seeing addition equations with three or more addends, they do not write equations with three or more addends.

Students consider composing and decomposing numbers to learn facts, develop computation strategies, and do mental mathematics. The understanding that addition equations can contain more than two addends is important. Once students have had experience working with three addends, using concrete materials and drawings, they should have opportunities to write and solve addition equations with three or more addends.

Notes

Operations and Algebraic Thinking
1.OA.B*

Understand and apply properties of operations and the relationship between addition and subtraction.

STANDARD 3 **1.OA.B.3:** Apply properties of operations as strategies to add and subtract.[2] *Examples: If 8 + 3 = 11 is known, then 3 + 8 = 11 is also known. (Commutative property of addition.) To add 2 + 6 + 4, the second two numbers can be added to make a ten, so 2 + 6 + 4 = 2 + 10 = 12. (Associative property of addition.)*

[2]Students need not use formal terms for these properties.

STANDARD 4 **1.OA.B.4:** Understand subtraction as an unknown-addend problem. *For example, subtract 10 – 8 by finding the number that makes 10 when added to 8. Add and subtract within 20.*

*Major cluster

Operations and Algebraic Thinking 1.OA.B

Cluster B: Understand and apply properties of operations and the relationship between addition and subtraction.
Grade 1 Overview

As students solve problems with addition and subtraction, they are connecting the counting they did in kindergarten to adding and subtracting numbers. Work with models such as ten frames and linking cubes support the strategy of using ten as a benchmark to solve addition and subtraction problems within 20 by decomposing and composing addends. Experiences in which the order of addends is reversed establishes a fundamental property (commutative) of addition and later multiplication. The order of the addends does not change the total (sum).

In developing an understanding of the relationship between addition and subtraction, students use fact families to see that combining two addends produces a total (sum), and if they know the total (sum) and one addend, they can either subtract (take away) or use addition to determine the missing addend. Connecting these meanings to problem situations helps students to more deeply understand the relationship between addition and subtraction as inverse operations (one "undoes" the other).

Standards for Mathematical Practice
SFMP 7. Look for and make use of structure.
SFMP 8. Look for and express regularity in repeated reasoning.

Through exploring and recognizing the properties of addition and subtraction, students begin to see the structure or patterns that help them to add and subtract numbers more efficiently. Recognizing that 7 + 3 = 3 + 7 (the commutative property) will help students to learn addition basic facts. Fact families that show the relationship between addition and subtraction, demonstrating both structure and patterns, will help students to use what they know about addition to do subtraction.

Related Content Standards

1.NBT.C.4   1.NBT.C.6   2.NBT.B.5   2.NBT.B.6   2.NBT.B.7   2.NBT.B.9

Notes
_____
_____
_____

Apply properties of operations as strategies to add and subtract.² Examples: If 8 + 3 = 11 is known, then 3 + 8 = 11 is also known. (Commutative property of addition.) To add 2 + 6 + 4, the second two numbers can be added to make a ten, so 2 + 6 + 4 = 2 + 10 = 12. (Associative property of addition.)

²Students need not use formal terms for these properties.

Within this standard, students explore and use patterns they see to begin to develop an understanding of important properties of addition and subtraction.

- **Identity property of addition:** Any number plus 0 equals the start number.

$$12 + 0 = 12 \quad \text{or} \quad 0 + 12 = 12$$

- **Identity property of subtraction:** Any number minus 0 equals the start number.

$$15 - 0 = 15 \quad \text{or} \quad 15 = 15 - 0$$

- **Commutative property of addition:** Reversing the order of the addends does not change the total (sum).

$$8 + 5 = 13 \quad \text{and} \quad 5 + 8 = 13 \quad \text{so} \quad 8 + 5 = 5 + 8$$

- **Associative property of addition is an extension of the commutative property:** I can change the order and grouping of three or more addends to find convenient sums (such as 10) in order to make the addition easier. Students do not use parentheses as this level. The focus is on looking for sums of 10.

$$4 + 8 + 2 = 4 + 10 = 14 \quad \text{or} \quad 6 + 8 + 4 = 6 + 4 + 8 = 18$$

What the TEACHER does:

- Present students with a variety of addition examples using concrete representations, such as ten frames, pictures, equations, and problems in which the order of the addends is reversed. The teacher does not explain the commutative property; rather, the teacher asks questions that support student observations of the pattern—the order of addends does not change the total.

  For example,

  - What do you notice about the dots on the tens frames? This progresses to what do you notice about the addends in these two problems?
  - What do you notice about the total?
  - Try this with two different addends? What do you notice about the total of these addends?
  - Do you think this will always be true?

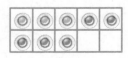 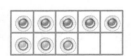

3 + 5   5 + 3

- Point out properties in other addition examples. For example, if students are using cubes to show all the ways they can make 7, facilitate discussions that help them to see that 4 green cubes plus 3 red cubes is equal to 3 green cubes plus 4 red cubes.

(Continued)

What the STUDENTS do:

- Use representations to solve addition and subtraction examples.
- Given specific situations (such as changing the order of the addends, adding or subtracting 0, or looking for tens when adding more than two numbers), students describe patterns and make generalizations.

  - The order of the addends does not change the total (commutative property).
  - When I add a number to 0, I get that number. When I add 0 to a number, I get the number I started with (identity element for addition).
  - When I subtract 0 from a number, the number doesn't change (identity element for subtraction).
  - When I have three or more addends, I can change the order and grouping of those addends to make the problem easier to solve.

- Explain their reasoning to others.
- Write equations for the examples they have modeled.
- Solve problems that use these properties.
- Model and recognize that when they add 10 to a one digit number, the digit in the tens place is 1, which represents a group of 10, and the digit in the ones place is the other addend.

What the TEACHER does (continued):

- Once students have an understanding of 0 as a number, introduce addition and subtraction examples that include 0. In this case, it may be more meaningful for students to begin with a problem situation and ask them to represent the problem with concrete objects and with equations.
- Ask students to describe the pattern they notice when they add 0 to a number or a number to 0. (The total is the non-zero addend.)
- Ask students to describe the pattern they notice when they subtract 0 from a number. (The difference is the same as the start number.)
- Provide students with opportunities to add a single digit number to 10 and 10 to a single digit number. Use double ten frames, hundreds charts, and place value charts with bundled straws or linking cubes. Model writing the equation for each example; ask students to give the total.

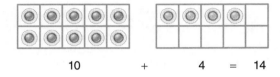

10   +   4   =   14

- Ask students to describe patterns they see when adding 10 to a single digit number. (There is a 1 in the tens place. The digit in the ones place is the number you added to 10.)
- As students begin to work with three or more addends, provide situations that include pairs of addends that make 10. Rather than advise students to look for groups of 10, have them represent the situations using ten frames and the commutative property so that they begin to develop strategies to look for and make tens. This lays the foundation for future work with using 10 and multiples of 10 as benchmarks.

 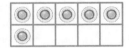

7 + 6 + 3 = 7 + 3 + 6

Addressing Student Misconceptions and Common Errors

Although subtraction is not commutative, it is important not to contribute to a potential student misconception by saying that you cannot take a larger number from a smaller number. It is appropriate to say that $8 - 5 \neq 5 - 8$.

It is possible to take a larger number from a smaller number. The result will be a negative number. Integers are not introduced until middle school.

Notes

Understand subtraction as an unknown-addend problem. For example, subtract 10 – 8 by finding the number that makes 10 when added to 8.

Given *change unknown* problem situations (Table 1), students begin to understand the relationship between addition and subtraction. For example, I had 8 markers. Mom gave me some more. Now I have 12 markers. How many did mom give me? Another way to think about this, "If I have 8, how many more will it take to make 12?"

$(8 + \Box = 12)$. This strategy is another way to solve $12 – 8 = \Box$.

Students often find learning subtraction facts to be more challenging than learning addition facts. Thinking about subtraction as finding a missing addend helps students connect what they don't know to what they do know and to begin to work with subtraction facts as part of a fact family. This strategy is known as the *think addition* strategy for learning subtraction facts. Although there are other strategies for learning subtraction facts, the think addition strategy reinforces both addition and subtraction facts.

$8 + 4 = \Box$ $8 + \Box = 12$ $12 – 8 = \Box$ $\Box + 4 = 12$ $12 – 4 = \Box$

What the TEACHER does:

- Give students examples of related addition and subtraction facts to model using objects, tens frames, part-part-whole chart, open number lines, and number sentences.
- Introduce the terms *addend*, *missing addend*, and *total*. Relate these terms to addition and subtraction equations. Provide multiple opportunities to identify the parts of addition and subtraction equations in different forms.

  - $8 + 5 = \Box$ addend + addend = total
  - $8 + \Box = 13$ addend + missing addend = total
  - $13 – 8 = \Box$ total – addend = missing addend

- Use the part-part-whole model to help students make the connection between addition and subtraction examples.

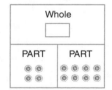 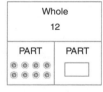

- Provide opportunities for students to practice addition and subtraction facts using fact families.

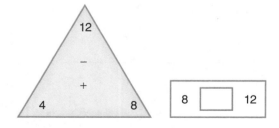

What the STUDENTS do:

- Use representations to model related addition and subtraction facts using objects, pictures, numbers, and words.
- Identify parts of addition and subtraction equations using the terms *addend*, *missing addend*, and *total*.

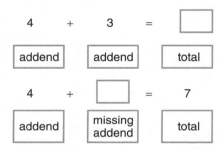

- Explain their reasoning to the teacher and to classmates.
- Use the relationship between addition and subtraction to practice basic facts.

Students may confuse the order of parts of addition and subtraction equations. Write the terms *addend, missing addend,* and *total* on large cards. Write an addition equation on the board and have students identify each part using the vocabulary cards. Write a related addition equation reversing the order of the addends and have students identify each part of the equation. Write a related equation with a missing addend and have students repeat identifying each part of the equation with the vocabulary cards. Write the related subtraction facts having students identify each part of the subtraction equation. Discuss what is similar in each equation.

Notes

GRADE 1

Operations and Algebraic Thinking
1.OA.C*

Add and subtract within 20.

STANDARD 5 **1.OA.C.5:** Relate counting to addition and subtraction (e.g., by counting on 2 to add 2).

STANDARD 6 **1.OA.C.6:** Add and subtract within 20, demonstrating fluency for addition and subtraction within 10. Use strategies such as counting on; making ten (e.g., $8 + 6 = 8 + 2 + 4 = 10 + 4 = 14$); decomposing a number leading to a ten (e.g., $13 - 4 = 13 - 3 - 1 = 10 - 1 = 9$); using the relationship between addition and subtraction (e.g., knowing that $8 + 4 = 12$, one knows $12 - 8 = 4$); and creating equivalent but easier or known sums (e.g., adding $6 + 7$ by creating the known equivalent $6 + 6 + 1 = 12 + 1 = 13$).

*Major cluster

Operations and Algebraic Thinking 1.OA.C

Cluster C: Add and subtract within 20.
Grade 1 Overview

Students in first grade continue to explore and make sense out of number combinations to 20, beginning with extending counting strategies to a larger range of numbers. Through carefully planned experiences, more sophisticated strategies become apparent. For example, once students know doubles in addition, they can begin to work with examples that can be modeled using doubles plus 1 or 2 more ($3 + 4$ can be thought of as $3 + 3 + 1$). Students should have many opportunities to model, draw conclusions, and share their thinking in order to deeply understand and make use of these strategies. Questions posed by the teacher can help students to move from concrete models and pictures to equations and using strategies to practice basic facts.

Standards for Mathematical Practice
SFMP 2. Reason abstractly and quantitatively.
SFMP 3. Construct viable arguments and critique the reasoning of others.
SFMP 4. Model with mathematics.
SFMP 7. Look for and make use of structure.

As students move from counting strategies to more sophisticated strategies, such as making tens, doubles, and doubles plus 1 or 2, they notice patterns and the structure of how numbers fit together. In doing so, they are beginning to reason about the numbers, their meaning, and how the properties of addition can help them to learn facts and to add and subtract efficiently. The use of concrete materials to represent and build these ideas is crucial to developing understanding and eventually fluency with facts. As students begin to make sense and use strategies, explaining their thinking to peers helps to clarify questions they may have and deepen understanding.

Related Content Standards
K.OA.A.2   K.OA.A.5   2.OA.B.2

Notes

Relate counting to addition and subtraction (e.g., by counting on 2 to add 2).

Before experiences with more sophisticated strategies, first graders continue to develop the counting strategies they used in kindergarten, including

- Counting all (addition)—start with 1 and count to find the total number of objects.

    o 8 + 4.   Start from 1, count up 8, and count up 4 more: 1, 2, 3, 4, 5, 6, 7, 8 . . . 9, 10, 11, 12

- Counting on (addition)—count from the start number rather than starting at 1.

    o 8 + 4.   Start at 8 . . . 9, 10, 11, 12

- Counting all (subtraction)—remove the appropriate number of items and count the remaining items starting with 1.

    o 12 – 8.   Start with 12 objects. Remove 8 and count the remaining items 1, 2, 3, 4

- Counting back (subtraction)—start with the total, count back the number being subtracted.

    o 12 – 8.   Start at 12 and count back 8, one number at a time, 11, 10, 9, 8, 7, 6, 5, 4

- Count on (subtraction)—start with the change number and count on to reach the total.

    o 12 – 8.   Start with 8 and count up to 12 by ones (and later by larger numbers)
       8 . . . 9, 10, 11, 12

Although it is common for students who are first using counting strategies to count on their fingers to keep track, as students become fluent with counting and other strategies, the use of fingers should eventually be gently discouraged. Questions posed such as "Do you think you can find that total without using your fingers?" will encourage students to move beyond using counting strategies and using their fingers.

Students will vary in the time needed to develop understanding of the counting strategies and readiness for the more sophisticated strategies they will encounter in standard 1.OA.C.6. While introducing a strategy may be a whole class lesson, individualized activities that allow students to progress through the strategies at a rate determined by their understanding is important. Class discussions, about how students found the answer to an individual fact, will expose students who are still working with counting strategies to make connections to the more sophisticated strategies.

What the TEACHER does:

- Review and extend counting strategies with explicit activities using physical objects, number lines, and the hundreds chart for addition and subtraction facts with sums to 10. As students demonstrate understanding, increase the range to sums to 15 and later sums to 20.
- Provide a variety of materials including counters, ten frames, number lines, and the hundreds chart for students to use.
- Pose questions to help students make sense out of their thinking, to determine if their answer is reasonable, and to determine for which facts counting is efficient. For example, with 7 – 5, counting back is efficient. With 7 – 2, counting back is not efficient.
- Provide opportunities for students to discuss their thinking using objects, pictures, numbers, and words.
- Determine when individual students are ready to move to more sophisticated strategies included in standard 1.OA.C.6 through formative assessment protocols, such as noticing if students are still counting by 1, counting all or counting on, counting back, or clumping (counting by more than one at a time).

What the STUDENTS do:

- Use a variety of materials to continue to work on counting strategies to find sums and differences of basic facts through sums of 10.
- Explain their thinking using a counting strategy for finding the answer to an addition or subtraction fact with sums to 10.
- Look for patterns as they use counting strategies, including for which facts counting is efficient.

Watch for students who may double count a number when adding or subtracting. This may occur with physical objects, pictures, or using a hundreds chart. For example, if a student is adding $6 + 4$, she may begin with the 6 (6, 7, 8, 9) with a result of 9 rather than counting on to the 6 (7, 8, 9, 10). The same may happen in subtraction. If a student is counting to subtract $8 - 5$, he may count the 8 as part of the count (8, 7, 6, 5, 4) with a result of 4 rather than subtracting from the 8 (7, 6, 5, 4, 3) to get the accurate amount. Not only should this be pointed out to students, but it is essential also to provide more explicit experiences with concrete materials in which students are adding on to the given addend or subtracting from the total.

Notes

STANDARD 6 (1.OA.C.6)

Add and subtract within 20, demonstrating fluency for addition and subtraction within 10. Use strategies such as counting on; making ten (e.g., 8 + 6 = 8 + 2 + 4 = 10 + 4 = 14); decomposing a number leading to a ten (e.g., 13 – 4 = 13 – 3 – 1 = 10 – 1 = 9); using the relationship between addition and subtraction (e.g., knowing that 8 + 4 = 12, one knows 12 – 8 = 4); and creating equivalent but easier or known sums (e.g., adding 6 + 7 by creating the known equivalent 6 + 6 + 1 = 12 + 1 = 13).

As students become comfortable with counting on strategies they should begin to have opportunities to use other strategies so they do not become dependent on counting, which beyond adding or subtracting 1 or 2 is inefficient.

Students need experiences with physical counters and ten frames to develop conceptual understanding of strategies prior to skill drill, and practice. Although fluency requires accuracy with reasonable speed (about 3 seconds per fact), it is best reached with a foundation of conceptual understanding and efficient strategies. Premature drill and practice does not produce fluency.

What the TEACHER does:

- Provide a variety of explicit experiences using concrete materials to help students develop and use thinking strategies to explore addition and subtraction facts with sums to 10, focusing on using 10 as a benchmark number (Table 2).
- Ask students to find patterns as they work on developing these strategies. For example, adding or subtracting 0 results in the same start number. Adding 1 is counting to the next number. Patterns in more sophisticated strategies emerge as students work with ten frames, number lines, and the hundreds chart.
- Expect students to explain their thinking as they develop understanding of strategies and individual facts. Pose questions such as "How did you figure out that 6 + 5 = 11? What strategy did you use?" Oral explanations and demonstrating with models, such as a ten frame or number line, often make more sense than having students write out all of the steps.
- Once students show understanding of a strategy, provide practice experiences including tasks with concrete materials, games, and worksheets that include a reasonable number of facts.
- Use a variety of formative assessments protocols in addition to writing facts to assess student fluency with the facts.
- As students continue to work with facts with sums to 10, provide experiences extending the strategies to addition and subtraction facts with sums to 20 (Table 2).
- Continue to work on developing strategies using concrete materials and pictorial representations, and connect these representations to written facts.

What the STUDENTS do:

- Use a variety of materials to develop understanding of strategies in adding and subtracting numbers with sums to 10.
- Explain their strategy for finding the answer to an addition or subtraction fact with sums to 10, using objects, pictures, words, and numbers. Students should use strategies that are efficient and make sense to them. Not all students will use the same strategy.
- Demonstrate fluency for addition and subtraction facts with sums to 10.
- Extend use of strategies to facts with sums to 20, using concrete, pictorial, and symbolic representations.
- Explain their thinking for extended facts, using objects, pictures, words, and numbers.

(Note: Fluency with addition and subtraction facts with sums to 20 is not an expectation for Grade 1. However, students should have a variety of experiences working with extended facts in preparation for work in Grade 2.)

Addressing Student Misconceptions and Common Errors

Continue to watch for students who are double counting a number when adding or subtracting.

Notes

Operations and Algebraic Thinking
1.OA.D*

Work with addition and subtraction equations.

STANDARD 7 | **1.OA.D.7:** Understand the meaning of the equal sign, and determine if equations involving addition and subtraction are true or false. *For example, which of the following equations are true, and which are false?*

$$6 = 6, \quad 7 = 8 - 1, \quad 5 + 2 = 2 + 5, \quad 4 + 1 = 5 + 2.$$

STANDARD 8 | **1.OA.D.8:** Determine the unknown whole number in an addition or subtraction equation relating three whole numbers. *For example, determine the unknown number that makes the equation true in each of the equations.*

$$8 + \square = 11, \quad 5 = \square - 3, \quad 6 + 6 = \square.$$

*Major cluster

Operations and Algebraic Thinking 1.OA.D

Cluster D: Work with addition and subtraction equations.
Grade 1 Overview

As students work through the earlier standards in this domain, instruction focuses on using physical and pictorial representations to develop understanding of the operations of addition and subtraction, solving problems in various contexts, and developing strategies for efficient approaches to learning basic facts. This cluster makes the explicit transition to experiences with symbolic representation for addition and subtraction including meaning of the equal sign and linking previous work with related facts to solving related equations.

These standards are not linear. It is expected that while you are teaching previous standards and students are ready, they will start to write equations using numbers; then, you can begin to emphasize the ideas in this cluster.

Standards for Mathematical Practice
SFMP 2. Reason abstractly and quantitatively.
SFMP 4. Model with mathematics.
SFMP 6. Attend to precision.

Up to this point, students have been using concrete materials and pictorial representations to model mathematical ideas. However, numerals and other mathematical symbols are abstract models of mathematical ideas. As students connect previous work to writing equations and the meaning of the equal sign, they are becoming more sophisticated in representing their thinking. Students are attending to precision when they relate mathematical symbols to their meaning in developmentally appropriate ways (= represents the concept of *same as*; + represents addition; − represents subtraction; and □ [or a similar symbol] represents finding the unknown in an equation).

Related Content Standards
K.NBT.A.1   1.OA.A.1   1.OA.A.2   1.OA.B.4   2.OA.A.1   2.OA.C.3   2.OA.C.4

Notes

STANDARD 7 (1.OA.D.7)

Understand the meaning of the equal sign, and determine if equations involving addition and subtraction are true or false. For example, which of the following equations are true, and which are false?

$$6 = 6, \quad 7 = 8 - 1, \quad 5 + 2 = 2 + 5, \quad 4 + 1 = 5 + 2$$

Critical to this standard is the understanding that the equal sign (=) represents a relationship and not an action. Reading "=" as *same as* rather than *equals* is one way to reinforce this important concept.

What the TEACHER does:

- Develop the concept of the *same amount* as students use physical objects in joining and separating situations. Use the language *same amount* or *same as* with students throughout these experiences.
- Use a balance scale or illustration of a balance scale to reinforce the concept that = means both sides of the equation are balanced.
- Connect physical experiences to the corresponding symbols including numerals, operational signs (+ and −), and the equal sign (=).
- Provide examples in which the orientation of the expressions in an equation includes all possible combinations.

$$6 + 5 = 11 \quad 11 = 6 + 5 \quad 11 - 6 = 5 \quad 5 = 11 - 6$$
$$11 = 11 \quad 6 + 5 = 7 + 4$$

- Once students understand the meaning of the equal sign, provide them with true and false equations, so they can indicate which are correct and which are incorrect.

$$6 = 5 + 1 \text{ (true)} \qquad 6 + 2 = 9 \text{ (false)}$$

- Use formative assessment strategies including questions, activities, and student explanations to determine whether students understand that equals (=) indicates the same amount or balance between the two sides of the equation.

What the STUDENTS do:

- Transition from the use of concrete objects that represent equations to the use of mathematical symbols including numerals, operational symbols (+, −), and the equal sign (=).
- After writing equations, justify their thinking, using concrete materials or words to show that both sides of the equation show the same amount.
- Write equations in all orientations.
- Given a variety of correct and incorrect equations, students identify which are true and which are false and justify their thinking.

Addressing Student Misconceptions and Common Errors

Some students may develop the misconception that the equal sign indicates the answer comes next or calls for the action of doing the mathematical operation. When students use calculators, pressing the equal key results in the answer, which can also cause this misconception. Students should have experiences early on that reinforce that the equal sign indicates both sides of the equation represent the same amount. Using a balance scale or picture of a balance scale with the equal sign on the center helps students to understand that the equal sign means both sides are balanced. As teachers model writing equations or give students examples to solve, it is important to repeat that the equal sign means "the same as." It is appropriate in early experiences using the equal sign to have students read it as "is the same as." For example, students would read $10 - 7 = 3$ as "10 minus 7 is the same as 3."

Notes

Determine the unknown whole number in an addition or subtraction equation relating three whole numbers. For example, determine the unknown number that makes the equation true in each of the equations.

$$8 + \square = 11 \qquad 5 = \square - 3 \qquad 6 + 6 = \square$$

Students have been working with the concept of related addition and subtraction facts with previous standards (1.OA.B.4 and 1.OA.C.6). They should begin to write equations with unknowns as they solve problems (see Table 1). Later, given an equation with an unknown, students explain their reasoning as they find the missing value.

What the TEACHER does:

- As students solve problems by modeling with concrete materials or pictures, teachers begin by writing the equation from student descriptions of how they solved the problem.
- Give students opportunities to write the equation in addition to their models, based on the strategy they used to solve the problem.

  For example,

  > I had 8 crayons. My little brother broke some of them. Now I have 5 crayons that are not broken. How many crayons are broken? $8 - \square = 5$

- Give students equations with the unknown value in various positions. Ask students to find the missing number and explain their thinking.

  For example,

  > Find the unknown number that makes this equation true. $7 + \square = 10$

  > Explain how you found your answer.

- Use formative assessment strategies including questions, activities, and student explanations to assess if students can find the unknown value in an equation and can explain their thinking.

What the STUDENTS do:

- After solving various problems using concrete materials, write equations to represent their work symbolically.
- Solve for the unknown in various positions in addition and subtraction equations.
- Explain how they found the unknown value in an equation.

Addressing Student Misconceptions and Common Errors

Although students may be able to model problem situations with materials and pictures, the transition to writing equations using symbols may be more difficult for them, particularly when their reasoning requires finding a missing addend. Asking students to explain their reasoning as they solve the problem with materials will help them to connect what they have done with the materials to the symbolic equation. Be sure that students have multiple experiences solving equations in which the unknown is in different positions.

$$3 + 8 = \square \qquad 3 + \square = 11 \qquad \square + 3 = 11 \qquad 11 - 3 = \square \qquad 11 - \square = 8 \qquad \square - 3 = 8$$

Notes

_____

_____

_____

_____

Standard: 1.OA.C.6. *Add and subtract within 20, demonstrating fluency for addition and subtraction within 10. Use strategies such as counting on; making ten (e.g., 8 + 6 = 8 + 2 + 4 = 10 + 4 = 14); decomposing a number leading to a ten (e.g., 13 – 4 = 13 – 3 – 1 = 10 – 1 = 9); using the relationship between addition and subtraction (e.g., knowing that 8 + 4 = 12, one knows 12 – 8 = 4); and creating equivalent but easier or known sums (e.g., adding 6 + 7 by creating the known equivalent 6 + 6 + 1 = 12 + 1 = 13).*

Mathematical Practice or Process Standards:

SFMP 7. Look for and make use of structure.

SFMP 8. Look for and express regularity in repeated reasoning.

Through exploring and recognizing the properties of addition and subtraction, students begin to see the structure or patterns that help them to add and subtract numbers more efficiently. From this structure, students will develop strategies to help them become fluent in addition and subtraction within 10 and extend those strategies to working with sums to 20.

Goal:

Now that students are developing fluency with addition and subtraction facts through sums of 10, this lesson will extend their work to addition facts through sums of 20. Students will use double ten frames to develop strategies for finding sums of 11. Class discussion following exploration will focus students on various strategies.

Planning:

Materials: Double ten frames, two-color counters, recording sheets

Sample Activity: Today you are going to the market. You want to buy some apples and some oranges. Altogether you buy 11 pieces of fruit. Show how many of each piece of fruit you can buy. Use your double ten frames and the two-color counters to show how many of each fruit you can buy. Record each solution you find on a double ten frame recording sheet.

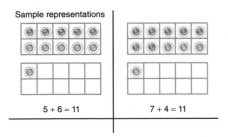

Sample representations

5 + 6 = 11   7 + 4 = 11

Allow students to work for 15 minutes. Use a document camera or projection device to show student recording sheets.

(Continued)

Questions/Prompts:

Call on students to discuss their representations in the following order. Have students discuss their ideas about the strategy that each representation illustrates.

Examples:

5 + 6	(doubles plus 1) (5 + 5 + 1)
6 + 5	(doubles minus 1) (6 + 6 − 1)
7 + 4	(make a ten—decompose 4 to 3 + 1) (7 + 3 + 1)
8 + 3	(make a ten—decompose 3 to 2 + 1) (8 + 2 + 1)
9 + 2	(count on 2 or make a ten) (9+1+1)
10 + 1	(count on 1) (10, 11)

Then discuss the reverse order of the addends; have students talk about how they can find the sums of those examples.

Differentiating Instruction:

Struggling Students: Students who are struggling need more time with a variety of concrete representations. They may still depend on counting on as the best strategy. Double ten frames and three colors of chips may help them see how to decompose a number to fill one ten frame by decomposing the second addend.

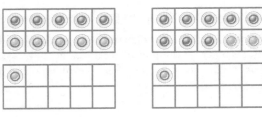

5 + 6 = 5 + 5 + 1   8 + 3 = 8 + 2 + 1

doubles plus 1   make a ten

Extension: Students who demonstrate understanding of these strategies should explain their thinking to others, may use alternate strategies, and can extend their work to sums of 12 and 13.

Notes

Standard:

Mathematical Practice or Process Standards:

Goal:

Planning:

Materials:

Sample Activity:

Questions/Prompts:

Differentiating Instruction:

Struggling Students:

Extension:

Standard:

Mathematical Practice or Process Standards:

Goal:

Planning:

Materials:

Sample Activity:

Questions/Prompts:

Differentiating Instruction:

Struggling Students:

Extension:

Standard:

Mathematical Practice or Process Standards:

Goal:

Planning:

Materials:

Sample Activity:

Questions/Prompts:

Differentiating Instruction:

Struggling Students:

Extension:

Standard:

Mathematical Practice or Process Standards:

Goal:

Planning:

Materials:

Sample Activity:

Questions/Prompts:

Differentiating Instruction:

Struggling Students:

Extension:

Operations and Algebraic Thinking
2.OA.A*

Represent and solve problems involving addition and subtraction.

STANDARD 1 **2.OA.A.1:** Use addition and subtraction within 100 to solve one- and two-step word problems involving situations of adding to, taking from, putting together, taking apart, and comparing, with unknowns in all positions, e.g., by using drawings and equations with a symbol for the unknown number to represent the problem (Table 1).

*Major cluster

Operations and Algebraic Thinking
2.OA.B*

Add and subtract within 20.

STANDARD 2 **2.OA.B.2:** Fluently add and subtract within 20 using mental strategies. By the end of Grade 2, know from memory all sums of two one-digit numbers (Table 2).

*Major cluster

Notes

Cluster A: Represent and solve problems involving addition and subtraction.
Grade 2 Overview

Students continue to work with solving addition and subtraction problems using the various situations in Table 1.

Problem situations include addition and subtraction within 100 and include two-step problems.

Standards for Mathematical Practice
SFMP 1. Make sense of problems and persevere in solving them.
SFMP 2. Use quantitative reasoning.
SFMP 3. Construct viable arguments and critique the reasoning of others.
SFMP 4. Model with mathematics.

Second graders continue to work with understanding the operations of addition and subtraction through experiences with all of the problem-solving situations in Table 1. This is a good opportunity to differentiate instruction as some students may still depend on making models and connecting those models to pictures, number lines, and other representations, which help them to make sense of problems and eventually link that understanding to mathematical notation (equations). Other students will begin to apply a variety of computational strategies shown in Table 2 and connect that thinking to equations. Problem situations now include sums to 100 as well as two-step problems. Students should have many chances to explain their thinking in small groups and to the entire class as well as to see the similarities and differences among their process and that of other students. As they relate what is happening in the problems to addition or subtraction, they begin to use quantitative reasoning by representing what is happening in the problem with mathematical symbols (decontextualize). Students should consistently ask themselves if their answers make sense.

As problems become more complex, including situations that use greater numbers and two-step problems, perseverance is an important characteristic of mathematical thinking comes into play. Guiding questions from the teacher support students in considering additional strategies or solutions paths if a chosen strategy is not leading to a reasonable solution.

Related Content Standards
K.OA.A.1   K.OA.A.2   1.OA.A.1   1.OA.B.3   1.OA.B.4   1.OA.B.8   1.NBT.C.4   1.NBT.C.5

Notes

STANDARD 1 (2.OA.A.1)

Use addition and subtraction within 100 to solve one- and two-step word problems involving situations of adding to, taking from, putting together, taking apart, and comparing, with unknowns in all positions, e.g., by using drawings and equations with a symbol for the unknown number to represent the problem (Table 1).

This cluster is an extension of the work in Grade 1 (Standard 1.OA.A.1). Students should continue to have access to materials including linking cubes, place value materials, ten frames, and counters to model problems. Some students may be ready to use pictorial representations. Encourage students to use materials or draw pictures in order to determine a strategy for solving a problem. Models and drawings may become more sophisticated as numbers in the problem situations are greater than in previous grades. For example, rather than drawing out all of the objects in a comparison problem, it will be easier for students to represent the information using a bar model and numerals to represent the number of objects. Problems should include addition and subtraction examples in which the numbers range up to a total (sum) of 100.

In Grade 1, problems were limited to one-step problems. This standard calls for solving two-step problems.

- Begin with problems in which the operation is the same in both steps.

> Marta had 8 quarters in her bank. On Monday, she added 3 more quarters. On Friday, she put in 6 more quarters. How many quarters are in Marta's bank now?
>
> $8 + 3 = \square$ $\qquad$ $\square + 6 = \bigcirc$ $\qquad$ (or $8 + 3 + 6 = \bigcirc$)

> Eduardo had 18 cookies. He gave 10 to Martina. Then he gave 6 to Fred. How many cookies does Eduardo have now?
>
> $18 - 10 = \square$ $\qquad$ $\square - 6 = \bigcirc$ $\qquad$ (or $18 - 10 - 6 = \bigcirc$)

- Progress to two-step problems that call for different operations.

> Tina had 12 pencils. She bought a package with 8 pencils. She gave 4 pencils to her little sister. How many pencils does Tina have?
>
> $12 + 8 = \square$ $\qquad$ $\square - 4 = \bigcirc$ $\qquad$ (or $12 + 8 - 4 = \bigcirc$)

> Anthony had 25¢. He lent 10¢ to Mark. Then Louise gave him the 5¢ she had borrowed earlier. How much money does Anthony have?
>
> $25¢ - 10¢ = \square$ $\qquad$ $\square + 5¢ = \bigcirc$ $\qquad$ (or $25¢ - 10¢ + 5¢ = \bigcirc$)

Because this is the first experience students have with two-step problems, keep the numbers small enough so the focus stays on understanding the problem situations and finding strategies to solve the problem and not on extending computational skills. It is appropriate for students to begin by using materials to represent the action in the problem and connect that to a written equation.

By the end of Grade 2, given a problem-solving situation, students should be able to determine the unknown in all positions (result unknown, change unknown, and start unknown), using a variety of strategies that make sense to them. Concrete and pictorial representations should be used in explaining their reasoning with explicit connections to writing equations. This includes problems with numbers to 100 and ultimately representing their work as a mathematical equation.

Be sure to ask students if their answer is reasonable. Labeling answers with the unit helps students to be sure their solution makes sense.

What the TEACHER does:

- Continue to provide students with experiences using the problem situations in Table 1.
- As students work with concrete representations to develop strategies to solve problems, it is the role of the teacher to make the connection to the written equation explicit.
- Give students opportunities to explain their strategies for solving problems and to compare how various strategies are similar. Some students may choose to represent their work with linking cubes; others may prefer an open number line. Some students may choose to subtract, while others may choose to think in terms of a missing addend. Having students discuss their thinking solidifies their understanding of the relationship between addition and subtraction, as well as making sense out of a variety of problem situations.
- To help students connect the concrete/pictorial representation to the symbolic representation, model how to write an equation for solving the problem based on student explanations.
- Increase the range of numbers in the problems.
- Use formative assessment protocols (activities, questions, discussion) to determine when students are ready to write mathematical equations independently.
- As part of determining if a solution is reasonable, expect students to label the answer to a problem with the count and unit. (Ex. 25 apples—25 is the count, apples is the label or unit)
- Introduce students to the term *sum* as a synonym for *total*.

What the STUDENTS do:

- Solve a variety of addition and subtraction problems, using concrete and pictorial representations, and explain their reasoning. For example,

  Anna had 25 game tokens. Anita gave her some more. Now Anna has 38 tokens. How many did Anita give to Anna?
- One student might use linking cubes and a part-part-whole chart.

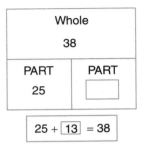

Explanation: "I know she started with 25 tokens and ended up with 38 tokens. I can count up from 25 to 38 to find out how many tokens Anita gave her. Anita gave her 13 tokens. $25 + \boxed{13} = 38$"

- Another student might use an open number line representation.

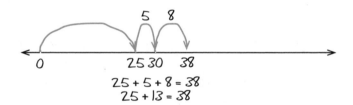

"I started at 25, jumped 5 to get to 30, and jumped 8 more to get to 38. Since $5 + 8 = 13$, I know that Anita gave her 13 tokens. $25 + \boxed{13} = 38$"

- Another student might represent her thinking with linking cubes.

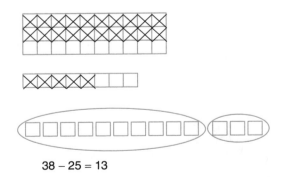

$38 - 25 = 13$

(Continued)

"If I start with the 38 and take away the 25 Anna had before she got some from Anita, I get the number of tokens Anita gave her. Anita gave her 13 tokens. $38 - 25 = \square$ "

- Given an equation based on concrete/pictorial representations, explain how the equation connects to their strategy. ($25 + \square = 38$ might be explained as "I put out 25 cubes and had to figure out how many more I need to have 38 cubes.")
- Write equations that represent the work they have shown with concrete materials or pictures.
- Determine if their answer is reasonable and justify their thinking to others.

Addressing Student Misconceptions and Common Errors

Teaching key words does not help students to develop an understanding of problem situations. Rather, by using concrete models and drawing pictures, students can relate their actions to whether the situation calls for addition or subtraction. In missing addend cases, students will determine what operation (addition or subtraction) makes the most sense to them, as either will result in a correct solution.

Students who struggle with two-step problems should work to identify missing information needed to solve the problem. While the question in the problem will focus on the final answer, identifying missing information will help students to recognize they need to perform an operation to find that information.

GRADE 2

Notes

Cluster B: Add and subtract within 20.
Grade 2 Overview

By the end of Grade 1, students should be fluent with addition and subtraction facts with sums to 10. In Grade 2, students extend work with the strategies to determine sums and differences to sums to 20 (Table 2). Students should have many opportunities to develop and use strategies that make sense to them, looking for patterns and similarities among facts and strategies.

Standards for Mathematical Practice
SFMP 2. Use quantitative reasoning.
SFMP 3. Construct viable arguments and critique the reasoning of others.
SFMP 4. Model with mathematics.
SFMP 7. Look for and make use of structure.
SFMP 8. Look for and express regularity in repeated reasoning.

Second-grade students continue to use concrete models and quantitative reasoning to extend ideas of addition and subtraction to become fluent with sums to 20. While they have had some experience with these strategies in Grade 1, the expectation is that by the end of Grade 2, students are fluent. Models such as ten frames, double ten frames, the hundreds chart, and place value materials will help students internalize the importance of making a ten, a critical structure in early mathematics learning. Models will help students find the sums and differences of more difficult facts. Students clarify their own reasoning and understanding by explaining their thinking and process to others.

Related Content Standards

K.OA.A.2   K.OA.A.3   K.OA.A.4   K.OA.A.5   1.OA.B.3   1.OA.B.4   1.OA.C.5   1.OA.C.6

Notes

STANDARD 2 (2.OA.B.2)

Fluently add and subtract within 20 using mental strategies. By the end of Grade 2, know from memory all sums of two one-digit numbers (Table 2).

Over the course of the year, students continue to develop and use strategies (Table 2) to determine sums and differences. As students become comfortable with a strategy, they use tasks, activities, and games to drill and practice facts.

What the TEACHER does:

- Review and extend strategies with explicit activities connected to facts using physical objects, number lines, and the hundreds chart for addition and subtraction facts with sums to 20 (Table 2).
- Provide a variety of materials including counters, ten frames, number lines, and hundreds chart for students to use.
- Provide opportunities for students to discuss their thinking, using objects, pictures, numbers, and words.
- Pose questions that help students make sense out of their thinking and determine if their answer is reasonable.

  For example, asking students to explain how they found the total (sum) for 9 + 6, students might decompose 6 to make a ten within the fact. An explanation might be, "I took one off the 6 and put it on the 9. Now I have 10 + 5, and that makes 15." (Think: 9 + 1 + 5)

- Use a balance of games, activities, and worksheets to drill and practice basic facts for which students have developed efficient strategies.
- Use a variety of formative assessment strategies to determine the level of student fluency.

What the STUDENTS do:

- Use a variety of materials to continue to work on strategies to find sums and differences of basic facts through sums of 20.
- Explain their strategy for finding the answer to an addition or subtraction fact with sums to 20, using materials, pictures, numbers, and words.
- Demonstrate understanding and application of strategies that make sense to them in finding sums to 20.
- Once students show strategic thinking, they use activities, games, and worksheets to practice basic facts.
- Show fluency (efficiency and accuracy based on understanding) with sums to 20. The recommended time is 3 seconds per fact.

Addressing Student Misconceptions and Common Errors

Watch for students who are making reasoning errors when working with concrete materials or objects as they begin to use more sophisticated strategies. Students may double count a number when adding or subtracting. This may occur with physical objects or pictures or using a hundreds chart. Students may decompose a number to make a ten and then incorrectly add the original addend on to the 10. The sooner such misconceptions are addressed through questions and use of concrete examples, the more likely the student is to self-correct with similar examples. Students do not have to be fluent with all of the mental strategies. They should have many opportunities to practice, explain, and compare strategies. Using the strategies that make sense to them will help students to be ready for drill and practice opportunities to become fluent with facts.

Notes

Operations and Algebraic Thinking 2.OA.C*

Work with equal groups of objects to gain foundations for multiplication.

STANDARD 3	**2.OA.C.3:** Determine whether a group of objects (up to 20) has an odd or even number of members, e.g., by pairing objects or counting them by 2s; write an equation to express an even number as a sum of two equal addends.
STANDARD 4	**2.OA.C.4:** Use addition to find the total number of objects arranged in rectangular arrays with up to 5 rows and up to 5 columns; write an equation to express the total as a sum of equal addends.

*Major cluster

Operations and Algebraic Thinking 2.OA.C

Cluster C: Work with equal groups of objects to gain foundations for multiplication.
Grade 2 Overview

Second graders begin to explore some general patterns that connect to their work with addition and subtraction. Standard 4 is also an informal introduction to the ideas of making groups (multiplication) that will be formally introduced in Grade 3.

Standards for Mathematical Practice
SFMP 2. Use quantitative reasoning.
SFMP 3. Construct viable arguments and critique the reasoning of others.
SFMP 4. Model with mathematics.
SFMP 7. Look for and make use of structure.
SFMP 8. Look for and express regularity in repeated reasoning.

Students continue to use concrete models and quantitative reasoning to extend ideas of addition to seeing the structure of mathematics as they explore what happens when they add combinations of even and odd numbers. They observe what happens to the sum in each situation, using quantitative reasoning to describe why they think this is happening (why is the sum always even when I add two even numbers?), and to make generalizations about each situation. The same process happens as students begin to explore arrays and use repeated addition to begin thinking informally about multiplication.

Related Content Standards
3.OA.A.1   3.NBT.A.3

Notes

STANDARD 3 (2.OA.C.3)

Determine whether a group of objects (up to 20) has an odd or even number of members, e.g., by pairing objects or counting them by 2s; write an equation to express an even number as a sum of two equal addends.

Students develop an understanding of even and odd numbers by using concrete materials to determine if a number can be broken into two parts, with the same number of objects in each part, or by pairing objects and looking to see if there are leftovers (odd) or not (even). They make connections from concrete materials to pictorial representations and later relate this concept to the doubles addition facts.

What the TEACHER does:

- Pose situations that allow students to explore whether a number can be decomposed into pairs of two with or without a leftover.

  There are 18 students going to the baseball game. Model with your cubes to show if each student will have a partner.

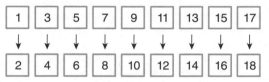

Each person has a partner.

  What if 15 students are going to the game? Will each person have a partner? Justify your answer by showing your thinking using the cubes.

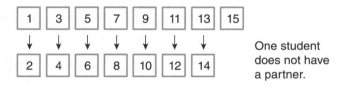

One student does not have a partner.

- When students are ready, they can answer similar questions using drawings rather than concrete objects.
- Expect students to explain their thinking.
- Introduce the vocabulary "even" and "odd" and explain that an even number can always be broken into pairs with no leftovers. An odd number will always have one leftover that cannot be paired with another object.
- Ask students to find other ways they can tell if a number is even or odd. (An even number can be broken into two equal addends—doubles. An odd number can never be represented with a doubles fact.)
- Continue to give students opportunities to recognize even and odd numbers extending the range of numbers beyond 20.

What the STUDENTS do:

- Use concrete materials to explore whether numbers can be divided into groups of 2 with none left over or if there will be a leftover.
- Understand the term *even* describes numbers that can be divided into groups of 2 with no leftovers.
- Understand the term *odd* describes numbers that when divided into groups of 2 will have one item leftover.
- Connect even numbers to the addition facts using doubles.

  o For example, 8 + 8 = 16, so 16 is even

- Recognize odd numbers are represented by addition facts using doubles plus 1.

  o For example, 7 + 8 = 15, so 15 is odd

- Extend the understanding of even and odd numbers by identifying if a number is even or odd for numbers greater than 20.

Addressing Student Misconceptions and Errors

Too often, the focus of even and odd numbers is on telling students (or having them recognize) that even numbers end in 0, 2, 4, 6, or 8 and odd numbers end in 1, 3, 5, 7, or 9. While these are interesting and efficient patterns, they do not define or provide a conceptual understanding of even and odd numbers. While this is not a misconception, it is important to emphasize the use of concrete experiences to develop a foundational understanding of the meaning of even and odd numbers.

Use addition to find the total number of objects arranged in rectangular arrays with up to 5 rows and up to 5 columns; write an equation to express the total as a sum of equal addends.

Second graders begin to extend their understanding of addition to equal groups and use repeated addition to determine the total number of items in a rectangular array that has up to 5 groups and up to 5 items in a group. A rectangular array is an arrangement of objects in rows and columns. As a foundational understanding for the operation of multiplication, a fundamental concept in Grade 3, students build arrays with concrete objects and pictures and determine the number of objects in a given array.

What the TEACHER does:

- Provide students with concrete and pictorial representations of rectangular arrays and ask them to determine the number of objects shown.

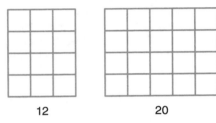

12   20

- Ask students to describe the picture (x columns and y rows). Expect students to explain how they determined the number of objects. Strategies include counting, skip counting, and repeated addition.
- Provide students with materials such as square tiles, cubes, and counters and allow them to explore other rectangular array configurations. For example, ask them to make an array with 8 objects.
- Expect students to explain their reasoning in describing the arrays they build.

  For example,

  "My array has 4 rows and 2 columns. I know there are 8 objects because I know that $4 + 4 = 8$."

- Describe an array and ask students to build it and determine the number of objects in the array.

  For example,

  "Use cubes to build an array that has 3 rows and 4 columns."

  "How many cubes are in the array? How did you find the number of cubes?"

- After students have had multiple experiences using concrete materials, provide them opportunities to draw arrays on grid paper and determine the number of objects in the array.

What the STUDENTS do:

- Use models to represent rectangular arrays with up to 5 rows and 5 columns and determine the total number of objects in the array.
- As the teacher presents physical models, students determine the number of objects and discuss their reasoning.
- Students are given a number (up to 25) and construct arrays using objects such as cubes or tiles. They describe the array and explain how they know the array has that number of objects. Strategies include counting, skip counting, and repeated addition.
- Given the dimensions of an array, for example 3 rows and 2 columns, students construct the array, determine the number of objects in the array, and explain how they arrived at that number.
- Repeat similar activities drawing the arrays on grid paper rather than using concrete objects.

Addressing Student Misconceptions and Common Errors

Students may miscount the number of objects in the array. Use arrays with smaller numbers (less than 10) gradually increasing the total number of items in the array.

Students may not think of a configuration with 1 row or 1 column as an array. Be certain they have some experiences seeing and constructing arrays with 1 row or 1 column.

Some students may have difficulty with repeated addition. Give students practice with skip counting and make connections to repeated addition.

Standard: 2.OA.A.1. *Use addition and subtraction within 100 to solve one- and two-step word problems involving situations of adding to, taking from, putting together, taking apart, and comparing, with unknowns in all positions, e.g., by using drawings and equations with a symbol for the unknown number to represent the problem (Table 1).*

Mathematical Practice or Process Standards:

SFMP 1. Make sense of problems and persevere in solving them.

SFMP 2. Use quantitative reasoning.

SFMP 3. Construct viable arguments and critique the reasoning of others.

SFMP 4. Model with mathematics.

When presented with comparison problem situations, students use concrete representations to model the problem and connect that representation to more abstract bar models. Through reasoning with the bar model, they determine the wanted information and connect it to the mathematical equation. These problems have multiple solution paths. Giving students a chance to explain their reasoning allows multiple ideas to be shared.

Goal:

This lesson focuses on comparison situations involving addition and subtraction within 100. Students begin with concrete representations of the information in simple problems (numbers < 20) and connect those representations to equations. More complex problems (numbers >20) are more easily represented in bar diagrams, and students make the transition from concrete models to bar diagrams to equations. This lesson focuses on the connection between concrete representations and bar models.

Planning:

Materials: Set of comparison problems, chips or counters, graph paper

Sample Activity: Present the students with the situation:

Martina has 15 coins fewer than Pat. Martina has 23 coins. How many coins does Pat have?

Students summarize the information in the problem, focus on the question, and model using chips or coins.

From the physical representation, students find the answer to the question. Students discuss their reasoning for the models they used. They write an equation to show the mathematical notation.

(Continued)

Questions/Prompts:

What do you know?

What do you want to find out?

How can you show this using chips?

How can you show what Pat has?

How will you use your model to show how to answer the question?

How can you show what you did using numbers and an equation?

Differentiating Instruction

Struggling Students: This is a comparison situation, and the word *fewer* may lead some students to think they need to subtract when actually they add to find the number of Pat's coins. Students who struggle to model this problem should be given a similar problem with smaller numbers. They may need more scaffolding to lay out Martina's coins and then explain in their own words what the problem tells them about the number of Pat's coins. Relate the model they build to the information in the problem, so they can check to see if the model is correct. These students may need support in writing the equation.

Extension: Give students similar problems and ask them to draw pictures or, if they are ready, to solve using an equation.

Notes

Standard:

Mathematical Practice or Process Standards:

Goal:

Planning:

Materials:

Sample Activity:

Questions/Prompts:

Differentiating Instruction:

Struggling Students:

Extension:

Standard:

Mathematical Practice or Process Standards:

Goal:

Planning:

Materials:

Sample Activity:

Questions/Prompts:

Differentiating Instruction:

Struggling Students:

Extension:

Standard:

Mathematical Practice or Process Standards:

Goal:

Planning:

Materials:

Sample Activity:

Questions/Prompts:

Differentiating Instruction:

Struggling Students:

Extension:

Reflection Questions: Operations and Algebraic Thinking

1. How does the use of problem situations help students to develop a conceptual understanding of addition and subtraction?

2. Discuss each problem situation in Table 1. As a group, develop a set of grade-level appropriate problems you can use for each situation. What are some developmentally appropriate models for your grade level? Refer to standards in this domain to determine the range of numbers with which students will be working at your grade level.

3. Discuss with colleagues who teach other grade levels in K–2 some strategies for introducing the problem types. How does this progress across grade levels? Use this information to build upon each other's work.

4. How do the properties of addition and subtraction help students to develop a deeper understanding of these operations as well as to become fluent with procedural skills?

5. What are some activities you can use to help students "discover" the properties, so they understand and use them? (Remember students do not need to know a property's formal name at this level.)

6. How does the expectation for fluency with facts develop across grade levels in this domain? Talk about strategies that students can use to help them become fluent with facts using understanding rather than rote memorization (Table 2).

Part 3

Number and Operations
in Base Ten

Number and Operations in Base Ten

Domain Overview

KINDERGARTEN

The work in kindergarten forms the foundation for students to develop an understanding of the base ten system. Special attention is focused on 10 and connections to the meaning of numbers from 11 to 19. Once students understand counts from 1 to 9, they can begin to think of the number 10 as 10 ones and the number 11 as ten ones and one more. This domain comprises the major work of kindergarten and will be developed across the entire school year and linked closely with the Counting and Cardinality and Operations and Algebraic Thinking domains.

GRADE 1

First graders build on kindergarten work and begin to think of ten ones as a unit called a ten. Students continue to form initial understanding using a variety of materials then move to drawings and then to symbolic notation, including <, >, and =. They will find sums to 100 with understanding by using materials and developing strategies. Subtraction with two-digit numbers includes only differences among multiples of 10 in first grade.

GRADE 2

In second grade, students extend place value understanding to working with a new unit comprising 10 tens or a group of 100. Using place value and properties of addition and subtraction, students become fluent with two-digit addition and subtraction including composing and decomposing groups of 10. They extend this work to addition and subtraction to 1,000 with careful scaffolding from concrete representations to pictorial representations and finally to working with abstract representations.

Table 2 illustrates common mental computation strategies that develop across K–2 and extend to more sophisticated addition and subtraction examples.

SUGGESTED MATERIALS FOR THIS DOMAIN

K	1	2	
✓	✓	✓	Objects for counting such as beans, linking cubes, counters, chips, coins, and straws
✓			Five frames (Reproducible 1)
✓	✓	✓	Ten frames (Reproducible 2)
	✓	✓	Double ten frames (Reproducible 3)
✓	✓	✓	Hundreds chart (Reproducible 4)
✓	✓	✓	Dot cards (Reproducible 5)
✓	✓		Numeral cards (Reproducible 6)
	✓	✓	Number line to 20 (Reproducible 7)
	✓	✓	Open number line (Reproducible 8)
✓	✓	✓	Part-Part-Whole chart (Reproducible 9)
	✓	✓	Straws or coffee stirrers and rubber bands for place value
	✓	✓	Linking cubes for place value
✓	✓	✓	Place value chart to tens (Reproducible 10)
		✓	Place value chart to hundreds (Reproducible 11)
	✓	✓	Greater than, Less than = cards (Reproducible 12)
		✓	*Base ten blocks

* Note that students should use materials such as linking cubes and straws that provide opportunities to physically put together and take apart tens and hundreds. Base ten blocks should only be used after students show competency with making tens and hundreds as they involve exchanging 10 ones for 1 ten or 10 tens for 1 hundred, which requires a higher level of understanding than actually putting together or taking apart objects to make ones, tens, and hundreds.

KEY VOCABULARY

K	1	2	
✓	✓	✓	**add** to combine or join together *related words: add, and, plus, join, put together, (+)*
	✓	✓	***associative property of addition** an extension of the commutative property, to change the order and group two addends to find convenient sums (such as 10) in order to make the addition easier. Note that students do not use parenthesis at this level. The focus is on looking for sums of 10. $4 + 8 + 2 = 4 + 10 = 14$ or $6 + 8 + 4 = 6 + 4 + 8 = 18$
	✓	✓	**bundle** to put individual units together to make a larger unit, for example, connecting 10 individual linking cubes to make a ten.
	✓	✓	***commutative property of addition** reversing the order of the addends does not change the total (sum) $8 + 5 = 13$ and $5 + 8 = 13$ so $8 + 5 = 5 + 8$
✓	✓	✓	**compare** to look for similarities or differences among numbers
	✓	✓	**compose** put a number together using other numbers $1 + 9$, $2 + 8$, $3 + 7$, $4 + 6$, $5 + 5$, $1 + 2 + 3 + 4$ are ways to compose 10

(Continued)

K	1	2	
	✓	✓	**decompose** separate a number into parts using other numbers 8 can be decomposed into 4 + 4, 3 + 5, 2 + 2 + 2 + 2
✓	✓	✓	**difference** the amount by which one number is greater or less than another number. The difference can be found by subtracting, comparing, or finding a missing addend.
✓	✓	✓	**equal** (=) same as in value or size
	✓	✓	**equation** a mathematical sentence in which one part is the same as, or equal to, the other part 3 + 5 = 8, 12 − 7 = 5, 11 = 8 + 3, 6 = 9 − 3
✓	✓	✓	**fewer** less than
✓	✓	✓	**greater** more than
		✓	**hundred** a group or bundle of 10 tens or 100 ones
✓	✓	✓	**hundreds chart** 10 by 10 grid with the counting numbers from 1 to 100 listed; used to develop and demonstrate patterns and strategies for counting, addition, subtraction, and place value
	✓	✓	*** identity property of addition** any number plus 0 equals the number 12 + 0 = 12 or 0 + 12 = 12
	✓	✓	*** identity property of subtraction** any number minus 0 equals the number 15 − 0 = 15 or 15 = 15 − 0
✓	✓	✓	**missing addend** given an equation in which the total (sum) and one addend is known, the unknown addend 5 + □ = 8 In this equation □ has a value of 3. It is the missing addend.
	✓	✓	**number line** a line used to show the position of a number in relation to other numbers (Reproducible 7)
	✓	✓	**open number line (empty number line)** a number line with no numbers or markers; used as a visual representation for recording and sharing strategies for adding or subtracting numbers (Reproducible 8)
	✓	✓	**part-part-whole model** a visual model for showing the relationship among numbers in addition and subtraction situations (Reproducible 9)
	✓	✓	**place value** the value of a digit is determined by its place in a number In 23, the 2 is in the tens place and has a value of 20; the 3 is in the ones place and has a value of 3.
✓	✓	✓	**subtract** to take one number away from another; to find the difference between two numbers *related words: subtract, minus, take from, take apart (−)*
		✓	**sum** the answer in an addition problem; total
✓	✓	✓	**ten** a group or bundle of 10 ones
✓	✓	✓	**ten frame** a graphic representation that is useful to help students to count, see number relationships, and learn basic facts (Reproducible 2)
		✓	**thousand** a group or bundle of 10 hundreds, 100 tens, or 1,000 ones
✓	✓	✓	**total (sum)** the result when two or more numbers are added together

* Students are not responsible for these vocabulary words; however, they should understand the mathematical concept.

Number and Operations in Base Ten
K.NBT.A*

Work with numbers 11–19 to gain foundation for place value.

STANDARD 1   **K.NBT.A.1:** Compose and decompose numbers from 11 to 19 into ten ones and some further ones, e.g., by using objects or drawings, and record each composition or decomposition by a drawing or equation; understand that these numbers are composed of ten ones and one, two, three, four, five, six, seven, eight, or nine ones.

*Major cluster

Number and Operations in Base Ten K.NBT

Cluster A: Work with numbers 11–19 to gain foundations for place value.
Kindergarten Overview

The focus of this cluster is on composing and decomposing numbers from 11 to 19 into 10 ones and some more ones. The idea of ten as a unit will not be introduced until Grade 1.

Standards for Mathematical Practice
SFMP 3. Construct viable arguments and critique the reasoning of others.
SFMP 4. Model with mathematics.
SFMP 7. Look for and make use of structure.

As they explore the meaning of place value with numbers from 11 to 19 as 10 ones and some more ones, students are having their first experience with the structure of mathematics. Place value is the foundation for all future work with whole numbers and decimal numbers. The use of concrete and pictorial models and later connecting those models to symbolic notation is fundamental to developing conceptual understanding. Students explain their reasoning and listen to the thinking of others to solidify their understanding.

Related Content Standards
1.NBT.B.2   2.NBT.A.1

Notes

Compose and decompose numbers from 11 to 19 into ten ones and some further ones, e.g., by using objects or drawings, and record each composition or decomposition by a drawing or equation (such as 18 = 10 + 8); understand that these numbers are composed of ten ones and one, two, three, four, five, six, seven, eight, or nine ones.

What the TEACHER does:

- Give students a variety of experiences with counting 10 ones and composing and decomposing ten using concrete materials.
- Progress to giving students a number from 11 to 19 (both orally and showing the numeral) beginning with numbers closer to 10. After students count out that number of objects, the teacher models putting a group of 10 together (composing 10) and counting the leftover objects. Students do the same. After doing several examples together, students continue to work independently.

- Model written equations showing a teen number composed (10 + 8 = 18) and decomposed (18 = 10 + 8). Connect the equation with the physical models and drawings. Provide students with number cards or situations in which they match the number with the correct equation. The final expectation is for students to write the equations. Students should have many opportunities to practice this through games and activities.

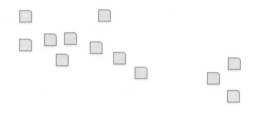

What the STUDENTS do:

- Experience putting together and taking apart numbers from 11 to 19 by forming a group of 10 ones and some more ones, using objects such as linking cubes, straws, double tens frames, or a cup of 10 and some ones.

Ways to represent 13:

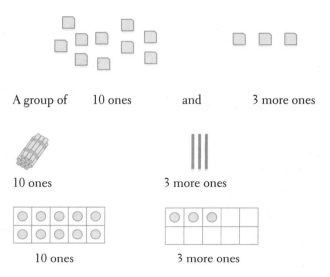

A group of   10 ones   and   3 more ones

10 ones   3 more ones

10 ones   3 more ones

- After many experiences with concrete materials, students use drawings to represent and explain their thinking.
- Students match representations (either concrete or pictorial) with numerals.
- Students continue to work with a variety of representations, including concrete models, drawings, and numerals, to develop a deep understanding of a teen number being composed of a ten ones and some more ones. Since this concept is the foundation for future work developing place value in Grades 1 and 2, the concept should be developed over the entire year.

Addressing Student Misconceptions and Common Errors

Kindergarten students have several new concepts with which to grapple as part of this standard including the notion of 10 ones being grouped together. Watch for those who struggle with this important place value concept. The concept that 1 group of 10 ones and some more ones can represent the same idea as the number they originally counted will be a stretch for some students, and they will need many opportunities to compose groups of 10 with concrete materials. The other concept that may present a challenge is the teen number names. A group of 10 and one more has the name "eleven"; a group of 10 and two more is called "twelve"; a group of 10 and three more is called "thirteen." Students entering kindergarten with little number experience may need much more practice with the representations and connecting representations to the number names.

Notes

Standard: K.NBT.A.1. *Compose and decompose numbers from 11 to 19 into ten ones and some further ones, e.g., by using objects or drawings, and record each composition or decomposition by a drawing or equation (such as 18 = 10 + 8); understand that these numbers are composed of ten ones and one, two, three, four, five, six, seven, eight, or nine ones.*

Mathematical Practice or Process Standards:

SFMP 4. Model with mathematics.
SFMP 6. Attend to precision.
SFMP 7. Look for and make use of structure.

Students use a variety of concrete materials to model the numbers between 11 and 19. They put 10 ones together to make a set of 10 and will have some leftover ones. After making physical models, students describe their representations with words and equations.

Goal:

This is students' first experience with place value, a fundamental structure of the whole number system. Students develop the concept of decomposing a number into a group of 10 ones and some more ones.

Planning:

Materials: Small cups, plastic sandwich bags, counters of all types (such as beans, chips, shells, buttons, teddy bear counters, etc.), numeral cards from 8 to 19. Put each type of counter and a set of numeral cards at workstations around the classroom.

Sample Activity:

Introduce the activity demonstrating that students will turn over a numeral card; count out that number of counters. If there are more than 9 counters, they take 10 counters and put them in a cup or in a plastic bag. They describe their representation and write an equation to represent the number. For example, if they draw 13, they would count out 13 chips. Count 10 of the chips and put them in a cup. They would describe their representation as 10 ones and 3 ones. They would write the equation as 13 = 10 + 3

Questions/Prompts:

How many counters do you have?
  (13)

Are there more than 10? (If yes) What should you do with 10 of the counters?
  (Put them in the cup.)

Describe what you have using words.
  (10 ones and 3 more ones)

How can you write that using numbers?
  ($13 = 10 + 3$)

Differentiating Instruction:

Struggling Students: Prerequisite skills to be successful with this activity include counting to 19 and using physical materials to represent each number. If students are unable to successfully represent numbers to 19, they will need more practice with that skill before they are ready for this standard. Scaffold the range of numbers beginning with a range of 8–13. Provide extra support in describing and writing the equation.

Extension: Students who are successful with this activity can decompose the teen numbers with drawings and then just by writing the equations. They might also begin to work with numbers to 25 filling two cups or plastic bags each with 10 ones for numbers from 20 to 25.

Standard:

Mathematical Practice or Process Standards:

Goal:

Planning:

Materials:

Sample Activity:

Questions/Prompts:

Differentiating Instruction:

Struggling Students:

Extension:

Number and Operations in Base Ten
1.NBT.A*

Extend the counting sequence.

STANDARD 1 **1.NBT.A.1:** Count to 120, starting at any number less than 120. In this range, read and write numerals and represent a number of objects with a written numeral.

*Major cluster

Number and Operations in Base Ten 1.NBT.A

Cluster A: Extend the counting sequence.
Grade 1 Overview

This cluster extends earlier work with standard K.CC.A.1 in which students rote counted to 100. Building on previous counting experiences, students count on from any number less than 120. They read, write, and represent any number to 120.

Standard for Mathematical Practice
SFMP 6. Attend to precision.

Students first learn numbers by rote counting. They build vocabulary with numbers to 120.

Related Content Standards

K.CC.A.1   2.NBT.A.2

Notes

STANDARD 1 (1.NBT.A.1)

Count to 120, starting at any number less than 120. In this range, read and write numerals and represent a number of objects with a written numeral.

The main difference between this standard and previous experiences with rote counting is that as students extend the range of counting numbers, focusing on the patterns evident in written numerals. This is the foundation for thinking about place value and the meaning of the digits in a numeral. Students are also expected to read and write numerals to 120.

What the TEACHER does:

- Begin by having students continue to count with objects and write the numeral for each count of objects.
- Give students a number to count on to within a range of numbers. For example, students should be able to count on from 25 to 50 starting with 25, 26, 27, 28 . . .
- Use the hundreds chart (Reproducible 4) for activities that provide opportunities for students to recognize written numerals and begin to recognize patterns on the hundreds chart. For example,
  - o All of the numbers in a column have the same digit in the ones place
  - o All of the numbers in a row have the same digit in the tens place
  - o The number that follows a given number is one more than the number (42 is one more than 41)
  - o The number that precedes a given number is one less than the number (40 is one less than 41)
- Provide activities and tasks that explicitly expect students to see the difference between reversed numbers, such as 25 and 52.

What the STUDENTS do:

- Count on from a number ending at any number up to 120.
- Recognize and explain patterns with numerals on a hundreds chart.
- Understand that the place of a digit determines its value. For example, students recognize that 24 is different from and less than 42.
- Explain their thinking with a variety of examples.
- Read and write numerals to 120.

Addressing Student Misconceptions and Common Errors

It is not expected that students develop an understanding of place value with this standard. However, watch for students who reverse digits in writing the numeral or do not demonstrate an understanding that 21 does not have the same value as 12. When reversals occur, have students model each number, using straws or linking cubes to reinforce the place value of digits and to help students differentiate between the numbers.

> Notes

Number and Operations in Base Ten
1.NBT.B*

Understand place value.

STANDARD 2 **1.NBT.A.2:** Understand that the two digits of a two-digit number represent amounts of tens and ones.

Understand the following as special cases:

a. 10 can be thought of as a bundle of ten ones—called a "ten."

b. The numbers from 11 to 19 are composed of a ten and one, two, three, four, five, six, seven, eight, or nine ones.

c. The numbers 10, 20, 30, 40, 50, 60, 70, 80, 90 refer to one, two, three, four, five, six, seven, eight, or nine tens (and 0 ones).

STANDARD 3 **1.NBT.A.3:** Compare two two-digit numbers based on meanings of the tens and ones digits, recording the results of comparisons with the symbols >, =, and <.

*Major cluster

Number and Operations in Base Ten 1.NBT.B

Cluster B: Understand place value.
Grade 1 Overview

This cluster underlies the critical foundation of understanding place value in preparation for understanding addition and subtraction beyond basic facts. Students think of whole numbers in terms of the value of the digits (tens and ones) and recognize that the digit in the tens place represents that many groups of 10, and a digit in the ones place represents that many ones.

Standards for Mathematical Practice
SFMP 2. Reason abstractly and quantitatively.
SFMP 3. Construct viable arguments and critique the reasoning of others.
SFMP 4. Model with mathematics.
SFMP 5. Use appropriate tools strategically.
SFMP 6. Attend to precision.
SFMP 7. Look for and make use of structure.

As they explore the meaning of place value with numbers from 11 to 19 as a group of 10 and some ones, students experience the structure of mathematics. Place value is the foundation for all future work with whole numbers and decimal numbers. The use of concrete models and pictorial models and explicitly connecting them to symbolic notation is fundamental to developing conceptual understanding. Students explain their reasoning and listen to the thinking of others to solidify their understanding.

Related Content Standards

K.NBT.A.1   KCC.C.7   2.NBT.A.1   2NBT A.4

Notes

STANDARD 2 (1.NBT.B.2)

Understand that the two digits of a two-digit number represent amounts of tens and ones.

This standard outlines a helpful progression for developing an initial understanding of place value, the concept that the location or place of a digit within a two-digit or three-digit numeral determines the value of that digit.

Understand the following as special cases:

a. 10 can be thought of as a bundle of ten ones—called a "ten."

Students begin to unitize or consider 10 ones as a group or unit called a ten. Rather than seeing 10 individual cubes, they can link those cubes and make a group of 1 ten.

What the TEACHER does:

- Use activities with ten frames, bundling straws, linking cubes, and counters that expect students to bundle or group 10 ones to make a ten.
- Develop student vocabulary to see a ten as a unit composed of 10 ones.
- Introduce students to the place value chart with ones and tens (Reproducible 10). A unit or group of 10 always belongs in the tens place. Individual ones always belong in the ones place.

What the STUDENTS do:

- Given objects such as counters, linking cubes, or ten frames, students bundle or group 10 ones to make a ten.
- Develop vocabulary to refer to a group of 10 as 1 ten.
- Differentiate between 1 ten (a bundle) and 10 ones.

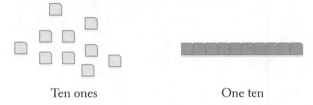

Ten ones   One ten

b. The numbers from 11 to 19 are composed of a ten and one, two, three, four, five, six, seven, eight, or nine ones.

Students build on previous work in kindergarten (K.NBT.A.1) where they composed and decomposed numbers from 11 to 19 into 10 ones and some more ones. This standard expects that students will understand that the 10 ones, from their previous experiences, are now thought of as a bundle or group of 10. It is a unit, that is, *1* ten. Through experiences using a variety of materials such as ten frames, bundling straws, and linking cubes, students see a teen number, such as 16, as 1 ten plus 6 ones.

What the TEACHER does:

- Give students between 11 and 19 concrete objects, which they represent as 1 ten and some ones. Tasks should require putting the 10 ones together, such as bundling straws or linking cubes, and placing the bundle of 10 in the tens place on a place value chart.
- Pose questions that reinforce the concept that when 10 ones are grouped or bundled, they now make up a new unit called 1 ten.

What the STUDENTS do:

- Given a number of objects between 11 and 19, group them into 1 group of ten and some ones.
- Describe the grouping, using place value language. For example, 17 is 1 ten and 7 ones.

c. The numbers 10, 20, 30, 40, 50, 60, 70, 80, 90 refer to one, two, three, four, five, six, seven, eight, or nine tens (and 0 ones).

Once students have a firm grasp of the concept of teen numbers being made up of 1 ten and some ones, they continue to explore with multiples of ten (10, 20, 30, 40, 50, 60, 70, 80, 90) as groups of ten with no ones leftover. For example, 40 is 4 groups or bundles of ten and no ones. This prepares students for understanding place value with numbers greater than 20. Although not explicit in this standard, there is an expectation that once students understand multiples of 10 through 90 as a specific number of tens and no ones, they begin to work with other numbers, describing them in terms of place value. For example, 57 is 5 tens and 7 ones or 57 ones.

What the TEACHER does:

- Build on experiences with groups of ten by giving students tasks in which they bundle 20, 30, 40 . . . objects into groups of ten. Placing bundles of ten on a place value chart reinforces the concept that these numbers represent bundles of tens and no ones. For example, 30 is represented by 3 tens and 0 ones.
- Provide multiple experiences with a variety of concrete objects including ten frames, linking cubes and counters that are placed in cups or baggies labeled ten, or bundling straws into groups of ten.
- Focus discussion on describing concrete representations using words. For example, 3 bundles of straws would be described as 3 tens and 0 ones.
- Use formative assessment protocols, including tasks, student explanations, and worksheets, to determine if students understand unitizing and can describe multiples of 10 up to 90 as a number of tens and no ones.
- Begin to provide experiences with other numbers up to 100. Give students a number of objects such as linking cubes, which are placed in the ones place on a place value chart (Reproducible 10). Ask students to connect as many groups of 10 as possible and move the rod of 10 cubes to the tens place. Any leftover cubes would remain in the ones place.
- Ask students to describe what they have represented on the place value chart. For example: 35 cubes would be represented as 3 tens and 5 ones.
- Guide students to make explicit connections between concrete materials and pictorial representations for place value. As students orally describe a number in terms of place value, they begin to connect that understanding to the written numeral.

4 tens   3 ones   43

What the STUDENTS do:

- Use concrete materials to represent numbers including 10, 20 30, . . . 90 as groups of ten with no ones.
- Place concrete representations on a place value chart to reinforce that the number is made up of tens and no ones.
- Describe the decade numbers using words that include the number of groups of ten to reinforce understanding ten as a unit that is different from ones. For example, 20 is 2 tens; 30 is 3 tens.
- Use concrete materials to represent any number from 10 to 99 by making as many groups of ten as possible and placing those groups in the tens place on a place value chart. Place any leftover single items in the ones place.
- Describe the representation using words.
- Write the numerals with emphasis on identifying how the written number shows the number of tens and the number of ones.
- Connect words to the written numeral. For example, 3 tens and 2 ones is written as 32.

Continue to watch for students who reverse digits. These students need more opportunities to decompose numbers into groups of ten and ones using concrete materials and then to put the items in the correct places on a place value chart. They describe the number in terms of tens and ones and then write the numeral below the concrete representation.

Observe students counting tens and ones separately. For example,

 Students who count this as 10, 20, 1, 2, 3 rather than 10, 20, 21, 22, 23 need more practice with counting.

Some students may have difficulty differentiating number words that sound alike, for example, *fifty* and *fifteen*. These number words can be spelled out and added to a word wall showing pictures, numbers, and words.

40   forty   14   fourteen

Notes

Compare two two-digit numbers based on meanings of the tens and ones digits, recording the results of comparisons with the symbols >, =, and <.

Once students show an understanding of place value for tens and ones, they begin to compare two numbers by determining the number of tens and the number of ones in each number. After experiences with comparing using concrete materials, including ten frames and place value charts, students move to the hundreds chart and number lines. They generalize that the number with the most tens is greater. If the number of tens is the same, the number with more ones is greater. Comparative language including greater than, more than, less than, fewer than, equal to, and same as is developed. When students become facile with using appropriate vocabulary, the mathematical symbols should be introduced.

What the TEACHER does:

- Provide students with a variety of concrete materials and place value charts for representing two 2-digit numbers for making comparisons. Present the numbers orally as well as using written numerals.
- Pose questions such as "Which is greater?" "Which has more?" "Which is less?" or "Which has fewer?" to familiarize students with appropriate vocabulary.
- Facilitate conversations in which students explain their thinking.
- Use formative assessment protocols to evaluate if students are using the number of tens and, if necessary, the number of ones in making comparisons.
- After concrete and pictorial experiences, ask students to compare two 2-digit numbers written as numerals.
- Once students demonstrate understanding by describing the comparison, introduce the mathematical symbols for these relationships (<, >, =).

What the STUDENTS do:

- Use concrete materials such as objects on place value charts, tens frames, hundreds chart, and number lines to compare two 2-digit numbers.
- Describe the comparison using terms including greater than, more than, less than, fewer than, equal to, and same as.
- Justify their reasoning as they compare numbers. For example, "I know 45 is more than 42 because they both have 4 tens, but 5 ones in 45 is more than 2 ones in 42."
- Compare two 2-digit numbers written as numerals.
- Use the mathematical symbols <, >, and = to represent comparisons symbolically.

Addressing Student Misconceptions and Common Errors

Students who recognize two-digit numbers but do not understand that the position of the digit determines its value need additional work with concrete representations. Give each student a number and ask them to represent that number on their place value chart. They work with a partner to determine which number is greater. They use cards with <, >, or = (Reproducible 12) and put the correct sign between their charts. Only when students show understanding with materials and pictorial representations should they begin to connect those representations to using numerals.

It is important for students to associate the symbols < and > with their real meaning. Rather than use aids such as alligators or Pac-Man, it may help students who confuse the symbols to think that the open end of the symbol is always closest to the greater number and the closed end is always pointed to the lesser number. It is also important to give students opportunities to change the order of the numbers to see how it impacts the symbols and their meaning.

Example: $35 < 65$ or $65 > 35$

Notes

Number and Operations in Base Ten
1.NBT.C*

Use place value understanding and properties of operations to add and subtract.

STANDARD 4　**1.NBT.C.4:** Add within 100, including adding a two-digit number and a one-digit number, and adding a two-digit number and a multiple of 10, using concrete models or drawings and strategies based on place value, properties of operations, and/or the relationship between addition and subtraction; relate the strategy to a written method and explain the reasoning used. Understand that in adding two-digit numbers, one adds tens and tens, ones and ones; and sometimes it is necessary to compose a ten.

STANDARD 5　**1.NBT.C.5:** Given a two-digit number, mentally find 10 more or 10 less than the number, without having to count; explain the reasoning used.

STANDARD 6　**1.NBT.C.6:** Subtract multiples of 10 in the range 10–90 from multiples of 10 in the range 10–90 (positive or zero differences), using concrete models or drawings and strategies based on place value, properties of operations, and/or the relationship between addition and subtraction; relate the strategy to a written method and explain the reasoning used.

*Major cluster

Number and Operations in Base Ten 1.NBT.C

Cluster C: Use place value understanding and properties of operations to add and subtract.
Grade 1 Overview

Once a deep understanding of place value concepts has been established, students use concrete materials to develop and understand the process for adding and subtracting up to 100. Students also develop mental strategies for finding 10 more or 10 less than a number up to 100. Subtraction with two 2-digit numbers is limited to subtracting multiples of 10.

Note that students may be working across the three standards in this cluster over time. It is not expected that mastery of standard four has been accomplished before working with standard five. In fact, the generalizations students develop in mentally adding and subtracting ten will prove very useful as students add and subtract with two-digit numbers.

Standards for Mathematical Practice
SFMP 1. Make sense of problems and persevere in solving them.
SFMP 2. Reason abstractly and quantitatively.
SFMP 3. Construct viable arguments and critique the reasoning of others.
SFMP 4. Model with mathematics.
SFMP 5. Use appropriate tools strategically.
SFMP 6. Attend to precision.
SFMP 7. Look for and make use of structure.
SFMP 8. Look for and express regularity in repeated reasoning.

Throughout their experiences using place value to add and subtract, students should use all of the Standards for Mathematical Practice. Whenever possible, provide students with problem contexts for addition and subtraction (Table 1). Students use abstract and quantitative reasoning to ask themselves if answers make sense by reflecting on the value of numbers and using strategies that employ number sense. Students model using various representations and, use tools such as concrete materials and place value charts followed by pictorial and lastly symbolic representations.

As students extend their previous understanding of ten as a unit, they see the structure of the place value system and identify that the concept of tens — whether 10 ones, 10 tens, or 10 hundreds — is repeated reasoning. Students will continue to build on these ideas in Grade 3 with all four operations.

Related Content Standards

1.OA.A.1　1.OA.A.2　2.OA.A.1　2.NBT.A.1　2.NBT.B.5　2.NBT.B.6　2.NBT.B.7　2.NBT.B.8

Add within 100, including adding a two-digit number and a one-digit number, and adding a two-digit number and a multiple of 10, using concrete models or drawings and strategies based on place value, properties of operations, and/or the relationship between addition and subtraction; relate the strategy to a written method and explain the reasoning used. Understand that in adding two-digit numbers, one adds tens and tens, ones and ones; and sometimes it is necessary to compose a ten.

There are several important components embedded in this standard. Students begin to develop understanding and skill with adding beyond the basic facts through the use of concrete representations. They progress to making generalizations and developing their own strategies for adding one- and two-digit numbers.

Previous work with Standard 1.NBT.B.2, making groups of ten and using place value charts, should be extended to working with two addends. Note the careful scaffolding of examples for students in Table 3.

Include problems that provide a context for addition as often as possible (Table 1). Equations should be written both horizontally and vertically.

Encourage students to make estimates before adding to determine if their answers are reasonable.

It is important to remember that the goal of this standard is to have students develop strategies and make sense of adding one- and two- digit numbers. It is not expected that students master the standard algorithm for addition at this time.

What the TEACHER does:

- Provide problem contexts to have students model addition using concrete materials, such as linking cubes, ten frames, and straws with place value charts.
- Use the progression of examples (Table 3) to scaffold level of complexity as students work to make sense out of adding one- and two-digit numbers and make generalizations about what is happening. Note that understanding develops over time. Be sure that students have ample experiences with concrete, pictorial, and numerical representations for each type of problem before moving on. Encourage students to use a variety of strategies and explain their thinking.
- Provide experiences using open number lines and the hundreds chart to help students develop strategies for adding and subtracting using the examples above. Connect student strategies with concrete experiences.
- Pose questions that require students to think about the strategies they are using to add making connections to place value. For example, if students are adding 35 + 24, you might ask,
  - What did you do first? (Note the various strategies in the following student responses)
  - (Student A) I used the hundreds chart and added 10 to 35 to get to 45
    The teacher then asks why the student did that and then ask, what did you do next?
  - (Student B) I added the 5 and the 4
    The teacher then asks why the student did that and then ask, what did you do next?
  - (Student C) I added 3 and 2
    The teacher would follow with questions to ask about the meaning of the 3 and the 2 to be sure the student understands that they represent 3 tens and 2 tens.
- Facilitate conversations or activities in which students explain their thinking.

What the STUDENTS do:

- Model addition examples with sums to 100 using concrete materials, pictures, and lastly numerals.
- Uses mental computation strategies to develop conceptual understanding and number sense around adding one- and two-digit numbers (Table 3).
- Record addition examples accurately using both vertical and horizontal formats.
- Explain their reasoning to classmates.

Students who do not know basic facts may be inaccurate computing with two-digit numbers. As those students continue to work on facts, physical models will help in adding accurately. Be sure that all students have ample experience with adding physical models on place value charts, counting on by benchmark numbers (tens and ones), using a hundreds chart, and using ten frames as appropriate. Make explicit connections among written physical models, strategies, and written formats.

Regrouping (composing tens from ones) when adding two-digit numbers is included in this standard. It is appropriate for students to use physical models for these examples and explain their reasoning, explicitly connecting physical models with symbolic notation (written equations).

Notes

GRADE 1

Given a two-digit number, mentally find 10 more or 10 less than the number, without having to count; explain the reasoning used.

This standard builds on students' work with place value and requires them to understand and apply the concept of ten by mentally finding 10 more or 10 less.

What the TEACHER does:

- Give the students a variety of situations in which they need to add or subtract 10 from a given number. For example,
  - Mason has 38 crayons. Dee gives him 10 more. How many crayons does Mason have now?
  - There are 45 pencils on the table. 10 pencils roll off the table. How many pencils are left on the table?
- Ask students to explain their thinking. Appropriate answers might include
  - I found 38 on the hundreds chart and went down one row and landed at 48
  - I know 10 more than 38 is 48 because 48 has one more 10 than 38
  - I found 45 on the hundreds chart and moved up one row, so 35 is 10 less than 45
- Provide games and activities in which students have a number and need to find 10 more or 10 less than the number.
- Ask students to explain their strategies.

What the STUDENTS do:

- Use a variety of materials and strategies to add or subtract 10 from a number in the range of 1 to 100.
- Explain their reasoning using place value understanding and patterns on the hundreds chart.
- Mentally calculate to find 10 more or 10 less than a given number.

Addressing Student Misconceptions and Common Errors

Since understanding the concept of 10 more or 10 less leads to understanding additional place value concepts, students who depend on counting or using their fingers have not met this standard. Students who cannot determine 10 more or 10 less than a number from 1 to 100 need more experience with concrete materials, such as linking cubes or bundles of straws. Finding patterns on the hundreds chart is also helpful, but the language can be confusing for some students (i.e., I go up a row to find 10 less and down a row to find 10 more).

Notes

STANDARD 6 (1.NBT.C.6)

Subtract multiples of 10 in the range 10–90 from multiples of 10 in the range 10–90 (positive or zero differences), using concrete models or drawings and strategies based on place value, properties of operations, and/or the relationship between addition and subtraction; relate the strategy to a written method and explain the reasoning used.

The expectation of this standard is for students to subtract multiples of 10 from greater multiples of 10, using understanding of subtraction and a variety of strategies. Connections among concrete, pictorial, and eventually written equations should be explicit.

What the TEACHER does:

- Provide concrete materials (linking cubes, bundling straws) and place value charts for students to use in solving a variety of subtraction problems (Table 1) involving subtracting multiples of 10 from multiples of 10.
- Ask students to look for patterns and explain their work. Appropriate questions might include, "What happens when you take some tens from more tens?" "What is happening with the digit in the ones place?" "What patterns do you notice?" "Can you explain how to subtract groups of ten from groups of ten?" "How would you write this using numbers?"
- Provide games and activities in which students need to subtract tens from tens. Once students understand this concept and can describe their actions, using dimes is a good context for additional problems and helps students to recognize and apply the concept of a dime as 10 cents.

What the STUDENTS do:

- Use a variety of materials and strategies to subtract groups of ten from more tens. Once students can successfully describe their work with concrete materials, move to pictures and then to words.
- Look for and describe patterns they find as they work with various representations.
- Explain their reasoning using place value understanding and patterns on the hundreds chart.
- Calculate subtracting multiples of 10 from multiples of 10 both mentally and using written equations.

Addressing Student Misconceptions and Common Errors

Some students may subtract the digits in the tens place but ignore the digits in the ones place. Ask them to describe what they are subtracting in terms of place value. For example, in subtracting 70 – 40, students should say they are taking 4 tens from 7 tens (or 7 tens minus 4 tens). Have them put concrete models on the place value chart and then subtract or physically remove the 4 tens from the 7 tens. They describe the difference as 3 tens. Ask them how to write 3 tens (30) and how many ones are in that number. They should explain why there are 0 ones and why it is necessary to put the digit 0 in the ones place.

Notes

Standard: 1.NCT.C.4. *Add within 100, including adding a two-digit number and a one-digit number, and adding a two-digit number and a multiple of 10, using concrete models or drawings and strategies based on place value, properties of operations, and/or the relationship between addition and subtraction; relate the strategy to a written method and explain the reasoning used. Understand that in adding two-digit numbers, one adds tens and tens, ones and ones; and sometimes it is necessary to compose a ten.*

Mathematical Practice or Process Standards:
SFMP 1. Make sense of problems and persevere in solving them.
SFMP 2. Reason abstractly and quantitatively.
SFMP 3. Construct viable arguments and critique the reasoning of others.
SFMP 4. Model with mathematics.
SFMP 7. Look for and make use of structure.
Students will solve problems and model adding two 2-digit numbers with no regrouping. Students will explain their reasoning, describing what they did to solve the problem. After using physical representations, they will link the models to writing the addition equation.

Goal:
This lesson extends work with modeling addition of numbers to 100 (Table 3). Students will model addition with no regrouping, focusing on adding tens and adding ones (in whatever order makes sense to them). Students will describe their work and compare with others, adding strategies they have used.

Planning:

Materials: Linking cubes, straws for bundling, place value chart with tens and ones (Reproducible 10)

Sample Activity: Problem: Charlie had 33 stickers. Hank gave him 25 more. How many stickers does Charlie have now?
Students represent Charlie's stickers as 3 bundles of ten and 3 ones on the place value chart. Directly below, they show 2 bundles of ten and 5 ones to show what Hank gave him. They then count the number of tens and the number of ones to find the total number of stickers. Students explain their work to classmates (or demonstrate and explain their reasoning using a document camera). Discussion includes other strategies used to solve the problem. After many examples of modeling using concrete materials, students can write the equation in both horizontal and vertical form.

Questions/Prompts:

What do you know? What do you want to find out?

How can you show Charlie's stickers using the counters?

Where do these belong on the place value chart?

How can you show the stickers that Hank gave to Charlie?

Where do these belong on the place value chart?

How many stickers does Charlie have now?

Differentiating Instruction:

Struggling Students: Be sure students are representing the two-digit addends accurately, showing tens and ones and placing them correctly on the place value chart. If students are struggling, use smaller numbers (perhaps limited to teen numbers at first) and then move into twenties.

These students may need many additional concrete examples before making the connection to the written equation.

Extension: Students who accurately model addition and subtraction can work with a variety of addition situations from Table 1. They can also work with greater numbers. As students show understanding, they can work on solving problems with pictures and equations.

Standard:

Mathematical Practice or Process Standards:

Goal:

Planning:

Materials:

Sample Activity:

Questions/Prompts:

Differentiating Instruction:

Struggling Students:

Extension:

Standard:

Mathematical Practice or Process Standards:

Goal:

Planning:

Materials:

Sample Activity:

Questions/Prompts:

Differentiating Instruction:

Struggling Students:

Extension:

Standard:

Mathematical Practice or Process Standards:

Goal:

Planning:

Materials:

Sample Activity:

Questions/Prompts:

Differentiating Instruction:

Struggling Students:

Extension:

Number and Operations in Base Ten
2.NBT.A*

Understand place value.

STANDARD 1 **2.NBT.A.1:** Understand that the three digits of a three-digit number represent amounts of hundreds, tens, and ones; e.g., 706 equals 7 hundreds, 0 tens, and 6 ones. Understand the following as special cases:

   a. 100 can be thought of as a bundle of ten tens—called a "hundred."

   b. The numbers 100, 200, 300, 400, 500, 600, 700, 800, 900 refer to one, two, three, four, five, six, seven, eight, or nine hundreds (and 0 tens and 0 ones).

STANDARD 2 **2.NBT.A.2:** Count within 1000; skip-count by 5s, 10s, and 100s.

STANDARD 3 **2.NBT.A.3:** Read and write numbers to 1000 using base-ten numerals, number names, and expanded form.

STANDARD 4 **2.NBT.A.4:** Compare two three-digit numbers based on meanings of the hundreds, tens, and ones digits, using >, =, and < symbols to record the results of comparisons.

*Major cluster

Number and Operations in Base Ten 2.NBT.A

Cluster A: Understand place value.
Grade 2 Overview

Students extend their understanding of place value to hundreds and to thousands by bundling 10 tens to make a hundred and later extend that understanding to bundling 10 hundreds to make 1 thousand. It is important to scaffold the work of this cluster so that students understand the concept of 1 hundred and then multiple hundreds. Conceptual understandings and skills built in previous grades should be explicitly connected to the new ideas in Grade 2 including place value, counting, and comparing numerals to 1,000.

Standard for Mathematical Practice
SFMP 2. Reason abstractly and quantitatively.
SFMP 3. Construct viable arguments and critique the reasoning of others.
SFMP 4. Model with mathematics.
SFMP 5. Use appropriate tools strategically.
SFMP 6. Attend to precision.
SFMP 7. Look for and make use of structure.
SFMP 8. Look for and express regularity in repeated reasoning.

In second grade, students continue to develop a deep understanding of place value and use that understanding to add and subtract within 1,000. This cluster focuses on the development of place value up to and beyond 100. Students should use the structure of building tens out of 10 ones, building hundreds out of 10 tens, and building a thousand out of 10 hundreds. This is the structure of our base-ten place value system. It is built on repeated reasoning that every time you have 10 of a particular item, you group it to make the next place value unit. Students use precision in describing their work with appropriate vocabulary and reading numbers accurately. They explain their reasoning to classmates throughout the cluster and compare their thinking with that of their peers.

Related Content Standards

K.NBT.A.1   KCC.C.7   1.NBT.B.1   1.NBT. B.2   1.NBT.B.3

Understand that the three digits of a three-digit number represent amounts of hundreds, tens, and ones; e.g., 706 equals 7 hundreds, 0 tens, and 6 ones. Understand the following as special cases:

a. 100 can be thought of as a bundle of ten tens—called a "hundred."

Students begin to unitize or consider 10 tens as a group or unit called 1 hundred.

What the TEACHER does:

- Review earlier place value experiences using concrete materials. Ask students to model and describe what happens when they have 10 ones. Reinforce the concept that 10 ones can be bundled into 1 ten.
- Introduce the next place on the place value chart (Reproducible 11).
- Develop student vocabulary to see a hundred as a unit composed of 10 tens.
- Give students bundles of 10 straws or linking cubes and have them make groups of 100.

What the STUDENTS do:

- Given bundles of tens, students group them into bundles of 100 and place them in the appropriate place on the place value chart.
- Understand the vocabulary that 1 hundred is made up of 10 tens.

Addressing Student Misconceptions and Common Errors

Although students may correctly place concrete representations on the hundreds chart and be able to read the number represented accurately, they may become confused when writing the numeral since there are no objects in the tens or ones place, as in the number 405 or 450. Provide students with numeral cards that include the digit 0 so that students can put the 0 in the tens place and ones place to represent that there are no objects in those places. This should help them transition between the concrete representation and the written numeral.

b. The numbers 100, 200, 300, 400, 500, 600, 700, 800, 900 refer to one, two, three, four, five, six, seven, eight, or nine hundreds (and 0 tens and 0 ones).

Once students understand the concept that 10 tens can be bundled to make 1 hundred, they explore multiples of 100 using pictures, numbers, and words. Although not explicitly stated, representing, describing, and reading all numbers from 1 to 999 are included in this standard.

What the TEACHER does:

- Give the students bundles of 10 straws to group into one hundred.

10 tens

1 hundred

What the STUDENTS do:

- Use concrete materials to bundle groups of 10 to represent numbers including 100, 200, 300, . . . 900 as bundles of 1 hundreds with no tens and no ones.
- Place concrete representations on a place value chart to reinforce that the number is made up of hundreds and no tens and no ones.
- Describe the multiples of 100 using words that include the number of groups of a hundred to reinforce understanding a hundred as a unit that is different from tens and ones. For example,

  200 is 2 bundles of 10 tens. 300 is 3 bundles of 10 tens.

(Continued)

(Continued)

What the TEACHER does (continued):

- Build on experiences of bundling 10 tens into 1 hundred by giving students tasks in which they bundle more tens into 2 hundreds, 3 hundreds. Placing bundles of hundred on a place value chart reinforces the concept that these numbers represent bundles of 1 hundred with no tens and no ones. For example, 300 is represented by 3 hundreds, 0 tens, and 0 ones (Reproducible 11).

hundreds	tens	ones

- Pose questions that reinforce the concept that each group of 10 tens makes 1 hundred. Ask students to describe the number of straws in terms of the number of hundreds. For example, 5 bundles of 100 would be 500.
- Connect physical and pictorial representation with written numerals for multiples of 100. Discuss why the digit 0 must be in the tens place and ones place.
- Use formative assessment protocols, including tasks, student explanations, and worksheets to determine if students understand unitizing and can describe multiples of 100 up to 900 as a number of hundreds with no tens and no ones.
- Begin to provide experiences with other numbers up to 999. Extend experiences of bundling hundreds with some leftover tens. Put the straws on the place value chart and have students describe the number and write the numeral.
- Extend experiences to numbers that would include tens and ones so students need to bundle to make as many hundreds as possible and as many tens as possible with some ones leftover.
- Explicitly connect work with concrete materials and place value charts to pictures, verbal descriptions, and writing numbers.
- Guide students to make explicit connections between concrete materials and pictorial representations for place value. As students orally describe a number in terms of place value, they also connect that understanding to the written numeral.
- Give a number from 100 to 999 for students to construct using straws and describe the value of each place.

What the STUDENTS do (continued):

- Use concrete materials to represent any number from 1 to 999 by making as many groups of hundreds as possible and placing those in the hundreds place on a place value chart. Place any leftover tens in the tens place and ones in the ones place.
- Describe the representation using numbers and words. For example,

| 4 hundreds | 5 tens | one | |
| 400 | 50 | 1 | = 451 |

- Write the numerals and identify how the written number shows the number of hundreds, tens, and ones.
- Connect words to the written numeral. For example, 3 hundreds, 2 tens, and 4 ones is written as 324 and read as three hundred twenty-four.

Watch for students who reverse digits. These students need additional opportunities to decompose numbers into groups of hundreds, tens, and ones and put them in the correct place on a place value chart. Describing the number in terms of hundreds, tens, and ones should be followed by writing the numeral below the concrete representation.

Observe students who may be counting hundreds, tens, and ones separately.

For example,

they count as   100,   200,   300 . . .   10, 20 . . .   1,   2,   3

rather than counting as 300, 20, 3 . . . 323.

These students need additional practice relating the representation or picture to the accurate word name for the number.

Notes

Count within 1000; skip-count by 5s, 10s, and 100s.

As students work with numbers to 1,000, they count on within a range of numbers from 1 to 1,000 and skip count building on earlier experiences with place value. Skip counting lays the foundation for future work with multiplication by forming groups of a given size.

What the TEACHER does:

- Give students a number and ask them to count on or back from that number. For example, given 567, students should count the next few numbers . . . 567, 568, 569, 570.
- Relate the counts to number line representations.

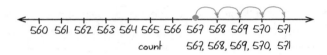

count 567, 568, 569, 570, 571

- Give students a number and ask them to count back from that number. For example, count back from 567.
- Describe place value patterns as they count. For example, when I count forward from 342, the hundreds and tens places stay the same as the ones place increases by 1 with each count. When I reach 349, the tens place in the next number increases by 1 because I can now make a group of ten.
- Relate patterns and previous experiences to skip counting by 5, 10, and 100 within a range of numbers from 1 to 1,000. For example, skip count by 5s from 150 to 175.
- Ask students to describe patterns in place value as they skip count.

What the STUDENTS do:

- Count forward from a given number from 1 to 1,000.
- Count back from a given number from 1 to 1,000.
- Relate counting to number line representations.
- Describe place value patterns as they count. For example, when I count forward from 342, the hundreds and tens places stay the same as the ones place increases by 1 with each count.
- Skip count by 5, 10, 100 and describe any patterns they notice.

Addressing Student Misconceptions and Common Errors

Students who have difficulty counting within 1,000 need more experience counting on with concrete, pictorial, and number line representations. Begin with lesser numbers in the range of 100–200. Point out patterns in the ones and tens places. Watch for students who confuse the next number in the tens place. For example, counting 127, 128, 129 . . . 1?? An extended hundreds chart with counts from 100 to 200 (use a hundreds chart and add 1 to the hundreds place in each numbers) will also be helpful.

Notes

Read and write numbers to 1000 using base-ten numerals, number names, and expanded form.

Once students experience making 1 hundred from 10 tens using concrete representations, they connect the physical representation by writing the appropriate digit under each place on the place value chart, identifying the place value name for each digit, writing the number in expanded form, and then saying the number name. Scaffolding this work with numbers from 100 and extending to 200, 300, . . . is important for struggling students.

What the TEACHER does:

- Provide students with a number of straws or similar material and ask them to bundle as appropriate making hundreds, tens, and ones and placing them on the place value chart.
- Give students numeral cards to place the correct numeral that represents the number in each place on the place value chart.
- Ask students to identify the place value name for each digit.

Hundreds	Tens	Ones
2 hundreds	4 tens	3 ones
2	4	3

What the STUDENTS do:

- Given a collection of straws or stick counters, students work in pairs to bundle them in as many groups of 100 as possible, bundling leftovers into groups of 10 until no more groups of 10 can be made.
- Place the bundles of straws on a place value chart.
- Use numeral cards to put the appropriate numeral under the straws in each place on the place value chart.
- Identify and read the number of hundreds, tens, and ones. For example, 134 would be read as 1 hundred, 3 tens, and 4 ones.
- Write and read the number represented in expanded form (100 + 30 + 4).
- Read the number name the physical model represents (one hundred thirty-four).
- Read number names without physical models.

- Following many experiences, students write and read the name of the number represented in expanded form.

2 hundreds   4 tens   3 ones

200   +   40   +   3

243

- Link place value, written numerals, and expanded form to reading the number name. First, experiences should be connected to the physical model, eventually moving to reading number names written as numerals.

Addressing Student Misconceptions and Common Errors

Watch for students who do not have the conceptual understanding that the place in which a digit is located determines the value of that digit. For example, a student reads 134 as one hundred thirty-four but when writing it in expanded form writes 1 + 3 + 4, or when asked the value of each digit, responds that the values are 1, 3, and 4. Provide these students with expanded numeral cards, including hundreds, tens, and ones, and place those cards in appropriate places under the physical models on the place value chart.

Some students may become confused with 0 as a place holder for a place that contains no objects such as 408 or 480. These students need more experience placing numeral cards below the appropriate place using physical models on the place value chart. Be sure to include multiple examples that have 0 items in the tens and/or ones place.

Compare two three-digit numbers based on meanings of the hundreds, tens, and ones digits, using >, =, and < symbols to record the results of comparisons.

Once students show an understanding of place value through hundreds, they begin to compare two numbers by determining the number of hundreds in each number. Begin with experiences comparing concrete representations, place value charts, and moving to number lines. Students generalize that the number with the most hundreds is greater. If the number of hundreds is the same, the number with more tens is greater. If the number of hundreds and tens is the same, the number with more ones is greater.

What the TEACHER does:

- Provide students with a variety of concrete materials and place value charts for representing two 3-digit numbers using tens and ones for making comparisons. Present the numbers orally as well as the written numerals (Reproducible 11).
- Pose questions such as "Which is greater?" "Which has more?" "Which is less?" "Which has fewer?" to familiarize students with appropriate vocabulary and symbols (Reproducible 12).
- Facilitate conversations in which students explain their thinking.
- Use formative assessment protocols to evaluate student understanding of using the number of hundreds, tens, or ones if necessary, to make comparisons.
- After concrete and pictorial experiences, ask students to compare two 3-digit numbers written as numerals.
- Ask students to demonstrate understanding by describing the comparison and demonstrate understanding of the symbolic representation using <, >, and = symbols.

What the STUDENTS do:

- Use concrete materials such as objects on a place value chart, a 100 chart, and number lines to compare two 3-digit numbers.
- Describe the comparison using terms including greater than, more than, less than, fewer than, equal to, same as.
- Justify their reasoning as they compare numbers. For example, "I know 245 is more than 242 because they both have 2 hundreds and 4 tens but 5 ones in 245 is more than 2 ones in 242."
- Compare two 3-digit number written as numerals.
- Use the mathematical symbols <, >, and = to represent comparisons symbolically.

Addressing Student Misconceptions and Common Errors

Watch for students who can read and write three-digit numbers but do not understand that the position of the digit determines its value. These students need more experience with concrete representations and may need to begin with review of the value of places in two-digit numbers. Students should relate numerals to their concrete representations, determining the greater (or lesser) number-based explicit work with concrete representations, beginning in the greatest place value and, if necessary, moving to tens and ones. Students who say, for example, that 78 is greater than 125 because 7 and 8 are greater than 1, 2, or 5 need more work with comparing physical models emphasizing the value of each place.

It is important for students to associate the symbols < and > with their real meaning. Rather than use aids such as alligators or Pac Man, it may help students who confuse the symbols to remember that the open end of the symbol is always closest to the greater number and the closed end is always closer to the lesser number. It is also important to give students opportunities to change the order of the numbers to see how it impacts the symbols and their meaning.

Example: 335 < 365   365 > 335

Notes

Number and Operations in Base Ten
2.NBT.B*

Use place value understanding and properties of operations to add and subtract.

STANDARD 5 **2.NBT.B.5:** Fluently add and subtract within 100 using strategies based on place value, properties of operations, and/or the relationship between addition and subtraction.

STANDARD 6 **2.NBT.B.6:** Add up to four two-digit numbers using strategies based on place value and properties of operations.

STANDARD 7 **2.NBT.B.7:** Add and subtract within 1000, using concrete models or drawings and strategies based on place value, properties of operations, and/or the relationship between addition and subtraction; relate the strategy to a written method. Understand that in adding or subtracting three-digit numbers, one adds or subtracts hundreds and hundreds, tens and tens, ones and ones; and sometimes it is necessary to compose or decompose tens or hundreds.

STANDARD 8 **2.NBT.B.8:** Mentally add 10 or 100 to a given number 100–900, and mentally subtract 10 or 100 from a given number 100–900.

STANDARD 9 **2.NBT.B.9:** Explain why addition and subtraction strategies work, using place value and the properties of operations.[1]

[1] Explanations may be supported by drawings or objects

*Major cluster

Number and Operations in Base Ten 2.NBT.B

Cluster B: Use place value understanding and properties of operations to add and subtract.
Grade 2 Overview

This cluster focuses on applying place value understanding and properties of addition and subtraction. Students apply various strategies based on number sense, mental mathematics, and the relationship between addition and subtraction to extended addition and subtraction examples and problem situations with sums to 100. Students also begin to explore adding and subtracting three-digit numbers, using concrete representations including composing and decomposing ones, tens, and hundreds to regroup when necessary. The cluster culminates with the expectation that students can explain their reasoning based on place value, strategies, and number sense.

Standard for Mathematical Practice
SFMP 1. Make sense of problems and persevere in solving them.
SFMP 2. Reason abstractly and quantitatively.
SFMP 3. Construct viable arguments and critique the reasoning of others.
SFMP 4. Model with mathematics.
SFMP 5. Use appropriate tools strategically.
SFMP 6. Attend to precision.
SFMP 7. Look for and make use of structure.
SFMP 8. Look for and express regularity in repeated reasoning.

Students should have opportunities to demonstrate all of the Standards for Mathematical Practice throughout this cluster. Problems given in meaningful contexts will help students to apply their understanding of when to add or subtract as well as when to estimate to determine if their answer is reasonable. Abstract and quantitative reasoning are demonstrated as students apply appropriate strategies (Table 3) and connect physical models to abstract symbols. Although many of these situations are best modeled using the place value representations from previous clusters, strategies such as counting using benchmark numbers (i.e., tens and hundreds) may be more efficient. Students attend to precision as they describe their reasoning and compare it to alternate approaches of their classmates. The structure of place value and the relationship among places is critical to understanding the processes of addition and subtraction.

Related Content Standards:

1.OA.A.1   1.OA.A.2   1.NBT.C.4   1.NBT.C.5   1.NBT.C.6   2OA.A.1   2.NBT.A.1   3.NBT.A.1   3.NBT.A.3

Fluently add and subtract within 100 using strategies based on place value, properties of operations, and/or the relationship between addition and subtraction.

In first grade, students used various representations to add with sums to 100 and to subtract multiples of 10 from multiples of 10. In second grade, they review these models and focus on computing mentally or in writing using various strategies. Previous work with place value and physical models can be extended to include more examples with composing tens in addition and decomposing tens in subtraction. Note the careful scaffolding of examples for students in Table 3. Include problems that provide a context for adding or subtracting as often as possible. Equations should be written both horizontally and vertically. Students use number sense and a variety of strategies that make sense to them to add and subtract. Encourage students to make estimates before adding or subtracting to determine if their answers are reasonable. Note that students are not expected to use the standard algorithm for addition and subtraction until Grade 4.

What the TEACHER does:

- Review addition with sums to 100, giving students problem contexts to model addition using concrete materials, such as linking cubes, ten frames, and bundling straws on place value charts. Make explicit connections between models and written equations.
- Scaffold the level of complexity as students work to make sense out of adding two 2-digit numbers and make generalizations about what is happening. Note that understanding develops over time. Encourage students to use a variety of strategies and explain their thinking (Table 3).
- When completing examples requiring regrouping (composing numbers from ones to tens) provide ample experience with place value materials. Make explicit connections with ways to write equations for these examples.

What the STUDENTS do:

- Solve addition examples with sums to 100, using a variety of strategies including physical models, mental computation, using benchmark numbers, place value charts, number lines, and hundreds chart.
- Use mental computation strategies to develop conceptual understanding and number sense adding 2-digit numbers.
- Explain their reasoning to classmates.
- Listen to the explanations of classmates and compare their strategies to those of others.
- Use physical models and place to explore subtraction with sums to 100.
- Explore other strategies for subtraction using benchmark numbers, number lines, and the hundreds chart.
- Write equations for subtraction with sums to 100.
- Explain their reasoning to classmates.

Add two 2-digit numbers, regrouping tens to ones.

tens	ones	
		36
		25
		5 tens 11 ones =
		6 tens 1 one

- Provide experiences using open number lines and the hundreds chart, using benchmarks of tens to help students develop strategies for adding.

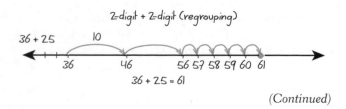

2-digit + 2-digit (regrouping)

36 + 25

36 + 25 = 61

(Continued)

What the TEACHER does (continued):

- Facilitate conversations and activities in which students explain their thinking.
- Present a variety of subtraction problems using sums to 100 that provide students with opportunities to apply properties and their understanding of place value with concrete materials, mental computation strategies, and models such as open number lines and benchmarks. Scaffold the complexity of examples as described on Table 3.

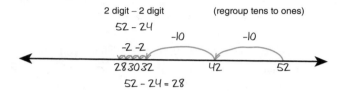

- Ask students to model subtraction examples using various strategies.
- Pose questions that help students to explain their work and their reasoning.

Addressing Student Misconceptions and Common Errors

Second-grade students do not need to have facility using the standard algorithm adding and subtracting. They should focus their work on developing and using efficient strategies that make sense. Although some students may be ready to write equations, composing tens when regrouping in addition and decomposing tens when regrouping in subtracting may be challenging to other students. Concrete representations, number lines, and hundreds charts will help students to develop a deeper understanding of the process of regrouping than only following rote procedures.

Notes

Add up to four two-digit numbers using strategies based on place value and properties of operations.

This standard extends the work from 2.NBT.B.5 to adding strings of two-digit numbers with up to four addends. Students apply understanding of place value, mental mathematics strategies, and properties of addition.

What the TEACHER does:

- Provide students with problem situations in which they add three 2-digit numbers using concrete materials, place value charts, and mental mathematics strategies that include using the commutative, associative, and identity properties.
- Extend this work to adding strings of four 2-digit numbers using similar strategies.

What the STUDENTS do:

- Use a variety of strategies to add up to four 2-digit numbers.
  - Example: $24 + 17 + 33$
    - Associative property:
      Add $17 + 33$ to get 50. Add 24 to 50 which equals 74
    - Place value:
      Add the tens $20 + 10 + 30 = 60$
      Add the ones $4 + 7 + 3 = 14$
      Add the two sums $60 + 14 = 74$

- Explain their thinking to classmates.
- Listen to the reasoning of others and find similarities with their own strategies.

Addressing Student Misconceptions and Common Errors

Students who struggle with adding strings of numbers should begin with three addends with no regrouping. If necessary, they can use physical models to help keep track of the sums. Move to examples using four addends with no regrouping. As students are ready, include examples with regrouping. Encourage students to use strategies that make sense to them. Help students using inefficient strategies to make connections to more efficient strategies. Note that some strategies are more difficult to follow when written out and make more sense when explained orally.

Notes

Add and subtract within 1000, using concrete models or drawings and strategies based on place value, properties of operations, and/or the relationship between addition and subtraction; relate the strategy to a written method. Understand that in adding or subtracting three-digit numbers, one adds or subtracts hundreds and hundreds, tens and tens, ones and ones; and sometimes it is necessary to compose or decompose tens or hundreds.

This standard extends the work of standard 2.NBT.B.6 to sums to 1,000 including adding and subtracting. Students need ample experience with physical models building on previous place value understanding. Table 3 shows scaffolding ideas for regrouping (composing in addition and decomposing in subtraction). While many students will be ready to transfer understanding to written equations, work with the standard algorithm is not an expectation until Grade 4.

What the TEACHER does:

- Provide problem contexts to have students model addition with sums to 1,000 using concrete materials, such as bundling straws, with place value charts.
- Use the progression of examples (Table 3) to scaffold level of complexity as students work to make sense adding two-digit numbers to three-digit numbers then move to adding three-digit numbers to three-digit numbers (Table 3).
- Note that understanding develops over time. Be sure that students have ample experiences with concrete representations and place value charts for each type of problem before moving on.

What the STUDENTS do:

- Model addition examples using concrete materials, then pictures, and lastly numerals.
- Use mental and written computation strategies to develop conceptual understanding and number sense around adding two-digit numbers and three-digit numbers with sums to 1,000 (Table 3).
- Use estimation strategies to determine if their answers are reasonable.
- Explain their reasoning to classmates.
- Listen to the reasoning of classmates and compare strategies.
- Model subtraction examples using concrete materials, pictures, and lastly numerals.
- Use mental and written computation strategies to develop conceptual understanding and number sense around subtracting two-digit numbers and three-digit numbers with sums to 1,000 (Table 3).
- Use estimation strategies to determine if their answers are reasonable.
- Explain their reasoning to classmates.
- Listen to the reasoning of classmates and compare strategies.

- Encourage students to use a variety of strategies and explain their thinking.

(Continued)

- Provide experiences using open number lines and benchmark numbers to help students develop strategies for adding.

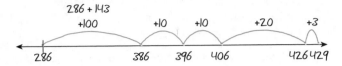

286 + 143

- Pose questions that require students to think about the process they are using to add, making connections to place value.
- Facilitate conversations or activities in which students explain their thinking.
- Provide problem contexts to have students model subtraction with sums to 1,000, using concrete materials, such as bundling straws, with place value charts.
- Use the progression of examples to scaffold level of complexity as students work to make sense subtracting two-digit numbers from three-digit numbers and move to subtracting three-digit numbers from three-digit numbers (Table 3).
- Note that understanding develops over time. Be sure that students have ample experiences with concrete representations and place value charts for each type of problem before moving on.

252 – 127

hundreds	tens	ones	
			252
			−127
1	2	5	

10 ones

- Encourage students to use a variety of strategies and explain their thinking.
- Provide experiences using open number lines and benchmark numbers to help students develop strategies for subtraction.

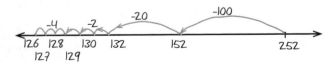

252 – 126

- Pose questions that require students to think about the process they are using to subtract, making connections to place value.
- Facilitate conversations or activities in which students explain their thinking.

Students who do not know basic facts may be inaccurate in computation. Although those students should continue to work on facts, physical models will help in accurate addition and subtraction. Be sure that all students have ample experience with adding physical models on place value charts, using benchmark numbers (hundreds, tens, and ones) on an open number line. Make explicit connections from written physical models and strategies to written formats.

Although regrouping (composing hundreds from tens and tens from ones) when adding two 3-digit numbers and (decomposing from hundreds to tens and from tens to ones) when subtracting two 3-digit numbers is included in this standard, it is appropriate for students to use physical models for these examples and explain their reasoning. Explicit connections to written equations will help students make the transition from concrete and pictorial representations to symbolic notations.

Notes

Mentally add 10 or 100 to a given number 100–900, and mentally subtract 10 or 100 from a given number 100–900.

This standard builds on students' work with place value and requires them to understand and apply the concept of ten and hundred by mentally adding or subtracting 10 or 100. Extended hundreds charts and open number lines are good models for this standard.

What the TEACHER does:

- Give the students a variety of situations in which they need to add or subtract 10 or 100 from a given number. For example,
  - The second grade class has collected 256 paper clips for its make-a-thousand project. Lucy brings in a box of 100 paper clips to add to the collection. How many paper-clips do they now have?
  - John finds 10 more paper clips on the floor. How many paperclips do they have now?
- Ask students to explain their thinking. Appropriate answers might include
  - I started at 256 on the open number line. I jumped 100 more and ended at 356.
  - I know to start at 356 on the open number line. I counted up 10 more steps and ended at 366.
- Provide games and activities in which students have a number and need to find 10 or 100 more, or 10 or 100 less, than a given number.
- Ask students to explain their strategies.

What the STUDENTS do:

- Use a variety of materials and strategies to add or subtract 10 or 100 from a three-digit number in the range of 100 to 900.
- Explain their reasoning using place value understanding and patterns.
- Mentally calculate finding 10 or 100 more or 10 or 100 less than a given number.

Addressing Student Misconceptions and Common Errors

Second graders should see the pattern of adding (or subtracting) 1 to the digit in the tens place when adding (or subtracting) 10. A similar pattern of adding (or subtracting) 1 to the digit in the hundreds place occurs when adding (or subtracting) 100. Students may find this confusing when they are adding 10 to numbers that have the digit 9 in the tens place or subtracting 10 from numbers that have the digit 0 in the tens place. Using a number line or portions of a hundreds chart will help them to visualize what happens when they are working with these numbers. If necessary, composing (to add) and decomposing (to subtract) with concrete materials will also help students to understand the concept.

Notes

STANDARD 9 (2.NBT.B.9)

Explain why addition and subtraction strategies work, using place value and the properties of operations.[1]

[1] Explanations may be supported by drawings or objects

As students solidify their understanding of addition and subtraction to 1,000, they explain their strategies based on their knowledge of place value and the properties of addition and subtraction. Students demonstrate their understanding using place value materials, hundreds charts and extended hundreds charts, and open number lines. Although this is the last standard in this cluster, students should be expected to explain their thinking throughout the Number and Operations in Base Ten domain. Keep in mind fluency with a standard algorithm is not an expectation until Grade 4.

What the TEACHER does:

- Present a problem for students to solve. For example, the second graders placed 36 pumpkins on the fence for Halloween. The wind blew 17 off the fence. How many pumpkins were left on the fence?
- Give students time to solve the problem using concrete objects, pictures numbers, and words.
- Ask students to show their work to their classmates and explain their thinking. Find a variety of strategies to share.

    o Student 1: I looked at the hundreds chart and started at 36. I went back 10 and landed on 26. I then went back 7 more. I ended up at 19. There were 19 pumpkins on the fence.
    o Student 2: I put out 3 tens and 6 ones on my place value chart. I took away 1 ten and then needed to take away 7 more. I had to unbundle 1 ten because I needed more ones. I had a total of 16 ones and took 7 ones away. When I counted, there were 19 straws left. So there were 19 pumpkins left on the fence.
    o Student 3: I used an open number line. I started at 17, jumped 10, and landed on 27. I jumped 3 more to get to 30. I jumped 6 more to get to 36. So I jumped 10 + 3 + 6 or 19 in all. There were 19 pumpkins left.

What the STUDENTS do:

- Solve addition and subtraction problems using objects, pictures, words, and numbers.
- Ask themselves if their answers make sense.
- Explain their thinking to classmates and the teacher.
- Compare their strategies with those of classmates.

Addressing Student Misconceptions and Common Errors

Some students may still struggle with solving word problems in a variety of situations. Support their thinking by asking what they know, what they want to find out, and how they might solve the problem. It is really important for these students to ask themselves if their answer is reasonable. You may need to help by reversing the situation for them. In the above example, ask if putting 19 pumpkins with the 17 that fell off the fence would be the 36 they started with. Giving students opportunities to explain their thinking, even when incorrect, provides opportunities for them to self-correct.

Notes

Standard: 2.NBT.B.8. *Mentally add 10 or 100 to a given number 100–900, and mentally subtract 10 or 100 from a given number 100–900.*

Mathematical Practice or Process Standards:
SFMP 2. Reason abstractly and quantitatively.
SFMP 6. Attend to precision.
SFMP 7. Look for and make use of structure.
SFMP 8. Look for and express regularity in repeated reasoning.

Goal:
Students continue to develop understanding place value while making connections to efficient strategies for mentally adding or subtracting 10 or 100 to a given number from 100 to 900. Experiences are based on the structure of place value and regularity in repeated reasoning (patterns) as they use open number lines, place value charts, and hundreds charts to develop understanding.

Planning:

Materials: Place value chart to hundreds place, straws and rubber bands, hundreds chart, extended hundreds chart, open number lines, dice or spinners with digits 0 to 9, numeral cards from 0 to 9. Set up workstations around the classroom with either dice, spinners or cards, and various concrete materials. Include a recording worksheet (see next page).

Sample Activity:
Students work in pairs to play a game. They create a three-digit number using the dice, spinner, or cards and write that number down. They add 10 to the number and record their sum. They add 100 to the number and record their sum.
Reverse the order of the original three digits and repeat by adding 10 and adding 100.
A similar game can be played subtracting 10 and 100 from the original number.

Questions/Prompts:

What number will you make from the three digits you picked?

What digit is in the tens place?

What digit is in the tens place after you add 10 to the number?

What do you notice?

What digit is in the hundreds place?

What digit is in the hundreds place after you add 100 to the number?

What did you notice?

Differentiating Instruction:

Struggling Students: Students who need concrete models to complete this activity should have access to place value charts and bundled straws. Model the number with concrete materials. Watch to be certain they are putting 1 ten or 1 hundreds on the place value chart and counting correctly. If necessary, provide single-digit numeral cards to show the number in each place on the chart and then write that number on the recording sheet.

Extension: Some students may be ready to extend the activity to starting with four-digit numbers and adding 10, 100, or 1,000 to that number.

Add 10 and 100 Recording Sheet

My number	+ 10	+ 100
__ __ __	__ __ __	__ __ __
__ __ __	__ __ __	__ __ __
__ __ __	__ __ __	__ __ __

Subtract 10 and 100 Recording Sheet

My number	− 10	− 100
__ __ __	__ __ __	__ __ __
__ __ __	__ __ __	__ __ __
__ __ __	__ __ __	__ __ __

Standard:

Mathematical Practice or Process Standards:

Goal:

Planning:

Materials:

Sample Activity:

Questions/Prompts:

Differentiating Instruction:

Struggling Students:

Extension:

Standard:

Mathematical Practice or Process Standards:

Goal:

Planning:

Materials:

Sample Activity:

Questions/Prompts:

Differentiating Instruction:

Struggling Students:

Extension:

Reflection Questions: Number and Operations in Base Ten

1. Discuss how this domain relates to the previous domains in K–2.

2. Look at the related standards listed in each cluster overview. Make a chart with a sequence of standards across your grade level. Share your ideas with colleagues who teach the other grades in K–2. From this work, you can see how ideas grow from one grade to the next and within a specific grade level.

3. Table 3 provides a sequence of developing conceptual understanding for addition and subtraction computation. Discuss strategies your students can use to make sense of computation. What would this look like in the classroom? What materials can you use? What questions will you ask to help students to explain their thinking?

4. Select one of the examples below. Talk about the strategies students could use to solve this example. Discuss the concrete models students can use to develop conceptual understanding.

a. Kindergarten:
$6 + 3 =$
$7 - 4 =$

b. First grade:
$32 + 14 =$
$58 - 26 =$

c. Second grade:
$64 + 27 =$
$71 - 43 =$

Part 4

Measurement and Data

Measurement and Data

Domain Overview

KINDERGARTEN

The study of measurement at the kindergarten level will apply directly to students' daily lives. Many children enter school already exposed to informal ideas about measurement. Experiences provided at this level will help children further develop concepts about what can be measured and how to measure it. Kindergartners will learn to describe measurable attributes of objects, such as length, weight, and height. Students will also compare objects and verbally describe the measurable attributes with words such as *how tall, how wide, how heavy*, and similar descriptive terms.

GRADE 1

First graders will learn what measurement is, how to measure length with nonstandard units, and how to align objects for comparison. Students will place nonstandard physical units such as cubes or straws end to end and count them to measure an object such as a student desk. Students will also learn to indirectly measure lengths and to iterate units. Iterating a unit means a single unit is repeated by placing multiple units of the same thing end to end, then, counting. For example, the length of a student desk can be measured with multiple straws placed end to end across the desk in a single line, then counted to find how many straws long the desk is. In addition, students will also learn to tell and write time in hours and half hours using analog and digital clocks. At this level, first graders will also learn to pose their own questions and collect, interpret, and analyze their own data.

GRADE 2

Second graders begin measuring with inches, feet, centimeters, and meters. In this domain, students learn that the measure of length is a count of how many units are needed to match the length of the object or distance being measured. Second graders will receive numerous experiences estimating and measuring length with a variety of tools including rulers, yardsticks, tape measures, and meter sticks and relate addition and subtraction to their study of length. Students will also works with time and money as well as represent and interpret data.

K	1	2	
✓			A variety of objects to measure or "weigh" such as stuffed animal toys, books, and a sheet of paper
✓	✓		A variety of nonstandard measurement tools such as counting cubes, string, straws, paper clips, pencils, and crayons
✓			A variety of objects to sort such as buttons, small toys, keys, coins, and color cubes,
✓			Attribute blocks
	✓	✓	A variety of objects to measure found in the classroom such as books, desks, bulletin board, and book shelves
	✓		Number cards with numbers 1, 2, 3, 4, 5, 6, 7, 8, 9, 10, 11, 12
	✓		Number cards with numbers 5, 10, 15, 20, 25, 30, 35, 40, 45, 50, 55, 60
	✓	✓	Individual student analog clocks to manipulate both small and big hands; whole class digital clock
	✓	✓	Individual student whiteboards/markers and paper/pencil to collect data
		✓	Measurement tools, such as rulers, yard sticks, meter sticks, measuring tapes
		✓	Concrete manipulatives, such as counting cubes to represent word problems
		✓	Number lines
✓	✓	✓	Dollar bills, coins (penny, nickel, dime, quarter)

KEY VOCABULARY

K	1	2	
	✓	✓	**analog clock** a clock with the numbers 1 to 12 around the face and rotating hands to show hours, minutes, and seconds
		✓	**analyze data** to interpret data: process of assigning meaning to the collected information and determining the conclusions
✓	✓	✓	**attributes** characteristic of an object such as color, size, thickness, or number of sides. K–2 measurable attributes include length and time
		✓	**bar graph** a graph using rectangular bars to show how large each value is. The bars can be horizontal or vertical
✓	✓	✓	**classify** to categorize, to arrange in groups by an attribute
✓			**color words** blue, yellow, green, orange, brown, tan, et cetera
	✓	✓	**data** information in numerical form that can be processed
✓	✓		**descriptive words** small, big, rough, smooth, bumpy, round, flat, more, less, same amount, tall, taller, heavy, lighter, more, most, same, different, less, least, shorter, about, and the like
	✓	✓	**digital clock** a clock that uses only numerals to show the time

(Continued)

(Continued)

K	1	2		
	✓	✓	**equation**	a mathematical sentence in which one part is the same as, or equal to, the other
✓	✓	✓	**estimate**	to roughly determine the size
	✓		**gap**	space, open distance between two measurements
		✓	**length**	the measure of distance from one point to another. units of length include inch, foot, yard, mile, millimeter, centimeter, meter, kilometer
✓	✓	✓	**length/height/weight**	measurement attributes
	✓	✓	**line plot**	a number line with an x placed above the corresponding value on the line for each piece of data
✓	✓	✓	**measure**	to find the size or amount of a particular attribute such as length, mass, time, money
		✓	**measurement units for length**	inch, foot, centimeter, meter, yard
✓	✓	✓	**money terms**	coin, dollar, penny, nickel, dime, quarter, value of
✓	✓		**nonstandard unit**	a unit used to measure that is made up of informal objects such as cubes, straws, paper clips.
		✓	**number line**	a model or representation using whole counting numbers; a line used to show the position of a number in relation to other numbers
	✓		**order**	to arrange in a particular sequence based on a specified attribute
	✓		**ordinal numbers**	numbers used to describe sequence or order (i.e., first, second, third...)
	✓		**overlap**	to coincide with; to cover
		✓	**picture graph**	a type of graph using pictures to represent data
	✓	✓	**predict**	to make a reasonable guess
✓	✓	✓	**sort**	to arrange or group by a given attribute such as size, shape, color
	✓		**time**	ongoing sequence of events, measured by clocks *related words: o'clock, hour, one-half hour, half past, day, night, week, month, year*
		✓	**unknown**	in an equation, the variable to be solved; e.g., in the equation $2 + n = 5$, n is the variable.

Measurement and Data
K.MD.A*

Describe and compare measurable attributes.

STANDARD 1 **K.MD.A.1:** Describe measurable attributes of objects such as length or weight. Describe several measurable attributes of a single object.

STANDARD 2 **K.MD.A.2:** Directly compare two objects with a measurable attribute in common, to see which object has "more of/less of" the attribute, and describe the difference. *For example, directly compare the heights of two children and describe one child as taller/shorter.*

*Additional cluster

Measurement and Data K.MD.A

Cluster A: Describe and compare measurable attributes.
Kindergarten Overview

This cluster will focus on measuring attributes, comparing, and classifying/sorting objects. Kindergartners will learn that an object has different attributes that can be measured, like the length of a sheet of paper or the height and weight of a can of food. Students will also describe the objects they measure, with vocabulary terms such as *taller, longer, shorter, heavier, lighter,* and similar descriptive terms.

Standards for Mathematical Practice
SFMP 2. Reason quantitatively and abstractly.

Students will use reasoning to compare objects to determine which object is longer.

SFMP 3. Construct viable arguments and critique the reasoning of others.

Kindergartners will describe measurable attributes of a single object and reason about how to compare its length.

SFMP 6. Attend to precision.
Students will attend to precision by aligning endpoints when comparing lengths.

Related Content Standards
1.MD.A.1   1.MD.A2   2.MD.A1   2.MD.A2

Notes

Describe measurable attributes of objects, such as length or weight. Describe several measurable attributes of a single object.

What the TEACHER does:

- Provide learning opportunities for students to identify and describe different measurable attributes of objects, such as height and weight. Kindergartners will need numerous experiences to explore how and why an object has several different measurable attributes.
- Help students understand that the length of an object is defined by the number of units, laid end to end, that make up the distance from one point to another. To measure length of objects, students begin by using nonstandard units such as counting cubes, string, straws, or paper clips. Provide a variety of objects for students to measure such as books, toys, a sheet of paper, and other objects that are familiar to students. Students may discover that a toy is 8 cubes long, a book is 9 cubes long, or a sheet of paper is 11 paper clips long. Make sure students understand that each object they measure is described with a number and a nonstandard unit.
- Help kindergartners learn that height is the distance from the lowest point to the highest point of an object or a person. Allow children to measure a variety of things they find in the classroom with nonstandard measurement tools such as string.
- Model measurement vocabulary such as "We discovered the *length* of our desks is 6 straws *long*." Ensure students have opportunities to talk with the teacher and each other to make sense of what they are learning. Be sure to provide numerous experiences to talk about and describe an object such as a book is heavy or the paper is light. Students could also describe the same book with other attributes such as the same book is also large and red. The paper is white and is a small sheet of paper.

What the STUDENTS do:

- Students should participate in discussions about appropriate nonstandard units to measure various attributes of objects. This dialog will help students understand that different kinds of units can be used to measure different attributes.
- Students will be actively engaged in measurement activities using nonstandard units with a variety of things to measure in different ways and a variety of tools to use for measuring.

Addressing Student Misconceptions and Common Errors

The term *biggest* may be a misconception for kindergartners as two students may claim their building block creations are the biggest. Teachers should engage students to compare their creations, helping students name measurable attributes, such as one student has a taller block creation (height) and the other student has a greater width. Students should talk about, label several attributes of the objects, and compare the creations using different attributes. Eventually, through dialog and discussions, students will be able to distinguish the meaning of "biggest."

Notes

STANDARD 2 (K.MD.A.2)

Directly compare two objects with a measurable attribute in common, to see which object has "more of/less of" the attribute, and describe the difference. For example, directly compare the heights of two children and describe one child as taller/shorter.

What the TEACHER does:

- Provide numerous experiences for students to directly compare two objects. Direct comparisons can be made when objects are put next to each other such as two blocks, two pencils, two shoes, and similar items. When making direct comparisons for length, students should match the ends of objects to get accurate measurement comparison. Ends of the objects must be lined up at the same point as shown below.

Comparing the unit to the object being measured indicates the number of units that are needed to match or cover the object. The number of units can be found by counting.

- Model vocabulary with phrases or a summary such as "We discovered the blue straw is *longer than* the orange one. The blue straw is 3 cubes *longer than* the orange one. The orange straw is *shorter* than the blue straw. The orange straw is 3 cubes shorter than the blue one. We noticed that there is *more of* the blue straw in the picture. The length of the orange straw is *less than* the blue straw."
- Ensure students have opportunities to talk with the teacher and each other to make sense of what they are learning.

What the STUDENTS do:

- Students should participate in discussions about comparing two objects. This dialog will help students not only understand the concept, but also it will allow students to use measurement comparison vocabulary.
- Students will be actively engaged in comparisons of two objects and will be able to see which object has more of or less than the other and describe the difference.

Addressing Student Misconceptions and Common Errors

Students may not understand conservation of length. This means that an object such as a pencil maintains the same size and length even if it is repositioned or moved. To understand this idea, students must realize that a pencil's length remains constant when it is placed in different orientations. For example, two pencils that are the same length remain equal in length when one pencil is placed ahead of the other one. Be sure to provide students with numerous experiences and discussions to master this principle that is a milestone for kindergarten children.

Notes

Measurement and Data
K.MD.B*

Classify objects and count the number of objects in each category.

STANDARD 3 **K.MD.B.3:** Classify objects into given categories; count the numbers of objects in each category and sort the categories by count.[3]

[3]Limit category counts to less than or equal to 10.

*Supporting cluster

Measurement and Data K.MD.B

Cluster B: Classify objects and count the number of objects in each category.
Kindergarten Overview

At this level, kindergartners will experience sorting by a variety of criteria as well as sorting rules that promote logical thinking and reasoning. Students will learn to distinguish between attributes and characteristics. Attributes are consistent to the definition and do not change; that is, a triangle has three sides. Characteristics may change such as the color of the triangle may be yellow, red, or blue. For this cluster, students will identify similarities and differences between objects (e.g., size, color, shape) and use the attributes to sort a collection of objects.

Standards for Mathematical Practice
SFMP 2. Reason abstractly and quantitatively.

Kindergartners sort by a variety of criteria and describe sorting rules that promote logical thinking and reasoning.

SFMP 6. Attend to precision.

Students will attend to precision with appropriate vocabulary to describe how piles of objects are sorted.

Related Content Standards

K.CC.B.5   1.MD.C.4

Notes

STANDARD 3 (K.MD.B.3)

Classify objects into given categories; count the numbers of objects in each category and sort the categories by count.[3]

[3]Limit category counts to less than or equal to 10.

What the TEACHER does:

- Provide numerous experiences for students to classify objects as this standard lays the groundwork for future data collection. In the later grades, students will use these foundational kindergarten skills to create and analyze graphical representations. Starting with a pile of ten or fewer objects, direct students to first sort by similarities and differences among the objects and then count the objects in each set. Try sorting with buttons, coins, small toys, and similar objects. Attribute blocks may also be used to sort by color, shape, size, and girth.
- Ensure students have opportunities to explain how the objects were sorted into groups and how they categorized or labeled each set.
- After sorting and counting, help students to compare the sorted groups of objects by modeling the use of the vocabulary terms *least, the same or alike,* and *most* to describe the categories.

What the STUDENTS do:

- Students will practice sorting collections of objects possibly with more than one way to sort. For example, with buttons, students can sort not only by color but also by size and maybe shape as not all buttons are round.
- Students will use descriptive words to describe how their collections have been sorted.

Addressing Student Misconceptions and Common Errors

Often times, students are able to sort but are not able to label each set. Through discussions, the teacher can help students think about and create a label for each set of items sorted. Counting may be an issue for some students as they point to one object and count 1, 2 before pointing to the next object in a set or collection. Teachers can review one to one correspondence and remind students, as they point to one object, only one number should be associated with the count.

Notes

Standard: K.MD.A.1. *Describe measurable attributes of objects, such as length or weight. Describe several measurable attributes of a single object.*

Mathematical Practice or Process Standards:
SFMP 3. Construct viable arguments and critique the reasoning of others.
Kindergartners will describe measurable attributes of a single object.

Goal:
Students will be engaged in nonstandard measurement activities with a variety of things to measure in different ways and a variety of tools to use for measuring. Students learn that all objects have attributes that can be measured.

Planning:

Materials: A variety of things to measure such as books, desks, shoes, and similar items; nonstandard measuring units such as paper clips, cubes, and similar items

Sample Activity:

- Explore how and why an object has several different measurable attributes. Start measuring with nonstandard units such as counting cubes, string, straws, or paper clips and provide a variety of objects for students to measure that are found in the classroom.
- Model measurement vocabulary such as, "We discovered the *length* of our desks is 20 cubes *long*. The *height* of our desks is 10 straws tall."

Questions/Prompts:

- Do students understand that length relates to how long an object is and that weight relates to how heavy an object is? Ask, *"How many cubes long is your sheet of paper?"*
- Do students understand different ways to measure attributes of objects? Ask, *"What two different ways can we measure this book?"*

Differentiating Instruction:

Struggling Students: Provide additional measurement experiences to help students explore different measurable attributes such as length, weight, height, and heaviness.

Extension: Provide experiences for students to *compare* different objects with different weights and lengths. For example, to weigh objects, group the students into partner pairs. One student places an object in the left-hand balance. The partner adds cubes until the scale is balanced. Partner one will count to find how many cubes and record. Partner two repeats, using a different object placed in the left balance scale. The students will explain which object is heavier and which is lighter.

Standard:

Mathematical Practice or Process Standards:

Goal:

Planning:

Materials:

Sample Activity:

Questions/Prompts:

Differentiating Instruction:

Struggling Students:

Extension:

Standard:

Mathematical Practice or Process Standards:

Goal:

Planning:

Materials:

Sample Activity:

Questions/Prompts:

Differentiating Instruction:

Struggling Students:

Extension:

Measurement and Data
1.MD.A*

Measure lengths indirectly and by iterating length units.

STANDARD 1   **1.MD.A.1:** Order three objects by length; compare the lengths of two objects indirectly by using a third object.

STANDARD 2   **1.MD.A.2:** Express the length of an object as a whole number of length units, by laying multiple copies of a shorter object (the length unit) end to end; understand that the length measurement of an object is the number of same-size length units that span it with no gaps or overlaps. *Limit to contexts where the object being measured is spanned by a whole number of length units with no gaps or overlaps.*

*Major cluster

Measurement and Data 1.MD.A

Cluster A: Measure lengths indirectly and by iterating length units.
Grade 1 Overview

First graders need to use direct comparisons, understanding that length is measured from one endpoint to another endpoint. By aligning objects, students can determine which is longer/shorter or taller/shorter as shown below.

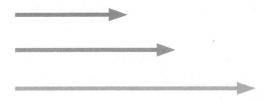

Standards for Mathematical Practice in This Cluster
SFMP 5. Use appropriate tools strategically.

Students use nonstandard tools to estimate and measure objects. They also compare lengths of three different objects.

SFMP 6. Attend to precision.

Students attend to precision using appropriate vocabulary to describe direct comparisons and the alignment of objects.

Related Content Standards

K.MD.A.1   K.MD.A.2   1.MD.A.2

Notes

Order three objects by length; compare the lengths of two objects indirectly by using a third object.

What the TEACHER does:

- Begin by teaching students to first predict by estimating how long or how tall an object will be. Provide multiple experiences for students to investigate a variety of objects using numerous nonstandard tools such as paper clips, straws, cubes, string, and similar items. Ask students to discuss their estimates and any unreasonable estimates they made with the measurement of their objects. Ensure that students measure the same object with several different sizes of units. Then, provide the students with three items to measure and compare length such as three different sizes of pencils or three completely different objects such as a crayon, a used pencil, and a pen. The height of three different students can also be compared. Teachers can also direct students to locate three things in the room that are the same size as the length of a book and three things shorter than the length of the book.
- Model vocabulary with examples such as "When we *measured* the *length* of our three different sizes of pencils, we found the yellow new pencil is the *tallest* pencil. The red pencil is *shorter* than the yellow pencil. The blue pencil is the *shortest* of all three pencils."
- Provide problem-solving experiences for students to share their thinking and reasoning with problems such as *"My mom wants to put my three hair ribbons in order from the shortest to the longest ribbon. She knows that the purple ribbon is longer than the pink ribbon. She also knows that the pink ribbon is longer than the yellow ribbon. In what order should she put my hair ribbons?"* Another problem could ask students to reason about which item is taller. Say, "Predict and then measure. Which item is taller: a bookcase or a teacher's desk?"

What the STUDENTS do:

- Students will use measurement vocabulary to first estimate, describe, and then compare the measurable attributes.

Addressing Student Misconceptions and Common Errors

Students may incorrectly align objects to be measured. This may result in an inaccurate comparison of the three items. Teachers can remind students to carefully check the object alignments.

> *Notes*

STANDARD 2 (1.MD.A.2)

Express the length of an object as a whole number of length units, by laying multiple copies of a shorter object (the length unit) end to end; understand that the length measurement of an object is the number of same-size length units that span it with no gaps or overlaps. Limit to contexts where the object being measure is spanned by a whole number of length units with no gaps or overlaps.

What the TEACHER does:

- Begin by modeling how to measure the length of a book or a desk with nonstandard units such as paper clips or cubes. Model placement of the cubes or clips end to end and count the cubes to find the number. The example below shows the length of a book is 11 cubes long.

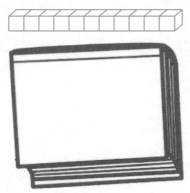

- Provide numerous items for students to measure. Before measuring, remind students to estimate how many objects it will take to measure an item. At first, give students specific items to measure along with the nonstandard unit objects to use. After measuring several items chosen by the teacher, allow students to pick their own nonstandard unit and their choice of items to measure. Let students measure a variety of items in the classroom.
- Encourage students to demonstrate their counting and measuring skills with each other. Ask them to estimate and predict before describing the item measured and the nonstandard object used to measure.

What the STUDENTS do:

- Students measure numerous items with different sizes of nonstandard units.
- First graders should learn that the smaller the unit, the more units will be needed to measure the object.

Addressing Student Misconceptions and Common Errors

Some students may leave a gap or space or overlap as the units are placed next to an item. Some students may simply think about measurement as merely a counting task. To correct these misconceptions, model and remind students that the length of an object is the number of units counted. Reiterate the idea that when using different sizes of nonstandard objects to measure the same item, the sizes of the objects must be taken into account rather than the amount of objects counted.

Notes

Measurement and Data
1.MD.B*

Cluster B

Tell and write time.

STANDARD 3 **1.MD.B.3:** Tell and write time in hours and half-hours using analog and digital clocks.

Measurement and Data 1.MD.B

Cluster B: Tell and write time.
Grade 1 Overview

This cluster is about reading a clock, orally telling time, and writing the time in hours or half hours. Students will be introduced to the measurement concept that sixty minutes equals one hour.

Standards for Mathematical Practice
SFMP 6. Attend to precision.

Students will attend to precision with specific vocabulary to describe and tell time such as half past the hour.

SFMP 7. Look for and make use of structure.

Students will use a clock to tell time noticing that sixty minutes is the same as one hour.

Related Content Standard

2.MD.C.7

Notes

STANDARD 3 (1.MD.B.3)

Tell and write time in hours and half-hours using analog and digital clocks.

What the TEACHER does:

- Start with a discussion of why learning to tell time is important. Generate a list of ideas from students including knowing when to get up each morning, getting to school on time, staying on schedule for recess, knowing when to eat lunch, and other experiences in their day. Demonstrate using an analog clock when each activity takes place. For example, show 7:00, noon, and other times in hours or half hours on a clock.
- Provide students with a progression of activities for learning how to tell time. Start by learning to tell time to the hour. Begin by using numbered cards one through twelve. Remind students of the sequential counting order, placing the cards for students to view and count.

1	2	3	4	5	6
7	8	9	10	11	12

- Demonstrate how the cards can be "converted into a clock face" to tell time. Show how to manipulate the cards sequentially into a clock circle as shown below, beginning with one and ending with twelve. Practice telling time to the hour with a small hand to show the time is exactly on the hour. Help students understand that a clock's hands move around the clock in one direction.

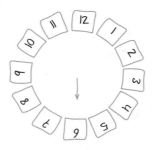

- As students begin to master telling time to the hour, use twelve more cards to create a second clock "circle." Number the cards 5, 10, 15, 20, 25, 30, 35, 40, 45, 50, 55, and 60. Manipulate these cards into a circle as shown.

What the STUDENTS do:

- Students must correctly tell and write the time using both an analog and digital clock.
- Students must use the correct vocabulary to describe time.
- Throughout the day, students will look at real analog and digital clocks to tell and write the time.

(Continued)

What the TEACHER does (continued):

- Beginning at one, ask students to count by fives with you as you touch each number on the clock until you get to the twelve. Explain that sixty minutes equals one hour. Show students that halfway between two hours on the clock is thirty minutes. Practice with numerous examples of telling time with a larger hand called the clock's minute hand. Join both clocks to focus telling time to the hour and thirty minutes after the hour. Talk about the ideas that when the clock shows time at the half hour, the hour hand is between numbers and not on a number and the hour is the number before where the hour hand is.

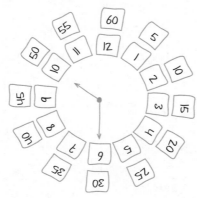

- Show students how to read time to the hour and half hour using a digital clock. Point out the use of the colon such as 1:00. Make the connection that time on the hour is written as it appears on a digital clock.
- Continue with a variety of ongoing experiences to practice telling and writing down the time. Create a time log recording bookmark for each student to write the time throughout the day at various hours and half hours.
- Model vocabulary by using statements such as "It is exactly 1 o'clock," "It is about 3 o'clock," "It is a little bit past 9 o'clock," or "It is almost 12 o'clock." Expect students to tell time to the hour with similar statements.
- Realize that learning to tell time is not a single event for students and is probably one of the most difficult first-grade concepts.

Addressing Student Misconceptions and Common Errors

Children may misunderstand the difference between the small hand and big hand of a clock face as well as the function of both hands. To correct this misconception, review time with a one handed clock to focus telling time to the hour and half hour.

Interpreting time to the hour with clock numbers may be confusing for some students. To counteract this confusion, explain that when telling time to the hour, the hand can directly point to the number or can be slightly ahead or behind a number. Discuss and show examples to the students. Use phrases such as "It is *about* 5 o'clock."

Notes

Measurement and Data
1.MD.C*

Represent and interpret data.

STANDARD 4 **1.MD.C.4:** Organize, represent, and interpret data with up to three categories; ask and answer questions about the total number of data points, how many each category, and how many more or less are in one category than in another.

*Supporting cluster

Measurement and Data 1.MD.C

Cluster C: Represent and interpret data.
Grade 1 Overview

This cluster engages first graders in collecting and using data to answer questions relevant to their lives. Students will form a question, collect data in a chart or table form, organize the data, and interpret the results to answer a question. Using three categories, first graders will summarize data by describing the categories with the most or least responses along with differences.

Standards for Mathematical Practice
SFMP 2. Reason abstractly and quantitatively.

Students will analyze and use reasoning to summarize and interpret data collected. They must make sense of the quantities counted in each category of their tables or charts.

SFMP 4. Model with mathematics.

First graders will pose questions and collect data to answer their questions. Students will organize and represent their data.

SFMP 6. Attend to precision.

Students will communicate by explaining what the information means with the data they collected.

Related Content Standards

K.MD.B.3   2.MD.D.10

Notes

Organize, represent, and interpret data with up to three categories; ask and answer questions about the total number of data points, how many in each category, and how many more or less are in one category than in another.

What the TEACHER does:

- Begin by posing a question such as "What is your favorite food?" Ask students to think about three categories for anticipated responses such as these choices: hamburger, macaroni and cheese, or pizza. Next, model how the data can be organized into a table. Ask the students to predict what they think the students in the class will choose. Show students how to write their names for their choice by category as shown below.

What Is Your Favorite Food?

Hamburger	Emily Sammy
Macaroni and Cheese	Megan Maria Teddy Roberto Isaiah Lynn Sean Angel
Pizza	LaTisha Matt Rebecca Kenya Suzanna

- Teach students to interpret the results by counting the names in each category. Discuss and answer questions such as "Which category has the most or least?" Help students learn to analyze the chart by reviewing the data and writing several sentences about the data collected. For example, students could write, "Most students in our class chose macaroni and cheese as their favorite food." "Our least favorite food was hamburgers. Only two students selected hamburgers." Have students compute to answer how many more students chose macaroni and cheese versus hamburgers.
- Ask students to pose their own questions to use to collect and interpret data. Expect them to create a table, and have everyone in the class respond by writing their names by the categories. Require students to write two sentences about their graph including analysis of the most and least in a category and a third sentence to tell how many more or less are in one category than another.
- Ensure students have opportunities to share the questions they posed and the interpretation and analysis of their data with each other.

What the STUDENTS do:

- Students will think about questions to pose and limit the responses to three top categories.
- Students will create a table or chart to use.
- First graders will collect the data by asking every student to sign his or her name in the chosen category.
- Students will analyze and interpret the data both verbally and in writing.
- First graders will use measurement vocabulary for analyzing data with terms such as *most*, *least*, *more than*, *less than*, and similar comparison words.

Addressing Student Misconceptions and Common Errors

Some students may pose a question that has too many choices such as "What is your favorite color?" To help with this error, ensure students limit the categories to only three choices. Some students may not realize they have not collected data from every student in the class. To help with this error, make sure students know the total number of classmates who will be answering the question. Some students may not be able to summarize with statements like, "The majority of the students like or have—," or similar statements. To help with this, review and discuss summary statements.

Standard: 1.MD.C.4. *Organize, represent, and interpret data with up to three categories; ask and answer questions about the total number of data points, how many in each category, and how many more or less are in one category than in another.*

Mathematical Practice or Process Standards:

SFMP 2. Reason abstractly and quantitatively.
Students will analyze and use reasoning to summarize and interpret data collected.

SFMP 4. Model with mathematics.
First graders will pose questions and collect data to answer their questions. Students will organize and represent their data.

SFMP 6. Attend to precision.
Students will communicate by explaining what the information means with the data they collected.

Goal:
Students will learn to pose questions, collect data, create a table or chart, analyze the information, and use measurement vocabulary to interpret the results.

Planning:

Materials: Pencil and paper

Sample Activity:
- Begin by posing a question such as "What is your favorite color?" Students will choose from three categories for anticipated responses such as the choices red, blue, or green.
- Next, model how the data can be organized into a table. Ask the students to predict what they think the students in the class will choose. Show students how to write their names for their choice by category.
- Teach students to interpret the results by describing how many in each category and how many more/less are in one category than in another.

Questions/Prompts:

- Are students able to collect all the information needed for their graph? Ask, *"How do you know you collected every student's data?"*
- Are students able to count how many objects are in each category? Ask, *"Which category has the most? Which category has the least?"*
- Are students able to figure out how many more objects are in one category than another? Ask, *"How many more in this category than that category?"*
- Are students able to analyze the information correctly?

Differentiating Instruction:

Struggling Students: Students may have difficulty counting the number of items in a category and making a summary statement about that category. Provide numerous opportunities for students to create charts and tables and share their conclusions about data collected.

Extension: Students can learn to create a bar graph to represent the data they collect. Ask students to graph the letters in their first names, the M&M's candies in a small bag, their favorite pets, their favorite television shows, and similar objects. Students can summarize the information in writing.

Standard:

Mathematical Practice or Process Standards:

Goal:

Planning:

Materials:

Sample Activity:

Questions/Prompts:

Differentiating Instruction:

Struggling Students:

Extension:

Standard:

Mathematical Practice or Process Standards:

Goal:

Planning:

Materials:

Sample Activity:

Questions/Prompts:

Differentiating Instruction:

Struggling Students:

Extension:

Standard:

Mathematical Practice or Process Standards:

Goal:

Planning:

Materials:

Sample Activity:

Questions/Prompts:

Differentiating Instruction:

Struggling Students:

Extension:

Measurement and Data
2.MD.A*

Measure and estimate lengths in standard units.

STANDARD 1	**2.MD.A.1:** Measure the length of an object by selecting and using appropriate tools such as rulers, yardsticks, meter sticks, and measuring tapes.
STANDARD 2	**2.MD.A.2:** Measure the length of an object twice, using length units of different lengths for the two measurements; describe how the two measurements relate to the size of the unit chosen.
STANDARD 3	**2.MD.A.3:** Estimate lengths using units of inches, feet, centimeters, and meters.
STANDARD 4	**2.MD.A.4:** Measure to determine how much longer one object is than another, expressing the length difference in terms of a standard length unit.

*Major cluster

Measurement and Data 2.MD.A

Cluster A: Measure and estimate lengths in standard units.
Grade 2 Overview

In this cluster, students will recognize the need for standard units of measure and use rulers, yardsticks, meter sticks, measuring tapes, and other measuring tools. Second graders will understand that linear measure involves an iteration of units with the idea that the smaller the unit, the more iterations they need to cover a given length.

Standards for Mathematical Practice
SFMP 5. Use appropriate tools strategically.

Students will measure an object with a ruler, yardstick, meter stick, or measuring tape.

SFMP 6. Attend to precision.

Students will use specific vocabulary to describe the measurement of objects.

SFMP 7. Look for and make use of structure.

Students will identify and select appropriate units to measure objects, discovering the relationship between the size of a unit and the number of units needed.

Related Content Standards

K.MD.A.1   1.MD.A.2

Notes
_____
_____
_____

Measure the length of an object by selecting and using appropriate tools such as rulers, yardsticks, meter sticks, and measuring tapes.

What the TEACHER does:

- Provide activities to teach students how to choose appropriate tools and units to measure an object in inches and feet or centimeters and meters. First, allow students to experiment by estimating and measuring a variety of things using different measuring tools with the outcome of selecting the best or the most appropriate tool. As a result of the experimentation, students will discover a relationship between the size of a unit and the number of units needed. When measuring a classroom length, for example, if the unit selected to measure the classroom is small such as measuring in inches, the more units it will take to measure the room. Students will notice that a yardstick is a more appropriate tool to measure the classroom's length.
- Model vocabulary usage with measurement terms.
- Provide time for student discussion about measurement tools and the ideas they are learning.

What the STUDENTS do:

- Students should experiment with a variety of tools and units to measure objects and things in their classrooms to discover the use of appropriate tools.
- Students should use the vocabulary associated with the measurement concepts they are learning.

Addressing Student Misconceptions and Common Errors

Some students may begin to measure starting with "1" on a ruler, yardstick, or meter stick. The teacher can use a large number line on the floor to demonstrate where the students must begin before "one" and relate this to all measuring done with linear measurement tools.

Notes

Measure the length of an object twice, using length units of different lengths for the two measurements; describe how the two measurements relate to the size of the unit chosen.

What the TEACHER does:

- Provide measurement activities to help students make a connection to the idea that the unit used to measure is as important as the attribute being measured. Allow students to experiment to measure an object using two different units such as inches and feet.
- Discuss the results in measuring the object in both inches and feet or in both centimeters and meters. Help the students describe how the two measurements relate to the size of the unit chosen.

What the STUDENTS do:

- Measure objects with two different units.
- Describe how the two measurements relate to each other and the size of the unit chosen.
- As a result of their experimentation, students should understand that larger units such as yards can be subdivided into equivalent units of feet and inches.

Addressing Student Misconceptions and Common Errors

Describing how two measurements relate to the size of the unit chosen is a very difficult concept for second graders to articulate. To address this, provide ongoing experiences and activities for students to learn to predict and measure. Allow students to talk about what they are noticing.

Notes

Estimate lengths using units of inches, feet, centimeters, and meter.

What the TEACHER does:

- Provide activities for students to estimate the lengths of objects in their environment such as a pencil, a book a sheet of paper, a desk, a bulletin board, a door, and similar items. Help students develop knowledge for a specific unit of measure; for example, to measure the length of a sheet of paper, the awareness of an inch is critical for estimating the paper's length in inches. Teaching students to estimate before measuring the length will help second graders develop a benchmark for how long something is.
- Model measurement and estimation vocabulary with terms such as *a little more than, a little less than, about,* and *close to.*
- Plan time for dialog and discussion about the importance of estimation and how it is used in daily life.
- Allow students to share their "benchmarks" of measurement for how long something is.

What the STUDENTS do:

- Students will estimate before measuring.
- Students will use measurement terminology.
- Students will measure an object two times using two different measures.

Addressing Student Misconceptions and Common Errors

Some students will estimate with "wild" estimate statements like, "I estimate our classroom to be one million yards long." Some children may estimate with a number that is not a close estimate and become frustrated to not give a correct answer. The teacher should provide additional estimating experiences along with a discussion about the purpose of estimation.

STANDARD 4 (2.MD.A.4)

Measure to determine how much longer one object is than another, expressing the length difference in terms of a standard length unit.

What the TEACHER does:

- Provide multiple activities for students to find the difference in length between two real objects. Have second graders select the objects to be measured, choose an appropriate tool and unit, measure both objects, and then determine the differences in lengths.
- Remind the students that direct comparisons can be made by measuring the difference in length between two objects by laying them side by side and selecting an appropriate standard length unit of measure. Help students make comparative statements to describe the differences between two objects such as, "This object is *shorter* by 2 inches" or "It is *longer* by 4 centimeters."

What the STUDENTS do:

- Select objects to measure to find how much longer one object is than another.
- Express the length difference of the two objects with centimeters, inches, meters, or yard.
- Use measurement terminology.

Addressing Student Misconceptions and Common Errors

Some second graders may think that the numbers of a ruler or yardstick are for counting the marks instead of the units or spaces between the marks. Some students might think that they can only measure lengths with a ruler starting at the left edge. To address this, engage students in discussions about measuring devices and demonstrate how to measure. Provide additional experiences for the students to use measuring devices correctly. Observe as students measure objects to determine specific measurement errors that may occur.

Measurement and Data
2.MD.B*

Relate addition and subtraction to length.

STANDARD 5　**2.MD.B.5:** Use addition and subtraction within 100 to solve word problems involving lengths that are given in the same units, e.g., by using drawings (such as drawings of rulers) and equations with a symbol for the unknown number to represent the problem.

STANDARD 6　**2.MD.B.6:** Represent whole numbers as lengths from 0 on a number line diagram with equally spaced points corresponding to the numbers 0, 1, 2, ..., and represent whole-number sums and differences within 100 on a number line diagram.

Measurement and Data 2.MD.B

Cluster B: Relate addition and subtraction to length.
Grade 2 Overview

Second graders will solve word problems by applying previously learned addition and subtraction skills to the concept of length. Students will write equations for measurement word problems using symbols for the unknown values and calculate the sum and differences represented in the equations.

Standards for Mathematical Practice
SFMP 1. Make sense of problems and persevere in solving them.

Students must interpret and solve measurement word problems using manipulatives or drawings.

SFMP 2. Reason abstractly and quantitatively.

Students must make sense of the quantities involved in each measurement problem, manipulating objects in a quantitative manner to solve the problems.

SFMP 4. Model with mathematics.

Students will apply addition and subtraction to solve problems.

SFMP 5. Use appropriate tools strategically.

Students will use a drawing, pencil and paper, concrete models, a ruler, and similar tools to solve measurement word problems.

Related Content Standard

2.NBT.B.7

Notes

Use addition and subtraction within 100 to solve word problems involving lengths that are given in the same units, e.g., by using drawings (such as drawings of rulers) and equations with a symbol for the unknown number to represent the problem.

What the TEACHER does:

- Provide a variety of experiences for students to apply the concept of length to solve addition and subtraction word problems with numbers within 100.
- Model several ways students can find solutions to word problems involving length by using concrete manipulatives or by using pictorial drawings to model the word problems. For example, Shannon built a train 23 inches long. Sammy built a train 15 inches long. How many inches longer is Shannon's train than Sammy's train? Write an equation to solve the problem. Students can model the problem with cubes as shown below and write an equation, such as $23 - 15 = n$ or $15 + n = 23$.

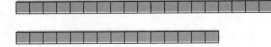

- Ensure that students use the same unit of measurement to solve the problems.
- Relate and connect this type of problem solving directly to standard 2.NBT.B.7.

What the STUDENTS do:

- Students use concrete models and/or pictures to make sense of a word problem and solve it.
- Students write an equation with a symbol for the unknown in the problem.
- Students explain verbally how the problem was solved.

Addressing Student Misconceptions and Student Errors

Some students may illustrate the problem by drawing a lovely picture that does not match the problem. Some students may not be able to solve and write an equation to show how they solved the problem. To address these issues, work with students to continue providing additional problems and examples. Use concrete objects rather than pictures to help students make sense of the problem versus allowing them to draw pictures. Listen to students' thinking as they attempt to solve the problems, correcting errors as you are interacting with the students.

Notes

STANDARD 6 (2.MD.B.6)

Represent whole numbers as lengths from 0 on a number line diagram with equally spaced points corresponding to the numbers 0, 1, 2, . . . , and represent whole-number sums and differences within 100 on a number line diagram.

What the TEACHER does:

- Begin by showing a number line. Model counting on or counting back by showing "jumps" using curved lines.

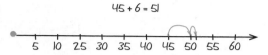

- Make a connection to whole number units on rulers, yardstick, meter sticks, and measuring tapes to number lines showing numbers starting at 0.
- Provide numerous teacher-created number line examples for students to represent addition and subtraction. Direct students to show their work of adding to, taking from, putting together, taking apart, and comparing using illustrated jumps, or hops, on the number line.
- After students understand adding and subtracting on the number line, incorporate word problems for students to solve.
- Dialog and discuss why a number line representation is a valuable tool for solving addition and subtraction.

What the STUDENTS do:

- Students represent addition and subtraction by eventually creating their own number lines using an individual whiteboard/marker, a piece of blank paper, or a sheet of graph paper. Students will mark and label the number line they personally draw with equal spaces and solve an addition or subtraction problem using the number line to model the solution.
- Students should explain how they solved the problems using the number line.

Addressing Student Misconceptions and Common Errors

Some students may solve the problems by modeling the jumps by ones on the number line, which is a tedious process. To help them, provide additional work using a hundreds chart to show groups of objects by fives and tens. Model and provide more experiences for the students to jump, or hop, on the number lines by fives and/or tens.

Notes

Measurement and Data
2.MD.C*

Work with time and money.

STANDARD 7   **2.MD.C.7:** Tell and write time from analog and digital clocks to the nearest five minutes, using a.m. and p.m.

STANDARD 8   **2.MD.C.8:** Solve word problems involving dollar bills, quarters, dimes, nickels, and pennies, using $ and ¢ symbols appropriately. Example: If you have 2 dimes and 3 pennies, how many cents do you have?

*Supporting cluster

Measurement and Data 2.MD.C

Cluster C: Work with time and money.
Grade 2 Overview

In this cluster, students will tell and write time to the nearest five minutes. Students will also solve word problems involving dollars or cents. Second graders will first need to identify coin values and be able to add and subtract money before solving word problems.

Standards for Mathematical Practice
SFMP 1. Make sense of problems and persevere in solving them.
Students must interpret what the information in a word problem means and determine how to solve the problem.

SFMP 2. Reason abstractly and quantitatively.
Students must make sense of the quantities of the coins, e.g., three dimes and two pennies is thirty-two cents.

SFMP 6. Attend to precision.
Students will attend to precision with specific vocabulary to describe and tell time to the nearest five minutes.

SFMP 7. Look for and make use of structure.
Students will understand there are twenty-four hours in each day with two cycles of twelve hours in a day including a.m. and p.m. Students must also interpret the addition of mixed coins.

Related Content Standard
1.MD.B.3

Notes

STANDARD 7 (2.MD.C.7)

Tell and write time from analog and digital clocks to the nearest five minutes, using a.m. and p.m.

What the TEACHER does:

- Relate telling time to everyday experiences at school, that is, the time school starts and ends, lunch time, and special activities such as recess time. Link telling time to their home experiences, that is, the time they get up, eat breakfast, leave for school, eat dinner, go to sleep, and so on.
- Connect the concept of counting by fives to telling time by five minute intervals on a clock.
- Provide a variety of experiences for students to tell time to the nearest five minutes. Use individual hands—on clocks—to practice.
- Model terminology used for telling time such as five minutes before 2 o'clock. Model how to write the time using colon notation as 1:55.
- Teach second graders there are twenty-four hours in each day. Explore the two cycles of twelve hours in a day—a.m. and p.m.
- Provide continuous practice throughout the day. At various times, have students first tell then record the time on a recording sheet taped to students' desks. This helps check individual students' time-telling skills and understanding.

What the STUDENTS do:

- Students must connect previous learning of skip counting by fives to tell time to the five minute intervals.
- Second graders must know and explain there are twenty-four hours in a day with two twelve-hour cycles called a.m. and p.m.
- Students must look at an analog clock and a digital clock to tell the time and use descriptive terms such as *half past, five after*, and similar descriptive words.
- Student must write the time correctly using the colon notation, such as 1:05 p.m.

Addressing Student Misconceptions and Common Errors

Some students will likely be confused with the hour and minute hands. For the time of 3:45, they may tell the time as 9:15. To address the confusion, make sure they understand telling time to the hour using the smaller hand on an analog clock before focusing on time to the nearest five minutes.

Notes

Solve word problems involving dollar bills, quarters, dimes, nickels, and pennies, using $ and ¢ symbols appropriately. Example: If you have 2 dimes and 3 pennies, how many cents do you have?

What the TEACHER does:

- Provide experiences for students to touch and feel real money coins and dollars. Students will need numerous ongoing activities to recognize the coins and their values.
- Practice counting money by using the same coins, such as all nickels or all dimes, as students will be able to relate counting coins to skip counting. Then, continue with many different coins combined, such as nickels, dimes, and pennies. This skill is more difficult and will take lots of practice.
- When students have mastered coin recognition and values, try using a hundreds number chart to place the coins to show addition of the coins. For this standard's example, *"If you have 2 dimes and 3 pennies, how many cents do you have?"* Start with 2 dimes. Ask students to place the first dime on the number ten and the second dime on twenty. The three pennies can be placed as 21, 22, and 23. Two dimes and three pennies equals 23 cents. With distributed, ongoing practice, students may be able to mentally visualize the hundreds chart without actually using it to add coins together.
- After success with counting sets of coins, show students how to compare two sets of coins, make and recognize equivalent collections of coins (same amount but different arrangements), select coins for a given amount, and make change. Include a lesson on the symbols ($ and ¢).
- Explore making the same amount such as $2.25 using a variety of different coins and dollar bill combinations. Incorporate story problems daily for students to solve and connect different representations, including objects, picture, charts, or tables. Problems can be as simple as "I have one dollar and 82¢ in my pocket. What are some possible coins I could have in my pocket?" I could have 3 quarters, 1 nickel, and 2 pennies. What is another combination of coins I could have?
- Ensure students have opportunities to talk and make sense of the problems they are solving with coins. Help students communicate their thinking and justify their answers for each problem they solve.

What the STUDENTS do:

- Students recognize coins and their values.
- Students add with coins.
- Students solve word problems involving coins and dollars.
- Students use the symbol notations of $ and ¢.

Addressing Student Misconceptions and Common Errors

When counting coins, some second graders may ignore the coins' values and want to count each coin as an individual object, such as a dime and a penny are two coins. These students may not think about the coins value of 11 cents. Some students may believe the value of a coin is directly related to its size, such as a nickel is bigger than a dime and is worth more, or a penny is bigger than a dime, so it must also be worth more. To address these misconceptions, students may use a hundreds chart and coins. For example, using a penny and a dime, have students place a dime on the ten spot of a hundreds chart and the penny next to the dime on the chart to represent one more than a dime or 11 cents. Another misconception occurs when some students may inappropriately use the $ symbol such as 39$. Through discussion about the symbols, students can learn to use the symbols correctly.

Measurement and Data
2.MD.D*

Represent and interpret data.

STANDARD 9   **2.MD.D.9:** Generate measurement data by measuring lengths of several objects to the nearest whole unit, or by making repeated measurements of the same object. Show the measurements by making a line plot, where the horizontal scale is marked off in whole-number units.

STANDARD 10   **2.MD.D.10:** Draw a picture graph and a bar graph (with single-unit scale) to represent a data set with up to four categories. Solve simple put-together, take-apart, and compare problems[1] using information presented in a bar graph.

[1]Sizes are compared directly or visually, not compared by measuring.

*Supporting cluster

Measurement and Data 2.MD.D

Cluster D: Represent and interpret data.
Grade 2 Overview

Second graders will learn about data through the study of line plots, picture graphs, and bar graphs. Students will pose questions, collect data, and analyze and interpret the results. At this level, they will also solve simple word problems about the data.

Standards for Mathematical Practice
SFMP 1. Make sense of problems and persevere in solving them.

Students interpret and solve *put together, take apart, and compare problems* using information presented in a bar graph. They analyze and use reasoning to summarize and interpret data collected.

SFMP 2. Reason abstractly and quantitatively.

They must make sense of the quantities counted in each category of picture and bar graphs.

SFMP 4. Model with mathematics.

Students organize and represent their data.

SFMP 6. Attend to precision.

Students use specific vocabulary to describe graphical representations and communicate by explaining what the information means with the data they collected.

Related Content Standard

1.MD.C.4

Notes

Generate measurement data by measuring lengths of several objects to the nearest whole unit, or by making repeated measurements of the same object. Show the measurements by making a line plot, where the horizontal scale is marked off in whole-number units.

What the TEACHER does:

- Introduce students to graphically displaying a set of data on a number line called a line plot. First, draw the number line along with a horizontal numerical scale marked in whole number units. To show data on a line plot, students will place an X above the corresponding value on the line that represents each piece of data. Model data collection and a line plot display. Demonstrate how to analyze data and interpret the results.
- To focus on representing data using a line plot, remind second graders to use their previously acquired measurement skills to measure and record the lengths of eight objects in the classroom that are less than 10 inches long.
- Discuss vocabulary used with line plots such as data, number line, pieces of data, and plot.
- Have students display the data they collect with an X on their own line plots. For example, Maria collected the following data for eight objects: crayon—3 inches, pencil eraser—2 inches, scissors—6 inches, marker—4 inches, new pencil—6 inches, book—8 inches, flash card—3 inches, and pencil sharpener—3 inches.

```
          Maria's Objects Measured in Inches

        X
        X           X
    X   X   X       X       X
  _____
    1   2   3   4   5   6   7   8   9   10
```

- Ask students to talk about and share the data for the line plots they created. In the previous example, Maria may say that three objects in the room each measured 3 inches, two objects measured 6 inches. One object measured 2 inches, one object measured 4 inches, and one object measured 8 inches. A total of eight objects were measured.

What the STUDENTS do:

- Students measure objects to the nearest whole unit.
- Students create a line plot to display the data of the objects they measured.
- Students share the data on a line plot they created.

Addressing Student Misconceptions and Common Errors

Some students may mark Xs on the line plot as different sizes, some small and some large. Talk with students to help them understand that different sizes of Xs on the plot may make it difficult to analyze and interpret.

STANDARD 10 (2.MD.D.10)

Draw a picture graph and a bar graph (with single-unit scale) to represent a data set with up to four categories. Solve simple put-together, take-apart, and compare problems[1] using information presented in a bar graph.

[1]*Sizes are compared directly or visually, not compared by measuring.*

What the TEACHER does:

- Provide activities for students to collect data and represent it on both picture and bar graphs. Remind second graders how to set up to four categories of potential responses for a question they will pose.
- Model terminology used for this standard along with specific parts of a data display such as a title, a key, the x and y axis labels, and other parts.
- Review how to analyze and interpret the data students collected and represented in their graphs. Remind students how to answer questions such as how many in each category—which category has the least or greatest number of items and questions to focus on conclusions, comparisons, and generalizations about the data they collected and displayed.
- Ensure students have opportunities to talk about and share their data with each other.

What the STUDENTS do:

- Think about an interesting question to pose to the class. Choose categories for the possible responses.
- Collect data and represent the data in either a picture or bar graph format.
- Prepare to share a summary of the data and conclusions, comparisons, and generalizations.

Addressing Student Misconceptions and Common Errors

Some students may forget to label and title the graphs. Address this with students as a reminder. Some second graders may not be able to read a graph and simply need more practice. Teachers may want to reteach this critical lifelong skill. Some children may not be able to analyze the data in their graphs. Teachers may need to begin by helping students count the number in each category and make comparison statements or draw conclusions.

Notes

Standard: 2.MD.D.9. *Generate measurement data by measuring lengths of several objects to the nearest whole unit, or by making repeated measurements of the same object. Show the measurements by making a line plot where the horizontal scale is marked off in whole-number units.*

Mathematical Practice or Process Standards:

SFMP 2. Reason abstractly and quantitatively.

Students will analyze and use reasoning to summarize and interpret data collected.

SFMP 4. Model with mathematics.

Students will pose questions and collect data to answer their questions. Students will organize and represent their data.

Goal:

Students will measure objects to the nearest whole unit, create line plots, and share the data of the objects they measured.

Planning:

Materials: Objects for students to measure found in the classroom, paper and pencil to create a line plot.

Sample Activity:

- Provide experiences for students to measure objects to the nearest inch such as pencils, notebooks, and crayons.
- Show students how to create a line plot by drawing a number line with whole numbers marked. Have students plot their data points for the objects measured with an X above the number line.
- Ask students to share the data for the line plots they created.

Questions/Prompts:

- Can students accurately measure objects to the nearest inch?
- Can students correctly create a line plot for the data they collected?
- Can students accurately summarize their data?

Differentiating Instruction:

Struggling Students:

- Students may not accurately measure. Provide numerous experiences to develop this skill. For example, students can measure five to eight different sizes of sharpened pencils or a variety of different linker cube "trains."

Extension:

- Students can continue to measure a variety of objects to create additional line plots. Instead of the teacher selecting the items to measure, have students choose ten different objects to measure and then plot on the number line. Have the students share the data by interpreting and summarizing it.

Standard:

Mathematical Practice or Process Standards:

Goal:

Planning:

Materials:

Sample Activity:

Questions/Prompts:

Differentiating Instruction:

Struggling Students:

Extension:

Standard:

Mathematical Practice or Process Standards:

Goal:

Planning:

Materials:

Sample Activity:

Questions/Prompts:

Differentiating Instruction:

Struggling Students:

Extension:

Standard:

Mathematical Practice or Process Standards:

Goal:

Planning:

Materials:

Sample Activity:

Questions/Prompts:

Differentiating Instruction:

Struggling Students:

Extension:

Standard:

Mathematical Practice or Process Standards:

Goal:

Planning:

Materials:

Sample Activity:

Questions/Prompts:

Differentiating Instruction:

Struggling Students:

Extension:

Reflection Questions: Measurement and Data

1. Discuss how the study of measurement and data will apply directly to students' lives.

2. Explain why nonstandard unit measurement activities are critical for primary learners and must precede student use of standard measurement tools.

3. Think about why predicting by estimating the length or height of an object is a valuable experience for K–2 students. Why should students talk about their estimates and the mistakes they make with the measurement of their objects?

4. As a result of studying the measurement and data domain, which problem-solving experiences will you use to help students think and reason about measurement?

Part 5

Geometry

Geometry

Domain Overview

KINDERGARTEN

The study of geometry in kindergarten is essential as students must be able to recognize and visualize shapes in their surroundings. Many students are already exposed to shapes as they play, draw, color, build, and explore with toys and technology. These experiences help to develop spatial reasoning, which is important in daily life for interpreting and making drawings, forming mental images, visualizing changes, and generalizing about perceptions in the environment. Kindergartners will identify, name, and describe basic two-dimensional shapes, such as squares, triangles, circles, rectangles, and hexagons, presented in a variety of ways with different sizes and orientations as well as three-dimensional shapes, such as cubes, cones, cylinders, and spheres.

GRADE 1

At the first grade level, the study of geometry features reasoning with shapes and their attributes. Students will learn three important ideas through the exploration of geometric and spatial concepts. First, students will identify defining attributes of two-dimensional and three-dimensional shapes by building on their kindergarten experiences of sorting, analyzing, comparing, and creating a variety of two-dimensional and three-dimensional shapes and objects. Second, first graders will use two-dimensional and three-dimensional shapes to create a larger composite shape. Third, students will divide circles and rectangles into halves, fourths, and quarters. As result of their study, first graders will relate what they have learned to real-life situations.

GRADE 2

In second grade, students will be thinking about, describing, and analyzing shapes by investigating their sides and angles. They will also be building, drawing, describing, decomposing, and combining shapes to make other shapes. As a result of this learning, students will develop a foundational understanding for the future concepts of area, volume, congruence, similarity, and symmetry.

K	1	2	
✓	✓	✓	Two-dimensional and three-dimensional shapes—found in the classroom/school/ home such as soup, soda, jack in the box toy, pizza cardboard for circles
✓	✓	✓	Attribute blocks
✓	✓	✓	Pattern blocks
✓	✓	✓	Tangrams
✓	✓	✓	Geoboards
✓	✓	✓	Shapes—A variety of cut-out shapes including circles, triangles, pentagons, hexagons
		✓	Paper—for folding for equal partitioning
	✓	✓	Objects/things—to create three-dimensional shapes, such as straws, gumdrops, marshmallows, toothpicks, pipe cleaners, popsicle sticks, and similar objects

KEY VOCABULARY

K	1	2	
✓	✓	✓	**angles** two rays (<) that share an endpoint
✓	✓	✓	**attributes** sides, angles, color, shape, size, girth
	✓	✓	**closed shape** a shape that begins and ends at the same point; that is, a triangle
	✓	✓	**column** a vertical arrangement of objects
	✓	✓	**equal shares** equal sizes, equal size parts
		✓	**face** the flat surface of a three-dimensional shape
✓	✓	✓	**figure** a closed shape in two-dimensions or three dimensions
✓	✓	✓	**halves** half circle, half of, two halves
	✓	✓	**open shape** a shape made up of line segments with at least one line segment that isn't connected to anything at one of its endpoints
		✓	**partition** equal dividing
✓			**positional vocabulary** above, below, beside, + in front of, behind, next to, same, different
	✓	✓	**quarter** one fourth, quarter circle, quarter of, fourths
	✓	✓	**row** a horizontal arrangement of objects
✓	✓	✓	**side** a line segment of a many-sided figure
		✓	**surface** the area of faces and cured surfaces of a three-dimensional figure
		✓	**thirds** third of a circle, one third, three thirds
✓	✓	✓	**vertex/corner** in a two-dimensional figure, the point at which two line segments meet to form an angle; in a three-dimensional figure, the point at which three or more edges meet to form a corner.

(Continued)

(Continued)

K	1	2	
✓	✓	✓	**three-dimensional figures** figures with three dimensions: length, width, height.
✓	✓	✓	**cone** three-dimensional figure (⬡) with one curved surface, one flat surface (usually circular), one curved edge, and one vertex
✓	✓	✓	**cube** three-dimensional figure (⬡) with six congruent square faces
✓	✓	✓	**cylinder** three-dimensional figure (⬡) with one curved surface and two congruent circular bases
✓	✓	✓	**prism** three-dimensional figure (⬡) with two congruent and parallel faces that are polygons. The rest of the faces are parallelograms
✓	✓	✓	**sphere** three-dimensional figure (●) made up of all points equally distant from the center
✓	✓	✓	**two-dimensional shapes** shapes with two dimensions: length and width
✓	✓	✓	**circle** perfectly round shape (◯). A line that is curved so that its ends meet and every point on the line is the same distance from the center
✓	✓	✓	**hexagon** a six-sided flat shape with straight sides (⬡)
✓	✓	✓	**pentagon** a five-sided flat shape with straight sides (⬠)
✓	✓	✓	**quadrilateral** a four-sided polygon (▱)
✓	✓	✓	**rectangle** a four-sided shape made up of two pairs of parallel lines and four right angles (▭)
✓	✓	✓	**square** a four-sided shape with straight sides where all sides have equal length and every vertex is a right angle (◻).
✓	✓	✓	**trapezoid** a four-sided flat shape (▱) with straight sides that has a pair of opposite sides parallel
✓	✓	✓	**triangle** a figure having three sides and three angles (▲)

Geometry
K.G.A*

Identify and describe shapes (squares, circles, triangles, hexagons, cubes, cones, cylinders, and spheres).

STANDARD 1   **K.G.A.1:** Describe objects in the environment using names of shapes and describe the relative position of these object using terms such as *above, below, beside, in front of behind,* and *next to.*

STANDARD 2   **K.G.A.2:** Correctly name shapes regardless of their orientations or overall size.

STANDARD 3   **K.G.A.3:** Identify shapes as two-dimensional (lying in a plane, "flat") or three-dimensional ("solid").

*Additional cluster

Geometry K.G.A

Cluster A: Identify and describe shapes (squares, circles, triangles, hexagons, cubes, cones, cylinders, and spheres).
Kindergarten Overview

At the kindergarten level, students will learn that specific attributes (number of side, angles, etc.) define what a shape is called and other attributes (color, size, and orientation) do not. Using attributes, students identify and describe squares, circles, triangles, rectangles, hexagons, cubes, cones, cylinders, and spheres. For this cluster, students find and identify shapes around home and school. They recognize, compare, and sort the shapes based upon geometric attributes. A variety of experiences must be provided for students to locate both two-dimensional and three-dimensional objects as well as describe the positional location of the objects.

Standards for Mathematical Practice
SFMP 6. Attend to precision.

Kindergartners begin to develop mathematical communication skills and will learn to use clear, precise language in discussions with others and in their own reasoning. Learning about geometric properties allows students to develop the concepts and language they need to analyze and describe two-dimensional shapes and three-dimensional figures with precision.

SFMP 7. Look for and make use of structure.

The experience of discussing and thinking about attributes of shapes will help kindergartners begin to understand geometric structure.

Related Content Standards
1.G.A.1   1.G.A.2   1.G.3   2.G.1

Notes

Describe objects in the environment using names of shapes, and describe the relative position of these object using terms such as above, below, beside, in front of behind, and next to.

What the TEACHER does:

- Begin by providing a variety of experiences for students to investigate geometric ideas by allowing students to touch and manipulate objects such as pattern blocks and attribute blocks. Photographs of objects and construction-paper shapes can also be used. Ask students to explain how the shapes are alike and different. Help students define attributes by teaching things such as number of sides and vertices (corners). Then, take students on a shape hunt inside their own classrooms and schools to locate shapes. While locating shapes in the environment, teachers can ask questions such as what object, which way, how far, and where? To answer the questions, students will begin developing spatial thinking. For example, a teacher could point to a ball on the playground asking, "What shape is the ball?" Upon students' responding, "A sphere," the teacher could place the sphere below a swing asking a positional question such as "Where is the ball?"
- Model vocabulary with numerous examples and encourage students to use the geometric terms. Teachers can play games such as "I Spy." For example, "I spy a shape that is *above* the bulletin board. My shape is a clock. What kind of shape is my clock?"
- Help students use the geometry concepts learned with real-world applications appropriate to kindergarten. Try having students create a picture of a clown by drawing a large circle, then, drawing two triangles for eyes at the top of the circle. Next, students should draw a square under the eyes for a nose and finally draw a rectangle above the bottom of the circle for a mouth. (Precut construction paper triangles, squares, and rectangles with glue can also be used to create the clown picture.) Another idea to apply concepts in the real world is to ask the student to search for a missing object and then describe where it was with directional words such as "It was under the table."
- Ensure students have opportunities to talk with the teacher and each other to make sense of what they are learning. If students are not talking about the mathematics, they may not be actively engaged in their learning of kindergarten geometry.

What the STUDENTS do:

- Students will locate shapes in their classrooms and school building and say, "The bulletin boards are rectangles, or the globe on my teacher's desk is a sphere."
- Students should use positional words to describe the objects they locate in their classrooms, such as the cube we use as our toy box is *below* the light switch.

Addressing Student Misconceptions and Common Errors

When first learning about shapes, students may use informal names for shapes, such as calling a sphere a ball or a cube a box. Reinforce appropriate vocabulary by reminding students to use the correct mathematical name. Students may also incorrectly name the following shapes as triangles:

To help with this misconception, provide a variety of shapes for students to discuss and sort. Talk about how students can recognize examples and non-examples of shapes in the environment.

STANDARD 2 (K.G.A.2)

Correctly name shapes regardless of their orientations or overall size.

What the TEACHER does:

- Teachers should expose students to many shapes in many different orientations and sizes. Examples of shapes that are long and skinny should be provided to allow students to contrast rectangles with non-rectangles as well as triangles of different lengths with non-triangles.
- Help students begin developing explicit and sophisticated levels of thinking and communication. Help children learn to describe and define shapes in terms of attributes (properties). Discussions between teachers and students during and after sorting activities are essential in helping students think about geometric properties. To encourage reflection about geometric properties, teachers might ask students questions such as "What is your sorting rule, or why did you not include this shape in this group?" Teachers should always model correct terminology kindergartners need to express ideas about geometric properties.
- Allow students to build representations of shapes from physical models of line segments, such as sticks or straws. As the students discuss their constructions, the attributes of the shapes will arise.
- Examples of shapes beyond circles, squares, rectangles, and triangles should also be shared with students; otherwise, some students may incorrectly think that a rhombus is not a shape because it is not a shape they have learned or can name.

What the STUDENTS do:

- Students will learn through problem-solving experiences with opportunities to reason about the geometry they are learning. Students should apply what they are learning in meaningful contexts through activities and games such as this triangle sort:

Triangle (common example)	More Triangles (other examples)	Not a Triangle. Explain why not.

Addressing Student Misconceptions and Common Errors

Kindergarten students usually will not recognize a triangle that has been inverted or turned upside down. Students often say that an inverted triangle does not look like a triangle. Teachers can provide activities to talk about what a shape looks like and identify specific attributes that define a shape. Another way to address this misconception is to have students trace shapes.

Notes

Identify shapes as two-dimensional (lying in a plane, "flat") or three dimensional ("solid").

What the TEACHER does:

- Teachers will help students identify, analyze, sort, compare, and position shapes into collections of objects. Try arranging three objects for students to view such as a box, a cone, and a ball. Describe one of the objects, for instance, "all of its surfaces are flat." Have students tell which figure was described. In addition, provide opportunities for students to describe both two-dimensional and three-dimensional figures themselves.
- Instruction must include helping students name a picture of a shape as two-dimensional because it is flat and can be measured in only two ways (length and width) and an object as three-dimensional because it is not flat (it is a solid object/shape) and can be measured in three different ways (length, width, and height).
- Provide experiences for students to explore and discuss examples of two-dimensional and three-dimensional shapes in the classroom and school. Students should be able to differentiate between two-dimensional (flat) and three-dimensional (solid) shapes. Students should name a picture of a shape as two-dimensional because it is flat. Students should describe an object using the term *three dimensional* because it is not flat (it is a solid object/shape). Faces of three-dimensional shapes can be identified as specific two-dimensional shapes. For example, an investigation of cylinders should include familiar items such as cans and other objects such as glue sticks or lipstick containers. Students should examine and discuss different sizes and forms of objects in various orientations to learn that figures can be identified by their geometric properties rather than by appearance alone. Constructing two-dimensional shapes using computer graphics programs may provide a rich experience and a motivational way for students to explore the attributes of the shapes.

What the STUDENTS do:

- Students will locate shapes in their classrooms and describe the shapes using appropriate vocabulary.
- Students will identify whether the shapes are two-dimensional or three-dimensional and identify their properties clearly and precisely.

Addressing Student Misconceptions and Common Errors

Students may use incorrect terminology when describing shapes. For example, students may say a cube is a square. Teachers should help students learn that the two-dimensional shape is a part of the object (e.g., a square is a "face" of a cube).

Notes

Geometry
K.G.B*

Analyze, compare, create, and compose shapes.

STANDARD 4 **K.G.B.4:** Analyze and compare two-dimensional and three-dimensional shapes, in different sizes and orientations, using informal language to describe their similarities, differences, parts (e.g., number of sides and vertices/corners) and other attributes (e.g., having sides of equal length).

STANDARD 5 **K.G.B.5:** Model shapes in the world by building shapes from components (e.g., sticks and clay balls) and drawing shapes.

STANDARD 6 **K.G.B.6:** Compose simple shapes to form larger shapes. *For example, "Can you join these two triangles with full sided touching to make a rectangle?"*

*Supporting cluster

Geometry K.G.B

Cluster B: Analyze, compare, create, and compose shapes.
Kindergarten Overview

In this cluster, students will understand that specific attributes (number of sides, angles, etc.) define what a shape's name is and other attributes (color, size, orientation, etc.) do not. Using the attributes, students can identify and describe what shapes look like such as cubes, cones, cylinders, and spheres. At the kindergarten level, children need numerous activities to explore various forms of shapes including different types of triangles (equilateral, isosceles, scalene); different sizes (big and small); and different orientations (rotated upside down or to the right).

Standards for Mathematical Practice
SFMP 4. Model with mathematics.

Students will use basic shapes and spatial reasoning to model objects in their environment and to construct more complex shapes. Students should create their own representations using concrete objects and pictures.

SFMP 6. Attend to precision.

Kindergartners will begin to talk about and use geometric vocabulary and terms to analyze and describe shapes and figures. Position words to clearly indicate that the location of shapes will also be used.

SFMP 7. Look for and make use of structure.

Students will use examples and non-examples of geometric shapes.

Related Content Standards

1.G.1   1.G.2   1.G.3   2.G.1

Notes

Analyze and compare two and three-dimensional shapes, in different sizes and orientations, using informal language to describe their similarities, differences, parts (e.g., number of sides and vertices/corners) and other attributes (e.g., having sides of equal length).

What the TEACHER does:

- Through observations and sorting activities, provide students numerous opportunities to sort, compare, and analyze two-dimensional and three-dimensional shapes to notice similarities and differences. For example, when comparing triangles and squares, students should notice triangles have three sides, squares have four. Observations will help children begin to understand how three-dimensional shapes are composed of two-dimensional shapes; for example, the top and base of a cylinder is a circle or a face of a cube is a square.
- Expose students to concrete objects, pictorial representations, and technology to help develop understandings and descriptive vocabulary for both two-dimensional and three-dimensional shapes. When students first learn to describe a shape such as a square, they will likely say, "a square has corners." Teachers should use the mathematical terms "vertex/vertices" when describing corner/corners.
- Use manipulatives, such as geoboards, for students to create triangles, squares, and rectangles to use for comparisons and descriptions. Use attribute blocks for students to sort by size, shape, color, and girth (thickness and thinness). Talk about similarities/differences of the blocks. Pattern blocks can also be used as a sorting tool.
- Take students on a scavenger hunt to locate and discuss properties of two-dimensional and three-dimensional shapes in the classroom and school building.

What the STUDENTS do:

- Students will describe two-dimensional and three-dimensional shapes by telling the number of sides a shape has. This will help students identify the two-dimensional shapes of triangles, squares, and rectangles.
- Students will point to the location where two sides meet, called a corner or vertex. With numerous experiences in counting the vertices of a shape, the students will learn that the number of vertices is the same as the number of sides.
- Students will recognize that length of sides is important for squares and rectangles. Students should notice that the sides of squares are equal in length and that the lengths of opposite sides of rectangles are equal.
- Students will be able to sort two-dimensional and three-dimensional objects and explain how the objects were sorted.

Addressing Student Misconceptions and Common Errors

Kindergartners may not realize that triangles can be inverted or rotated. Some children may recognize the triangle shown below on the left as a triangle because it has a flat bottom but may believe the triangle on the right is not a triangle. Students may decide to name a triangle based on perception, not reasoning.

Kindergartners may not consider the properties of two-dimensional shapes and may believe the shapes below are rectangles.

With numerous experiences and discussions using a variety of shapes, students can correct the misconception and learn to identify triangles and rectangles of any form, size, or orientation.

STANDARD 5 (K.G.B.5)

Model shapes in the world by building shapes from components (e.g., sticks and clay balls) and drawing shapes.

What the TEACHER does:

- Discuss similarities and differences of two-dimensional and three-dimensional shapes and then take students on a scavenger hunt to locate two-dimensional and three-dimensional shapes in the classroom and school building. Students could also bring a shape from home to share with the class. The students will classify the shape and explain why it is two-dimensional or three-dimensional.
- Plan hands-on activities for kindergarten children to draw two-dimensional squares, rectangles, and triangles in a sandbox, with shaving cream on their desks, or with pencil and paper. Stencils and cutouts can also be used as tools to help students draw the shapes. Allow students to talk about and name the shapes they drew.
- Create experiences for students to build three-dimensional shapes with straws, toothpicks, pipe cleaners, popsicle sticks and gumdrops, marshmallows, or clay. Ask students to share, describe, and name their three-dimensional creations.

What the STUDENTS do:

- This standard asks students to use their background of knowledge and understanding of geometric attributes of shapes to draw two-dimensional triangles, rectangles, squares, and circles and build three-dimensional cubes, cones, spheres, and similar shapes.

Addressing Student Misconception and Common Errors

Some students may confuse the name of a two-dimensional shape with a related three-dimensional shape or the shape of its face. For example, students might call a cube a square. While exploring with two-dimensional flat shapes, start by using flat paper.

Notes

Compose simple shapes to form larger shapes. For example, "Can you join these two triangles with full sides touching to make a rectangle?"

What the TEACHER does:

- Provide experiences for students to manipulate two or more shapes to create a new shape. Use tangrams for students to learn to slide, rotate, flip, and arrange pieces. Exploring with the tangrams and pattern blocks allows students to join shapes to create new shapes. Students can also apply these ideas by using puzzles in which an outline is covered with the tangrams or pattern block shapes, such as an outline of an arrow or square.
- Focus on vocabulary by asking students to state the names of the shapes used to compose a larger shape; for example, "I used two triangles to make a rectangle," such as

What the STUDENTS do:

- Students will use their background of experience with puzzles to combine simple shapes to create pictures and larger shapes.
- Students will use geometric terminology to describe the shapes they have composed.

Addressing Student Misconceptions and Student Errors

Some students may be unable to visually see shapes from different perspectives and therefore struggle to "move" a shape by sliding, rotating, or flipping the shape to create another shape. Teachers may need to demonstrate how to join the shapes together or how to fill in the outline of a picture shown below with pattern blocks.

Notes

Standard: K.G.A.1. *Describe objects in the environment using names of shapes, and describe the relative position of these object using terms such as above, below, beside, in front of behind, and next to.*

Mathematical Practice or Process Standards:

SFMP 6. Attend to precision.

Kindergartners learn to use clear, precise language to describe basic shapes and their locations in the classroom.

SFMP 7. Look for and make use of structure.

Talking and thinking about attributes of shapes help kindergartners begin to understand geometric structure.

Goal:

Students are introduced to geometric shapes and learn to describe attributes or characteristics of each shape. A shape's name is connected to real-world objects such as the bulletin board is a rectangle. Words that describe the position of an object such as "the rectangular bulletin board is *below* the ceiling" are emphasized.

Planning:

Materials: (1) Construction paper circles squares, triangles, and rectangles cut in different sizes and real-world objects found in the classroom to connect a shape's name. (2) Real-world examples of cubes, hexagons, cylinders, and spheres. (3) Pattern blocks for the extension activity.

Sample Activity:

- Display a paper rectangle and tell students the name of the shape. Have students describe the shape such as it has four corners and four sides: two long and two short. Repeat display and dialogue with other shapes. Introduce several different example sizes and orientations.
- Plan a shape hunt to locate shapes and describe their positions with descriptive vocabulary such as the circle clock is above the teacher's desk or the sphere is the shape of our ball.

Questions/Prompts:

- Can students identify circles, squares, rectangles, triangles hexagons, cubes, cones, cylinders, and spheres? Ask, *"What real-world objects are shaped like a rectangle, a square, a circle, etc.?"*

- Can students describe the characteristics of the shapes, such as a rectangle has four sides, two long and two short, and it has four square corners (vertices)? Ask, *"How are a square and a rectangle the same? How are they different?"*

- Can students locate the shapes in their classroom? Using terms such as *above, below, beside, in front of, behind,* and *next to,* ask, *"Can you find an object in this room that is a circle and describe where it is located?"*

Differentiating Instruction:

Struggling Students:

- Display numerous examples of rectangles, squares, circles, triangles, hexagons, cubes, cylinders, and spheres with different sizes and different orientations. Ask students to discuss and sort. Talk about how students can recognize examples and non-examples of shapes in the environment. Reinforce positional vocabulary to describe the shape's location.

Extension:

- Play the pattern block game with a partner. Place a divider between two students sitting across from each other. Student one will create a design with blocks without letting the partner see it and then tell the partner how to place the pattern blocks to match the created design. Student one will use positional words to describe block placement. Take away the divider. Look at both designs to see if they match. Student two takes a turn.

Notes

Standard:

Mathematical Practice or Process Standards:

Goal:

Planning:

Materials:

Sample Activity:

Questions/Prompts:

Differentiating Instruction:

Struggling Students:

Extension:

Standard:

Mathematical Practice or Process Standards:

Goal:

Planning:

Materials:

Sample Activity:

Questions/Prompts:

Differentiating Instruction:

Struggling Students:

Extension:

Geometry
1.G.A*

Reason with shapes and their attributes.

STANDARD 1

1.G.A.1: Distinguish between defining attributes (e.g., triangles are closed and three-sided) versus non-defining attributes (e.g. color, orientation, overall size); build and draw shapes to possess defining attributes.

STANDARD 2

1.G.A.2: Compose two-dimensional shapes (rectangles, squares, trapezoids, triangles, half-circles, and quarter circles) or three-dimensional shapes (cubes, right rectangular prisms, right circular cones, and right circular cylinders) to create a composite shape, and compose new shapes from the composite shapes.[1]

[1]Students do not need to learn formal names such as "right rectangular prism."

STANDARD 3

1.G.A.3: Partition circles and rectangles into two and four equal shapes, describe the shares using the words halves, fourths, and quarters, and use the phrases half of, fourth of, and quarter of. Describe the whole as two of, or four of, the shares. Understand for these examples that decomposing into more equal shares creates smaller shapes.

*Additional cluster

Geometry 1.G.A

Cluster A: Reason with shapes and their attributes.
Grade 1 Overview

For this cluster, students will compose and decompose two-dimensional and three-dimensional figures and build an understanding of part-whole relationships as well as the properties of the original and composite shapes. First graders will combine shapes to begin recognizing the shapes from different perspectives and orientations and will describe the shapes' geometric attributes to determine how they are alike and different.

Standards for Mathematical Practice
SFMP 1. Make sense of problems and persevere in solving them.

Students will become problem solvers as they arrange shapes to create new composite shapes and as they recompose the pieces into different shapes.

SFMP 6. Attend to precision.

Students will use clear, specific definitions to define attributes and use terms such halves, fourth, and quarters to describe the partitioning of shapes.

Related Content Standards

K.G.1   K.G.2   K.G.3   K.G.4   K.G.5   K.G.6   1.G.2   1.G.3

Notes

Distinguish between defining attributes (e.g., triangles are closed and three-sided) versus non-defining attributes (e.g., color, orientation, overall size); build and draw shapes to possess defining attributes.

What the TEACHER does:

- Review previously learned geometry vocabulary with the following terms: *shape, two-dimensional* and *three-dimensional, rectangle, square, trapezoid, triangle, cube, cone,* and *cylinder.* Teach the new terms *open* and *closed figures* with student exploration with a variety of shapes. Begin classifying them according to specified attributes (sides, closed, vertices, edges, and faces).
- Explain to students that *defining attributes,* such as a number of sides, *define* the name of a shape. "For example, a triangle must have three sides and be a closed figure." Nondefining attributes do not identify what the shape is called, such as color, size, or orientation.
- Provide activities for first graders to draw or build a shape with specific attributes such as a square has four sides that are the same size. Play a game called "Name my shape." Begin with, "I am thinking of a shape. My shape is a three-sided closed figure. Can you name my shape? Tell your partner the name of my shape. Yes, it is a triangle. A triangle is a three-sided, closed figure. Now, let's draw our triangle on your individual student whiteboards." Ask students to explain and draw the difference between a closed and unclosed figure, such as

What the STUDENTS do:

- Students will build and draw two-dimensional shapes.
- Students will verbally describe the attributes of shapes by stating something like, "I know this shape is a square because my square's four sides are the same length; it has four corners. It is a closed figure."

Addressing Student Misconceptions and Common Errors

The vocabulary terms *closed* and *unclosed* (open) figures may confuse students. Through discussions and numerous examples, students will learn to correctly define each term.

Notes

STANDARD 2 (1.G.A.2)

Compose two-dimensional shapes (rectangles, squares, trapezoids, triangles, half-circles, and quarter circles) or three-dimensional shapes (cubes, right rectangular prisms, right circular cones, and right circular cylinders) to create a composite shape, and compose new shapes from the composite shapes.[1]

[1]Students do not need to learn formal names such as "right rectangular prism."

What the TEACHER does:

- Provide activities for students to combine shapes to create a new composite shape. Composite shapes and figures are created by joining two or more geometric shapes together to create a different shape. Pattern blocks can be used for student exploration and creation of composite shapes. For example, a student may discover that a rectangle may be created by using six triangles.

  Tangram puzzle shapes can be used to help students fill in a larger region such as a picture of a square or a candle.

What the STUDENTS do:

- Students will identify the name of the composite shape as well as the names of each shape that forms it.
- With exploration, students will be able to solve shape puzzles, create designs with shapes, and maintain a shape as a unit.

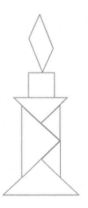

Addressing Student Misconceptions and Common Errors

Some students have difficulty visualizing filling in shape puzzles. Some students may not notice that two triangles make a rectangle as shown.

To help address the misconceptions, provide additional experiences for students to fill in shape puzzles with pattern blocks or tangrams. Remind students to flip, turn, and/or rotate the shapes to fit the puzzles.

Notes

Partition circles and rectangles into two and four equal shapes, describe the shares using the words halves, fourths, and quarters, and use the phrases half of, fourth of, and quarter of. Describe the whole as two of, or four of the shares. Understand for these examples that decomposing into more equal shares creates smaller shapes.

What the TEACHER does:

- In first grade, students have an informal understanding of sharing and equal shares. Teachers should start student exploration of fractional parts with halves and fourths with real things such as cookies, pies, and pizza and then move to circles and rectangles.
- Teachers must provide numerous experiences with different sizes of circles and rectangles to learn that decomposing equal shares into more equal shares results in smaller equal shares.
- Teachers must lead a discussion for first graders to learn that halves of two different wholes are not necessarily the same size.

What the STUDENTS do:

- Students should relate geometric figures to equal parts and name the parts as halves and fourths (or quarters). For example, students should visually notice that a rectangle can be partitioned into two equal triangles and that the same triangles can be recomposed to form the original rectangle.
- Students must explore and divide shapes to make the connection that as they create more parts, decomposing the shares from halves to fourths, the parts get smaller.

Addressing Student Misconceptions and Common Errors

Some students may incorrectly think the size of the equal shares is directly related to the number of equal shares; for example, there are four fourths in one whole and only two halves in one whole, so the fourths must be larger. Some students may mistakenly believe that a fourth is larger than a half because the number four is larger than the number two. Discussing and physically comparing one fourth to one half of the same whole along with a discussion will help students make sense of the misconception.

Notes

Standard: 1.G.A.3. *Partition circles/rectangles into 2 and 4 equal shapes, describe shares using the words halves, fourths, and quarters, and use phrases half of, fourth of, and quarter of. Describe the whole as two of, or four of the shares. Understand for these examples that decomposing into more equal shares creates smaller shapes.*

Mathematical Practice or Process Standards:
SFMP 6. Attend to precision.

Students will use clear, specific definitions to define attributes and use terms such as *halves, fourth,* and *quarters* to describe the partitioning of shapes.

Goal:
Students are introduced to fractions with equal shares of halves and fourths.

Planning:

Materials: Plastic or paper fraction circles with halves and fourths, construction paper circles and rectangular shapes cut in different sizes, pattern blocks, and real things such as crackers, candy bars, and similar objects to divide into fractions.

Sample Activity:

- Begin by exploring how many halves make a whole and fourths to make halves. Establish a connection to real-life fractions with concrete things such as graham crackers, candy bars, pizza, pie, or cake. Provide experiences for students to use the vocabulary terms *whole, halves,* and *fourths*.
- Allow students to divide shapes or objects into additional sections to create smaller individual pieces.
- Continue exploring fractions with other shapes such as squares, rectangles, hexagons, and similar objects.

Questions/Prompts:

- Are the student able to divide a circle into halves and fourths? Say, "Show me how to divide this circle into halves, now fourths."

- Are the students able to explain why when dividing a circle into fourths, the pieces are smaller than when dividing into halves? Say, "Tell me why when you divide a circle into four parts, the pieces are smaller than when you divide into two parts."

- Are the students able to use the correct terms with fractions? Ask, "When you cut a shape into two equal parts or four equal parts, what mathematics vocabulary terms can be used to describe the parts?"

Differentiating Instruction:

Struggling Students: Some students may incorrectly think the size of the equal shares is directly related to the number of equal shares; for example, there are four fourths in one whole and only two halves in one whole so the fourths must be larger. Make the connection by actually folding a rectangle into halves then cutting and folding a same-size rectangle into fourths then cutting. Compare the sizes.

Extension: Provide experiences for students to divide shapes into other fractions, such as thirds, sixths, or eighths. For example, fold a rectangular strip of paper into half. Fold that half again and again one more time. Ask students to think about how many sections the strip of paper will have. Ask them to cut the strip into eight parts. Fold another rectangular strip into thirds. Try pattern blocks to show halves with two red trapezoids, thirds with three blue rhombi, and sixths with six green triangles.

Standard:

Mathematical Practice or Process Standards:

Goal:

Planning:

Materials:

Sample Activity:

Questions/Prompts:

Differentiating Instruction:

Struggling Students:

Extension:

Geometry
2.G.A*

Reason with shapes and their attributes.

STANDARD 1 **2.G.A.1:** Recognize and draw shapes having specified attributes, such as a given number of angles or a given number of equal faces.[1] Identify triangles, quadrilaterals, pentagons, hexagons, and cubes.

[1]Sizes are compared directly or visually, not compared by measuring.

STANDARD 2 **2.G.A.2:** Partition a rectangle into rows and columns of same-size squares and count to find the total number of them.

STANDARD 3 **2.G.A.3:** Partition circles and rectangles into two, three, or four equal shares, describe the shares using the words halves, thirds, half of, a third of, etc., and describe the whole as two halves, three thirds, four fourths. Recognize that equal shares of identical wholes need not have the same shape.

*Additional cluster

Geometry 2.G.A

Cluster A: Reason with shapes and their attributes.
Grade 2 Overview

In this cluster, students will reason with shapes and their attributes by identifying shapes such as triangles, quadrilaterals, pentagons, hexagons, and cubes and drawing these shapes with specified attributes such as a given number of angles or faces. Students will partition a rectangle into rows and columns of same-size squares and partition circles and rectangles into halves, thirds, and fourths.

Standards for Mathematical Practice
SFMP 2. Reason abstractly and quantitatively.

Students are reasoning as they explain their thinking about shapes.

SFMP 4. Model with mathematics.

Students are drawing pictures to divide a rectangle into squares to show equal partitioning.

SFMP 5. Use appropriate tools strategically.

Students will either draw a shape or use a manipulative to describe a shape's specific attributes.

SFMP 6. Attend to precision.

Second graders will communicate mathematically by using clear and precise language in their discussions about shapes and their properties.

Related Content Standards
1.GA.1   1.GA.2   1.GA.3   2.GA.1   2.GA.2   2.GA.3

Notes

Recognize and draw shapes having specified attributes, such as a given number of angles or a given number of equal faces.[1] Identify triangles, quadrilaterals, pentagons, hexagons, and cubes.

[1]Sizes are compared directly or visually, not compared by measuring.

What the TEACHER does:

- Provide exploration time for second graders to investigate shapes and learn to identify, name, and draw the shapes based upon specific attributes. Regular (equal sides and equal angles) and irregular triangles, pentagons, and hexagons should be included in students' discoveries. Shapes should be explored in a variety of orientations and configurations.

- Plan an activity called *Guess and Draw My Shape*. Ask students to guess a shape and draw a shape you describe with *specified attributes*. For example, "What is the shape that has six sides? Draw it on your individual student whiteboard. Now, name my shape. Yes, it is a hexagon."

- Focus on mathematical vocabulary. Students should use the word *vertex* versus *corner* and *side (two-dimensional)* or *edge (three-dimensional)* versus *line*. Teachers should lead students in a discussion of the characteristics of two-dimensional and three-dimensional shapes to develop the concepts and vocabulary needed to recognize the shapes.

- Present opportunities for students to sort and classify two-dimensional and three-dimensional shapes. For example, for two-dimensional shapes, have students sort by the number of vertices. For three-dimensional shapes sort by the shapes of the faces. Play "Guess My Rule." If a document camera is available, have a student sort a collection of two-dimensional shapes versus three-dimensional shapes. Other students will observe the sorted shapes to determine the sorting rule.

What the STUDENTS do:

- Students should locate and describe examples of the two-dimensional shapes and three-dimensional shapes in the classroom and around the school building.

- Students should use the precise geometry vocabulary to describe the attributes of the shapes.

- Students should describe similarities and differences between two-dimensional and three-dimensional shapes.

Addressing Student Misconceptions and Common Errors

Some second graders may believe a shape can be changed by its orientation. To help with this misconception, it is critical to have primary learners touch and feel shapes. As they touch the shapes, students will discover the shape will not change regardless of the orientation.

Notes

Partition a rectangle into rows and columns of same-size squares and count to find the total number of them.

What the TEACHER does:

- Plan activities to connect equal sharing and partitioning with rectangles of various sizes to promote second graders' conceptual understanding of multiplication. Use square tiles to provide student discovery of how many tiles it will take to cover an entire rectangle. For example, students could equally partition a rectangle into smaller squares and then tell the number of squares by showing two rows of four columns. After exploration with the tiles, students can start drawing the examples.

What the STUDENTS do:

- Explore and demonstrate examples of rows and columns of a divided rectangle.
- Tell how the shape was partitioned into squares. Count to find the total number of squares.

Addressing Student Misconceptions and Common Errors

Some students may not be able to distinguish between a row and a column. Through discussion, students will learn to make a distinction between rows and columns.

Notes

STANDARD 3 (2.G.A.3)

Partition circles and rectangles into two, three, or four equal shares, describe the shares using the words halves, thirds, half of, a third of, etc., and describe the whole as two halves, three thirds, four fourths. Recognize that equal shares of identical wholes need not have the same shape.

What the TEACHER does:

- To introduce fractions with the area model, provide students with a variety of experiences. Explore the concept of fair shares. Give second graders a variety of different sizes of circles and rectangles cut from construction paper. Ask students to fold some of the shapes into halves, some into thirds, and some into fourths.
- Ensure students have opportunities to talk with the teacher and each other to make sense of what they are learning.

What the STUDENTS do:

- Recognize that when a circle is cut into four equal pieces, each piece will equal one fourth of its original whole. Students will describe the whole as four fourths. If a circle is cut into four equal pieces, each piece will equal one fourth of its original whole. The whole is described as four fourths.

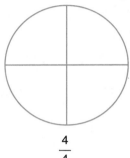

$$\frac{4}{4}$$

- Students should explore circles and rectangles partitioned in multiple ways to recognize that equal shares may be different shapes within the same whole.

Fourths

Addressing Student Misconceptions and Common Errors

- For some children, the idea that equal shares of identical wholes may not have the same shape is difficult to grasp. Some students may not understand that an area model may represent one out of two or three or four fractional parts without understanding the parts are equal shares. Additional experiences and discussions about equal shares with different shapes will help students begin to understand this confusing concept.

Notes

Standard: 2.G.A.1. *Recognize and draw shapes having specified attributes, such as a given number of angles or a given number of equal faces. Identify triangles, quadrilaterals, pentagons, hexagons, and cubes.*

[1]Sizes are compared directly or visually, not compared by measuring.

Mathematical Practice or Process Standards:
SFMP 2. Reason abstractly and quantitatively.

Students are reasoning as they explain their thinking about shapes.

SFMP 4. Model with mathematics.

Students are drawing pictures to show specified attributes such as angles.

SFMP 5. Use appropriate tools strategically.

Students will either draw a shape or use a manipulative to describe a shape's specific attributes.

SFMP 6. Attend to precision.

Second graders will communicate mathematically by using clear and precise language in their discussions about shapes and their properties.

Goal:
Students will draw, explore, and classify triangles, quadrilaterals, pentagons, hexagons, and cubes with specific attributes such as sides, angles, vertices, edges, and faces.

Planning:

Materials: Pattern block shapes, paper, and pencil to draw shapes.

Sample Activity:

- Sort and classify two-dimensional and three-dimensional shapes. For example, for two-dimensional shapes, have students sort by the number of vertices. For three-dimensional shapes, sort by the shapes of the faces.
- Play *Guess My Rule*. Sort a collection of two-dimensional shapes versus three-dimensional shapes. Ask students to determine the sorting rule.
- Play *Guess My Shape and Draw My Shape*.
- Ask students to guess a shape and draw a shape you describe with *specified attributes*. For example, "What is the shape that has six sides? Draw it."

Questions/Prompts:

- Look at these pattern blocks. Identify and name the shapes. *Can you describe the number of sides, angles, and vertices?*

- Look at this three-dimensional shape (cube). Identify by naming it. *Can you describe the number of faces, edges, and vertices?*

- *Can you identify the number of angles in a triangle, hexagon, and pentagon?*

Differentiating Instruction:

Struggling Students: Students may not be able to identify or explain attributes of shapes. Provide additional exploration experiences with concrete manipulatives and a discussion of *defining attributes* including sides, angles, and vertices.

Extension: Provide additional experiences to extend learning with quadrilaterals such as recognizing the differences between rhombuses, rectangles, and squares. Try another "Guess My Shape" game. Play with a partner.

1. Player one will draw a shape and write three clues about the shape and then tell player two what the clues are. My shape is a parallelogram. My shape has four equal length sides. My shape is both a rhombus and a rectangle. What is my shape?

2. Player two will re-create the shape by drawing it on paper and explaining the clues, stating it is a square.

Notes

Standard:

Mathematical Practice or Process Standards:

Goal:

Planning:

Materials:

Sample Activity:

Questions/Prompts:

Differentiating Instruction:

Struggling Students:

Extension:

Reflection Questions: Geometry

1. Explain why primary students must have opportunities to talk with other students and their teachers to make sense of the geometry they are learning.

2. Simple games and activities will help K–2 students learn geometry concepts. Discuss three activities for this domain you believe will help promote student understanding and applications.

3. Explain why vocabulary and terminology are critical to student success with the study of geometry.

4. Some students may have difficulty visualizing geometric shapes from different perspectives. Discuss why using real objects is superior to using paper worksheets.

Resources

Table 1 Addition and Subtraction Situations

SITUATION	PROBLEM	PHYSICAL MODEL	PART PART WHOLE	EQUATION(S)
Add to—result unknown Grades K, 1, 2	Frank had 5 pennies. Mark gave him 4 more. How many pennies does Frank have?			$5 + 4 = \square$
Take from—result unknown Grades K, 1, 2	Frank had 9 pennies. He spent 5 pennies on a jawbreaker. How many pennies does he have left?			$9 - 5 = \square$
Put together take apart—total unknown Grades K, 1, 2	Anna has 8 pennies and 3 nickels. How many coins does she have?			$8 + 3 = \square$
Put together take apart—addends unknown Grades K, 1, 2	Anna has 11 coins. Some are pennies and some are nickels. How many pennies and how many nickels could Anna have?	**Show table with different combinations of pennies and nickels that will total 11 (use illustrations of coins)**		$1 + 10 = 11$ $2 + 9 = 11$ $3 + 8 = 11$ $4 + 7 = 11$ $5 + 6 = 11$ $6 + 5 = 11$ $7 + 4 = 11$ $8 + 3 = 11$ $9 + 2 = 11$ $10 + 1 = 11$

SITUATION	PROBLEM	PHYSICAL MODEL	PART PART WHOLE	EQUATION(S)
Add to—change unknown Grades 1, 2	Frank had 5 pennies. Mark gave him some more. Now Frank has 9 pennies. How many pennies did Mark give to Frank?		Whole 1¢1¢1¢1¢1¢1¢1¢1¢1¢ Part — 1¢1¢1¢1¢ / Part — □	$5 + \square = 9$
Add to—start unknown Grades 1, 2 Mastery at Grade 2	Frank had some pennies in his piggy bank. Mark gave 4 more. Now Frank has 9 pennies. How many pennies did Frank have at the beginning?		Whole 1¢1¢1¢1¢1¢1¢1¢1¢1¢ Part — □ / Part — 1¢1¢1¢ 1¢	$\square + 4 = 9$
Take from—change unknown Grades 1, 2	Frank had 9 pennies. He spent some pennies on a jawbreaker. Now Frank has 4 pennies. How much did he spend on the jawbreaker?		Whole 1¢1¢1¢1¢1¢1¢1¢1¢1¢ Part — □ / Part — 1¢1¢1¢ 1¢	$9 - \square = 4$
Take from—start unknown Grades 1, 2 Mastery at Grade 2	Frank had some pennies in his bank. He spent 5 pennies on a jawbreaker. Now he has 4 pennies. How many pennies did Frank have in his bank?		Whole — □ Part — 1¢1¢1¢ 1¢1¢ / Part — 1¢1¢ 1¢1¢	$\square - 5 = 4$
Put together take apart—addend unknown Grades 1, 2	Anna has 11 coins. She has 8 pennies and the rest are nickels. How many coins are nickels?		Whole OOOOOOOOOOO Part — 1¢1¢1¢1¢ 1¢1¢1¢1¢ / Part — □	$11 = 8 + \square$

SITUATION	PROBLEM	PHYSICAL MODEL	BAR MODEL	EQUATION(S)
Compare—difference unknown Grades 1, 2	*How many more?* Marty has 12 dimes. Tony has 16 dimes. How many more does Tony have?			**12 + □ = 16** **16 − □ = 12**
Compare—difference unknown Grades 1, 2	*How many fewer?* Marty has 12 dimes. Tony has 16 dimes. How many fewer does Marty have?			**12 + □ = 16** **16 − □ = 12**
Compare—bigger unknown Grades 1, 2	*More version* Tony has 4 more dimes than Marty. Marty has 12 dimes. How many does Tony have?			**4 + 12 = □** **12 + 4 = □**
Compare—bigger unknown Grade 2	*Fewer version* Marty has 4 fewer dimes than Tony. Marty has 12 dimes. How many does Tony have?			**4 + 12 = □** **12 + 4 = □**
Compare—smaller unknown Grades 1, 2	*Fewer version* Marty has 4 fewer dimes than Tony. Tony has 16 dimes. How many does Marty have?			**16 − 4 = □** **□ + 4 = 16**
Compare—smaller unknown Grade 2	*More version* Tony has 4 more dimes than Marty. Tony has 16 dimes. How many does Marty have?			**16 − 4 = □** **□ + 4 = 16**

Table 2 Addition and Subtraction Fact Strategies

ADDITION STRATEGIES	EXPLANATION	EXAMPLES	MODEL
Count on 1 or 2 Grades: K, 1	Count on 1 or 2 more to an addend. First use with materials; eventually move to mentally counting on.	3 + 1 Student counts "three....four" 7 + 2 Student counts "seven....eight....nine"	
Add zero Grades: K, 1	Any addend plus zero equals the addend.	5 + 0 = 5	
Doubles Grades: K, 1	Add a number to itself.	4 + 4 = 8 6 + 6 = 12 9 + 9 = 18	
Doubles plus 1 or 2 Grades: 1, 2	Double the smaller addend and add 1 or 2.	4 + 5 Think 4 + 4 + 1 5 + 7 Think 5 + 5 + 2 6 + 8 Think 6 + 6 + 2	4+4+1 5+5+2 4+4+2
Doubles minus 1 or 2 Grades: 1, 2	Double the larger addend and subtract 1 or 2.	6 + 5 Think 6 + 6 − 1 7 + 5 Think 7 + 7 − 2	6+6-1 7+7-2
Combination for ten Grade: 1	Recognize number combinations that add to 10.	1 + 9 = 10 2 + 8 = 10 3 + 7 = 10 4 + 6 = 10 5 + 5 = 10	9+1 8+2 5+5 7+3 6+4 tens frames

ADDITION STRATEGIES

	EXPLANATION	EXAMPLES	MODEL
Add ten Grade: 1	Note and use patterns when adding 10 to a single-digit number.	10 + 7 = 17 8 + 10 = 18 3 + 10 = 13	10 + 7
Make a ten Grades: 1, 2	Decompose one of the addends to make a sum of 10 in the fact.	9 + 8 Think 9 + 1 + 7 7 + 5 Think 7 + 3 + 2	9 + 8 10 + 7

SUBTRACTION STRATEGIES

	EXPLANATION	EXAMPLES	MODEL
Count up 1 or 2 Grades: 1, 2	Begin with the addend and count up to get to the total.	Works with facts in which the difference is only 1 or 2. 9 − 7 Think seven ...... eight, nine so 9 − 7 = 2	7 ... 8 9
Count back 1 or 2 Grades: 1, 2	Begin with the total and count back one or two to get to the missing addend.	Works with facts subtracting 1 or 2. 9 − 2 Think nine ...... eight, seven so 9 − 2 = 7	7 8 9
Build to 10 (think addition) Grades: 1, 2	Add up to 10 and then add the rest of the way to find the difference.	17 − 9 Think 9 + 1 = 10 and 10 + 7 = 17 7 + 1 = 8 so 17 − 9 = 8	9 + 1 (1 7) 1 + 7 = 8 10 + 7 = 17
Back off from 10 Grades: 1, 2	Count back to 10 and then count back the rest of the way.	17 − 9 Think 17 − 7 = 10 I still need to take off 2 more 10 − 2 = 8	take away 2 more
Use related addition facts Grades: 1, 2	Once students know addition facts they can think of subtraction as finding a missing addend.	13 − 8 Think 8 + _____ = 13	take away 7 8 + 5 = 13

Table 3   Scaffolding Addition and Subtraction

As you plan examples for addition, keep in mind how to scaffold examples with regrouping. Some students may need this broken into smaller concepts while others may be able to make generalizations. What is particularly important is to give students the opportunity to solve each type of example by making sense of the numbers and using various representations.

Grade Level	Description	Example
K 1 2	1 digit + 1 digit	9 + 7
1	2 digit + 1 digit; no regrouping	23 + 6
1	Add 2 digit number + a multiple of 10	33 + 50
1	2 digit + 2 digit; no regrouping	33 + 25
1 2	2 digit + 1 digit with regrouping	35 + 7
1 2	2 digit + 2 digit regrouping	25 + 26
2	3 digit + 1 and 2 digit; no regrouping	372 + 7
2	3 digit plus 1 digit; regroup ones to tens	345 + 8
2	3 digit plus 2 digit; regroup ones to tens	356 + 38
2	3 digit plus 2 digit; regroup tens to hundreds	428 + 26
2	3 digit plus 2 digit; regroup ones to tens and tens to hundreds	567 + 48
2	3 digit + 3 digit; no regrouping	256 + 121
2	3 digit plus 3 digit; regroup ones to tens	234 + 126
2	3 digit plus 3 digit; regroup tens to hundreds	154 + 162
2	3 digit plus 3 digit; regroup ones to tens and tens to hundreds	274 + 247

As you plan examples for subtraction, keep in mind how to scaffold examples with regrouping. Some students may need this broken into smaller concepts while others may be able to make generalizations. What is particularly important is to give students the opportunity to solve each type of example by making sense of the numbers and using various representations.

Grade Level	Description	Example
K 1 2	Subtraction facts in two forms subtract missing addend	5 − 2 = 3 2 + ___ = 5
1	Subtracting multiples of 10 from multiples of 10	50 − 20 20 + ___ = 50
2	Subtract 1 digit from 2 digits; no regrouping	27 − 4 4 + ___ 27
2	Subtract 2 digits from 2 digits; no regrouping	78 − 45

(Continued)

Grade Level	Description	Example
2	Subtract 1 digit from 2 digits with regrouping	45 – 9
2	Subtract 1 digit from 3 digits; no regrouping	427 – 2
2	Subtract 2 digits from 3 digits; no regrouping	568 – 35
2	Subtract 1 digit from 3 digits; regroup tens to ones	342 – 7
2	Subtract 2 digits from 3 digits; regroup tens to ones	348 – 64
2	Subtract 2 digits from 3 digits; regroup hundreds to tens	639 – 275
2	Subtract 2 digits from 3 digits; regroup hundreds to tens and tens to ones	534 – 275
2	Subtract 3 digits from 3 digits; no regrouping	453 – 222
2	Subtract 3 digits from 3 digits; regroup tens to ones	453 – 226
2	Subtract 3 digits from 3 digits; regroup hundreds to tens	627 – 345
2	Subtract 3 digits from 3 digits; regroup hundreds to tens and tens to ones	732 – 556

Table 4 Sample Addition and Subtraction Strategies

Addition

Counting on Using Benchmarks

33 + 25

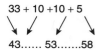

43...... 53.......58

Open Number Line

33 + 25

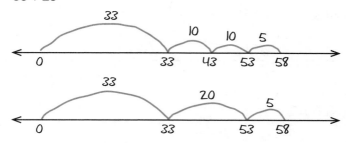

Place Value Model

33 + 28

Tens	Ones	
		33
		28
5 tens	11 ones (put 10 ones together to make 1 ten)	
6 tens	1 one	61

Subtraction

Counting Up

47 − 26

Think 26 + _____ = 47

26...36...46...47

26 + 10 + 10 + 1 = 47

26 + 21 = 47

Counting Back Using Benchmark Numbers

44 − 29

44 − 20 = 24

24 − 4 = 20

20 − 5 = 15

....

44 − 29 = 15

Open Number Line

44 − 29

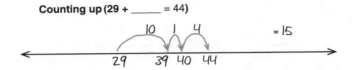

Counting up (29 + _____ = 44)

10   1   4   = 15

29   39   40   44

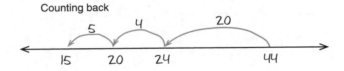

Counting back

5   4   20

15   20   24   44

Place Value Model

44 − 29

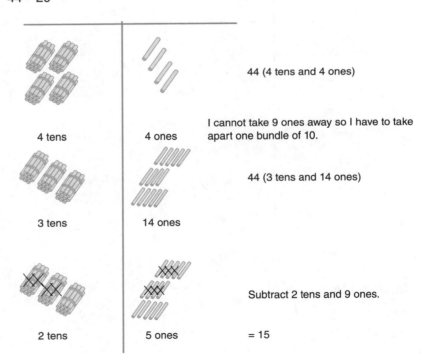

4 tens   4 ones   44 (4 tens and 4 ones)

I cannot take 9 ones away so I have to take apart one bundle of 10.

3 tens   14 ones   44 (3 tens and 14 ones)

2 tens   5 ones   Subtract 2 tens and 9 ones.

                                = 15

Table 5   Standards for Mathematical Practice

Standard for Mathematical Practice	What the teacher does	What the students do

1. Make sense of problems and persevere in solving them.	• Provides students with rich tasks that focus on and promote student understanding of an important mathematical concept.
	• Provides time for and facilitates the discussion of problem solutions.
	
	  o What are you asked to find?
	  o Have you solved similar problems before?
	  o What is your plan for solving the problem?
	  o Can you explain how you solved the problem?
	  o Does your answer make sense?
	  o Did you use a different method to check your answer?
		• Actively engage in solving problems by working to understand the information that is in the problem and the question that is asked.
		• Choose appropriate manipulatives or drawings to help make sense of the actions in the problem.
		• Use a variety of strategies that make sense to solve the problem.
		• Ask themselves if their solution makes sense.

2. Reason abstractly and quantitatively.	• Provides a variety of concrete materials and encourages their use to help students develop mathematical ideas.
	• Gives students problem situations and encourages varied solution paths.
	• Helps students use mathematical reasoning by asking questions such as
	
	  o Can you tell me what is happening here?
	  o How can you show what is happening in the problem using materials?
	  o Can you write a number sentence (equation) to match the story?
	  o What do the numbers in the number sentence mean?
		• Use various strategies, models, and drawings to think about the mathematics of a task or example.
		• Demonstrate mathematical understanding about the "numberness" of a given situation (quantitative reasoning).
		• Connect concrete examples with pictorial and symbolic representations as developmentally appropriate.

3. Construct viable arguments and critique the reasoning of others.	• Provides tasks that encourage students to construct mathematical arguments.
	• Expects students to explain their strategies and mathematical thinking to others.
	• Expects students to listen to the reasoning of others.
	• Helps students to compare strategies and methods by asking questions such as
	
	  o How can you prove that your answer is correct?
	  o What do you think about _____'s strategy?
	  o How is your method different than _____'s? How is it similar?
	  o What questions do you have for ____?
		• Explain their strategies and thinking orally or in writing, using concrete models, drawings, actions, or numbers.
		• Use number sense to determine if a solution is reasonable.
		• Listen to the thinking of others in the class.
		• Ask questions to one another and to the teacher to clarify their understanding.
		• Look for similarities among different ways to solve problems.

(Continued)

Table 5 (Continued)

Standard for Mathematical Practice	What the teacher does	What the students do

4. Model with mathematics.	• Provides a variety of materials for students to use as they work to make sense of mathematical ideas and solve problems.
	• Pose real world tasks that are developmentally appropriate for students.
	• Uses the progression of developing conceptual understanding through the use of concrete models, pictorial models, and when students are ready, symbolic representations.
	• Encourages students to use models as they create mathematical arguments and explain their thinking to others.
	• Asks students questions such as
	
	  o Can you show me how you solved this using a _____?
	  o Can you draw a picture or act out what is happening in the problem?
	  o Is this working or do you need to change your model?
		• Put the problem or situation in their own words.
		• Model the situation using concrete materials and an appropriate strategy (i.e., part part whole, bar model, place value chart).
		• Describe what they do with the models and how it relates to the problem situation.
		• Check to see if an answer makes sense and change the model when necessary.

5. Use appropriate tools strategically.	• Encourages students to use models in constructing mathematical arguments. • Provides a variety of concrete materials and encourages their use to help students develop mathematical ideas. • Helps students to link concrete to pictorial to numerical representations as developmentally appropriate.	• Select concrete materials that will help to develop conceptual understanding. • Begin to make the transition from concrete to pictorial representations when conceptual understanding is apparent. • Determine if mental computation, concrete models, or paper and pencil are the most efficient way to solve a problem or task.

6. Attend to precision.	• Supports students in developing an understanding of mathematical vocabulary by explicitly introducing terms and having them available for students to use (for example, by using a word wall).
	• Repeats a student's explanation using accurate vocabulary when necessary.
	• Supports student's precision by asking them the following questions:
	
	  o What does ____ mean?
	  o What labels could you use with your answer?
	  o What unit of measure would you use when you are measuring _____ ?
		• Communicate using grade level appropriate vocabulary.
		• Work to carefully formulate clear explanations.
		• State the meaning of symbols, calculates accurately and efficiently.
		• Chooses appropriate units of measure.
		• Labels accurately when measuring.

Standard for Mathematical Practice	What the teacher does	What the students do

7. Look for and make use of structure.	• Provides explicit situations in which students can use a strategy to develop understanding of a concept.
	• Supports student thinking by providing materials that are appropriate to the concept (for example, using 10 frames in learning addition and subtraction facts).
	• Asks questions that help student to see the structure of the mathematics and make generalizations:
	
	  o What happens when you add (or subtract) zero to a number?
	  o What should you do when you have ten or more ones?
	  o What is the difference between the value of 2 in 2 and in 20?
	  o How can you use what you know to explain why this works?
	  o What patterns do you see?
		• Look for patterns when developing conceptual understanding of place value, addition, subtraction, and other grade level concepts.
		• Recognize patterns related to properties of addition and subtraction.
		• Identify efficient strategies to use in a variety of situations using concrete materials and then generalizing to any similar situation.
		• Develop conceptual understanding by working to determine why numbers work the way they do.

8. Look for and express regularity in repeated reasoning.	• Provides a variety of examples that explicitly focus on patterns and repeated reasoning.
	• Asks students to fine tune their mathematical arguments with questions such as
	
	  o What do you notice about the totals of 3 + 5 and 5 + 3?
	  o If you think about the value of the numbers, can you find an easier way to think about the problem?
	  o How could this problem help you solve another problem?
		Notice repeated calculations and make generalizations.
		
		Continually evaluate the reasonableness of their answers and their thinking.
		
		Make generalization by seeing patterns based on properties or models and use these generalizations to develop conceptual understanding.

Table 6 Effective Teaching Practices

Practice	Purpose	What the teacher does	What the students do
1. Establish mathematics goals to focus learning.	• Sets the stage to guide instructional decisions. • Includes expecting students to understand the purpose of a lesson beyond simply repeating the standard.	Considers broad goals as well as the goals of the unit and the actual lesson including: • What is to be learned? • Why is the goal important? • Where do students need to go? • How can learning be extended?	• Make sense of new concepts and skills. • Experience connections among the standards and across domains. • Deepen their understanding and expect mathematics to make sense.
2. Implement tasks that promote reasoning and problem solving.	• Provides opportunities for students to engage in exploration and make sense of important mathematics. • Encourages students to use procedures in ways that are connected to understanding.	Chooses tasks that • are built on current student understandings. • have various entry points with multiple ways for the problems to be solved. • are interesting to students.	• Work to make sense out of the task and persevere in solving problems. • Use a variety of models and materials to make sense of the mathematics in the task. • Convince themselves the answer is reasonable.
3. Use and connect mathematical representations.	• Concrete representations lead students to developing conceptual understanding and later connect that understanding to procedural skills.	• Uses tasks that allow students to use a variety of representations. • Encourages the use of different representations, including concrete models, pictures, words and numbers, that support students in explaining their thinking and reasoning.	• Use materials to make sense out of problem situations. • Connect representations to mathematical ideas and the structure of big ideas including operational sense and place value.
4. Facilitate meaningful mathematical discourse.	• Provides students with opportunities to share ideas, clarify their understanding, and develop convincing arguments. • Talking and sharing aloud advances the mathematical thinking of the whole class.	• Engages students in explaining their mathematical reasoning in small group and classroom situations. • Facilitates discussion among students that supports making sense of a variety of strategies and approaches. • Scaffolds classroom discussions so that connections between representations and mathematical ideas take place.	• Explain their ideas and reasoning in small groups and with the entire class. • Listen to the reasoning of others. • Ask questions of others to make sense of their ideas.

Practice	Purpose	What the teacher does	What the students do
5. Pose purposeful questions.	• Reveals students' current understanding of a concept. • Encourages students to explain, elaborate, and clarify thinking. • Makes the learning of mathematics more visible and accessible for students.	• Asks questions that build on and extend student thinking. • Is intentional about the kinds of questions to make the mathematics more visible to students. • Uses wait time to provide students with time to think and examine their ideas.	• Think more deeply about the process of the mathematics rather than simply focusing on the answer. • Listen to and comment on the explanations of others in the class.
6. Build procedural fluency from conceptual understanding.	• Experiences with concrete materials allow students to make sense of important mathematics and flexibly choose from a variety of methods to solve problems.	• Provides opportunities for students to reason about mathematical ideas. • Expects students to explain why their strategies work. • Connects student methods to efficient procedures as appropriate.	• Understand and explain the procedures they are using and why they work. • Uses a variety of strategies to solve problems and make sense of mathematical ideas. • Do not rely on shortcuts or tricks to do mathematics.
7. Support productive struggle in learning mathematics.	• Productive struggle is significant and essential to learning mathematics with understanding. • Allows students to grapple with ideas and relationships. • Giving young students ample time to work with and make sense out of new ideas is critical to their learning with understanding.	• Supports student struggle without showing and telling a procedure but rather focusing on the important mathematical ideas. • Asks questions that scaffold student thinking. • Builds questions and lessons on important student mistakes rather than focusing on the correct answer. • Recognizes the importance of effort as students work to make sense of new ideas.	• Stick to a task and recognize that struggle is part of making sense. • Ask questions that will help them to better understand the task. • Support each other with ideas rather than telling others the answer or how to solve a problem.
8. Elicit and use evidence of student thinking.	• Eliciting and using evidence of student thinking helps teachers access learning progress and can be used to make instructional decisions during the lessons as well as help to prepare what will occur in the next lesson. • Formative assessment through student written and oral ideas are excellent artifacts to assess student thinking and understanding.	• Determines what to look for in gathering evidence of student learning. • Poses questions and answers student questions that provide information about student understanding, strategies, and reasoning. • Uses evidence to determine next steps of instruction.	• Accept that reasoning and understanding are as important as the answer to a problem. • Use mistakes and misconceptions to rethink their understanding. • Ask questions of the teacher and peers to clarify confusion or misunderstanding. • Self-assess progress toward developing mathematical undesrstanding.

Adapted from *Principles to Actions,* National Council of Teachers of Mathematics (2014)

Reproducibles

Reproducible 1. Five Frame

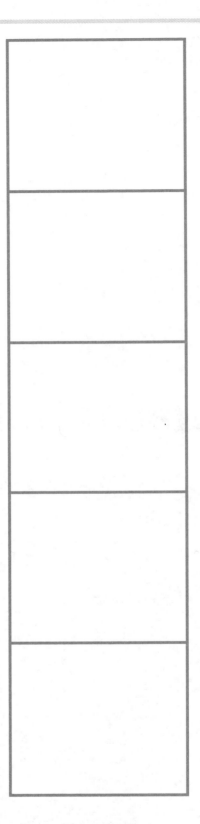

Reproducible 2. Ten Frame

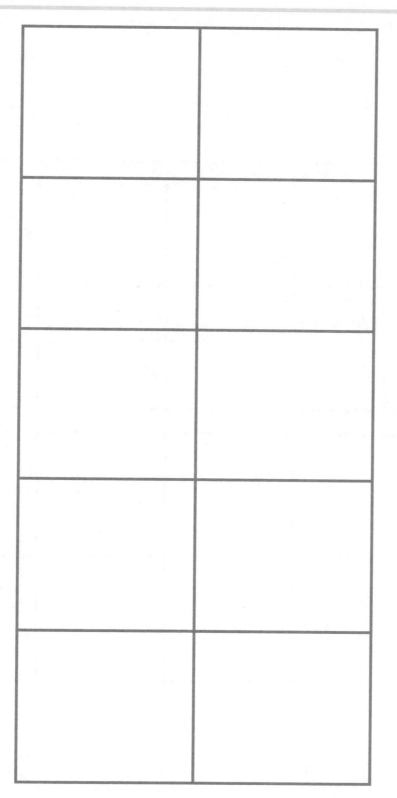

1	2	3	4	5	6	7	8	9	10
11	12	13	14	15	16	17	18	19	20
21	22	23	24	25	26	27	28	29	30
31	32	33	34	35	36	37	38	39	40
41	42	43	44	45	46	47	48	49	50
51	52	53	54	55	56	57	58	59	60
61	62	63	64	65	66	67	68	69	70
71	72	73	74	75	76	77	78	79	80
81	82	83	84	85	86	87	88	89	90
91	92	93	94	95	96	97	98	99	100

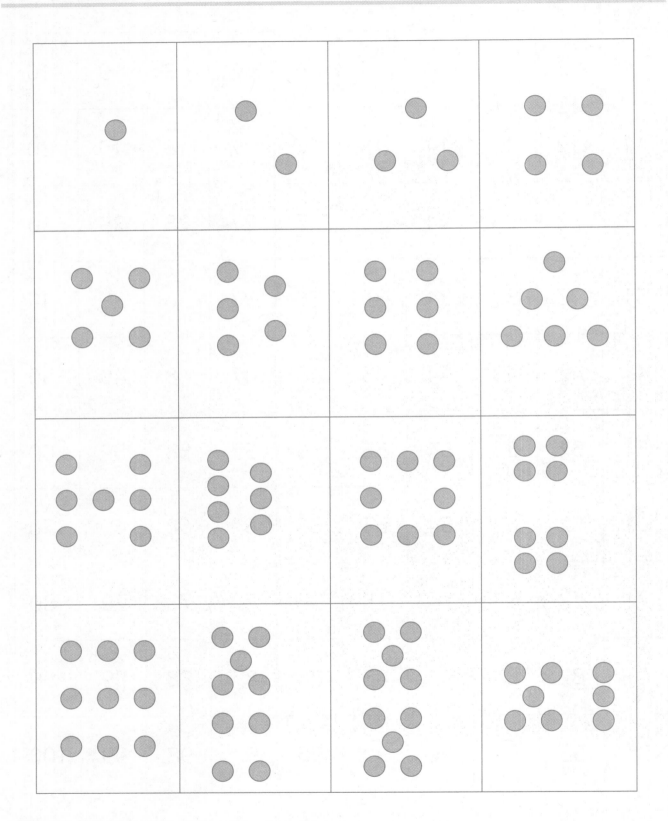

0	1 ✏	2 ☎☎	3 ★★★
4 ✈✈✈✈	5 🖐🖐🖐 🖐🖐	6 ☺☺☺ ☺☺☺	7 🕯🕯🕯🕯 🕯🕯🕯
8 🔔🔔🔔🔔 🔔🔔🔔🔔	9 🚩🚩🚩🚩🚩 🚩🚩🚩🚩		

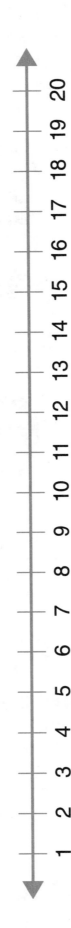

Whole

Part

Part

Reproducible 10. Place Value Chart (Tens/Ones)

tens	ones

online resources

Reproducible 11. Place Value Chart (Hundreds/Tens/Ones)

hundreds	tens	ones

greater than	**>**
less than	**<**
same as	**=**

Additional Resources

Online

http://www.achievethecore.org

Practical tools designed to help students and teachers see their hard work deliver results. Achievethecore.org was created in the spirit of collaboration and includes planning materials, professional development resources, assessment information, and implementation support.

http://www.corestandards.org

A complete copy of the common core standards or by grade level is available on this site. Includes other supporting resources including background on the development of the standards, videos, documents, faqs, and much more.

http://illuminations.nctm.org

A collection of high quality tasks, lessons, and activities that align with the common core standards and include the Standards for Mathematical Practice.

http://illustrativemathematics.org

A variety of videos, tasks, and suggestions for professional development accessible to all teachers.

http://ime.math.arizona.edu/progressions

The series of progressions documents written by leading researchers in the field summarizing the standards progressions for specific CCSS domains.

http://www.pta.org/parents/content.cfm?ItemNumber=2583

The *Parents' Guides to Student Success* were developed by teachers, parents, and education experts in response to the Common Core State Standards. Created for Grades K–high school in English language arts/literacy and mathematics, the guides provide clear, consistent expectations for what students should be learning at each grade in order to be prepared for college and career.

Books

Caldwell, J. H., Karp, K., & Bay-Williams, J., & Zbiek, R. M. (2011). *Developing essential understanding of addition and subtraction for teaching mathematics in pre-k–grade 2*. Reston, VA: NCTM. (ISBN 978-0-87353-664-6)

Hull, T. H., Harbin Miles, R., & Balka, D. S. (2012). *The common core mathematics standards: Transforming practice through team leadership*. Thousand Oaks, CA: Corwin. (ISBN-13: 978-1452226224)

National Council of Teachers of Mathematics. (1989). *The curriculum and evaluation standards for school mathematics*. Reston, VA: NCTM.

National Council of Teachers of Mathematics. (2001). *Principles and standards for school mathematics*. Reston, VA: NCTM.

National Council of Teachers of Mathematics. (2014). *Principles to actions: Ensuring mathematical success for all*. Reston, VA: NCTM. (*ISBN 978-0-87353-774-2*)

O'Connell, S., & SanGiovanni, J. (2013). *Putting the practices into action: Implementing the common core standards for mathematical practice, K–8*. Portsmouth, NH: Heinemann. (ISBN-13: 978-0325046556)

Richardson, K. (2012). *How children learn number concepts: A guide to the critical learning phases*. Bellingham, WA: Math Perspectives Teacher Development Center. (ISBN-13: 978-0984838196)

Schwartz, S. L., & Curcio, F. R. (2013). *Implementing the common core state standards through mathematical problem solving: Kindergarten–grade 2*. Reston, VA: NTCM. (ISBN 978-0-87353-723-0)

Van de Walle, J. A., Lovin, L. A. H., Karp, K. S., & Bay-Williams, J. M. (2013). *Teaching student-centered mathematics: Developmentally appropriate instruction for grades pre-K–2*. Upper Saddle River, NJ: Pearson Education. (ISBN13: 978-0132824828)

About the Authors

Linda M. Gojak is a past president of the National Council of Teachers of Mathematics. At Hawken School in Gates Mills, Ohio, Linda chaired the mathematics department and taught Grades 4–8 mathematics. As the director of the Center for Mathematics and Science Education, Teaching, and Technology (CMSETT) at John Carroll University, she plans and facilitates professional development for K–12 mathematics teachers. Linda has been actively involved in professional organizations, including the Mathematical Sciences Education Board, the Conference Board of the Mathematical Sciences, the Council of Presidential Awardees in Mathematics, and the MathCounts Board of Directors. She has served as president of the National Council of Supervisors of Mathematics and president of the Ohio Council of Teachers of Mathematics. Among her recognitions are the Presidential Award for Excellence in Mathematics and Science Teaching and the Christofferson-Fawcett Award for lifetime contribution to mathematics education.

Ruth Harbin Miles coaches rural, suburban, and inner-city school mathematics teachers. Her professional experiences include coordinating the K–12 Mathematics Teaching and Learning Program for the Olathe, Kansas, Public Schools for more than 25 years; teaching mathematics methods courses at Virginia's Mary Baldwin College; and serving on the Board of Directors for the National Council of Teachers of Mathematics, the National Council of Supervisors of Mathematics, and both the Virginia Council of Teachers of Mathematics and the Kansas Association of Teachers of Mathematics. Ruth is a co-author of five Corwin books, including *A Guide to Mathematics Coaching*, *A Guide to Mathematics Leadership*, *Visible Thinking in the K–8 Mathematics Classroom*, *The Common Core Mathematics Standards*, and *Realizing Rigor in the Mathematics Classroom*. As co-owner of Happy Mountain Learning, Ruth specializes in developing teachers' content knowledge and strategies for engaging students to achieve high standards in mathematics.

SUPPORTING
TEACHERS,
EMPOWERING
LEARNERS

YOUR MATHEMATICS STANDARDS COMPANIONS

The key to raising school- and district-wide achievement is purposeful, potent, standards-based instruction—all year long in every classroom. That's where the Your Mathematics Standards Companion series can help. Linda M. Gojak, Ruth Harbin Miles, and Lois A. Williams walk you step by step through what the standards mean and how to teach them. Ensure that every student in your school or district has the critical skills they need to succeed on test day, in school, and in life.

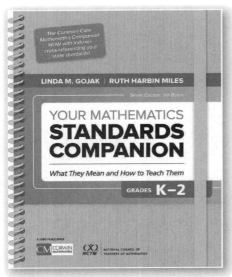

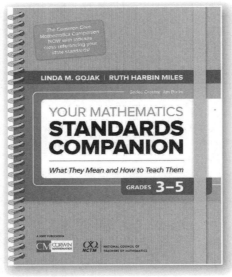

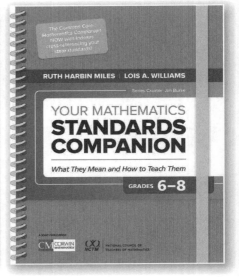

Grades K–2
ISBN: 978-1-5063-8223-4

Grades 3–5
ISBN: 978-1-5063-8224-1

Grades 6–8
ISBN: 978-1-5063-8225-8